Angle
Of
Attack

Air France 447 and
The Future of Aviation
Safety

Roger Rapoport
& Captain Shem
Malmquist

"The key to safety in any operation requires the identification of the hazards. Unrecognized, hazards kill. Once hazards come to light appropriate action must be taken to mitigate the associated risks. This timely and dramatic work shows how high altitude, thin air stalls were not recognized as the hazard they are, but now, experts have shown they do exist and have developed engineering and procedural remedies to prevent further tragedy. Take your time, read every word — we owe Rapoport and Malmquist a great debt of gratitude for their research and concern for the safety of all of us who fly."

Dr. Gary W. Helmer
Chief, Safety Division
National Transportation Safety Board

"Angle of Attack is a great resource for aeronautical professionals and anyone with an interest in aviation mishaps because it systematically exposes the failed defenses that can reside at each layer of the aviation system from top-level management down to pilots and the not-so-perfect, artificially intelligent systems that help them fly."

Dr. Chris Johnson
Director of Aviation Education and Research
Industrial & Systems Engineering
University of Wisconsin, Madison

"Rapoport and Malmquist do it again! A masterful piece of work that was hard to put down despite already knowing the accident. With deft ability, they take the reader down the inextricably intertwined paths of raw emotion and technical details of some of our most troubling and persistent global aviation safety problems. If you travel by air, or are interested in air safety, then this is simply a must-read!"

Capt. Shawn Pruchnicki (Ret.) MS ATP CFII
Chief Scientist for Human Factors Investigation and Education (HFIE)
Ohio State University Center for Aviation Studies

"The authors have written a book that is a must-read for anyone with an interest in aircraft accident investigation and aviation safety. Their exhaustive research highlights safety issues on nearly every page. Given Malmquist's vast aeronautical knowledge and years of experience, and Rapoport's dogged reporting, they virtually reconstruct what was going on that fateful night in the cockpit of AF447. As we have painfully learned, with many post crash-investigations, the industry has much to do to enhance safety. Some of the shortcomings include, more realistic simulation, in depth meteorology training, use of angle of attack indicators and crew dependence on automation. As we absorb the next generation of pilots we need to quickly fix these or watch an increasing accident rate."

Professor Walt Houghton
Central Florida Space Academy & Embry Riddle University,
McDill Air Force Base, Former Manager Vermont State Airports

"You don't have to be a pilot to find this book moving and absorbing, just an airline passenger. The authors clearly and vividly explain the series of small events that make the difference between the hundreds of thousands of flights that are safe and routine and the one that ends in tragedy."

Adam Hochschild
Author of Spain in Our Hearts and King Leopold's Ghost

"As a young Naval Aviator I learned to maximize the performance of my aircraft in every regime of flight through use of Angle of Attack. When I began my initial training in the B727 I asked about AOA, but was taken aback when my instructor said "we don't use that in the airlines." I asked why and was told "we just don't." Rapoport and Malmquist have again asked the question of why? Using Air France 447 as a backdrop, they have taken a detailed look at the current state of airline training, safety and the politics involved in how and why we fly like we do. Angle of Attack is a must-read for the professional aviator desiring to become a better pilot while developing a broader understanding of the airline industry."

Jeff Kilmer
B777 Captain and former chief international pilot FedEx

"As Angle of Attack makes clear, comprehension of meteorological conditions for aviation involves a multitude of data points which need to be orchestrated, communicated and coordinated by all the relevant entities within the global aviation community to ensure safer skies. This book proves conclusively that education by meteorologists is the key to fundamental understanding of the impact weather has on the elements of the aviation arena including pilots, dispatchers, air traffic controllers and other leaders in aviation."

Debbie M. Schaum
Associate Chair and Associate Professor
Applied Aviation Sciences

"What an excellent book! The authors have hit this one out of the ballpark. Both aviation enthusiasts and non aviation enthusiasts will enjoy this book. I highly recommend it."

Captain James Nielsen

"Roger Rapaport and Shem Malmquist focus this book on the issues related to training of new generation automated aircraft flight crews to deal with the rare and unexpected emergencies. Their subject matter expertise is admirable! Their analysis describes the problems related to the difficulty of replicating rare, hazardous flight conditions to facilitate training airline flight crews to handle unexpected challenges in high altitude flight emergencies and hazardous weather encounters. They have used the Air France 447 crash and some other crashes of automated airplanes as examples of accidents that might have been prevented if the crews could have had access to realistic training to prepare them for those rare events, and if their aircraft had been equipped with angle of attack indicators.This book is a must-read for professional pilots, aircraft designers, government regulators, and political decision makers. It will dispel many of the misconceptions and myths surrounding some of the seemingly improbable losses of newer, high technology aircraft and points the way to safer ways to design and equip the machines and train the crews who operate them."

Gregory Fox
Director of Safety Florida Institute of Technology ATPL pilot,
safety manager since 1971, 35 years safety regulator, and 20 years
check inspector on A320 and A340.

Angle of Attack:
Air France 447 and
the Future of Aviation Safety

Roger Rapoport and Captain Shem Malmquist

Curt Lewis Aviation Books
an imprint of Lexographic Press
33 W Huron St, 305
Chicago IL 60654

ISBN: 978-0-9847142-6-1

Cover design and production: James Sparling, Lexographic
Text design and production: Lexographic, Chicago

lexographicpress.com, first edition August 2017.

Set in Book Antiqua, 10.5 on 14pt

Printed in the United States of America

*This book is dedicated to the legendary aviation writer
Pierre Sparaco, who covered the Airbus story from the
company's inception. He opened many doors and shared many
profound insights into the Air France 447 story.*

Contents

x

Forward

Starting with the Air France 447 accident, the authors present a fascinating and heartbreaking human-interest story about one of the most important events in aviation history. They have also written the defining work on Angle of Attack technology and what it means to every pilot and passenger. Their analysis of worldwide aviation accident history shows how the use of AOA equipment instrumentation may have prevented aviation tragedies.

Additionally, they have considered the regulatory and training issues of AOA implementation that could prevent these aircraft stall-type accidents. Their scholarship is impeccable and they have written a book that is a must-read for airline executives, pilots and their passengers.

As an accident investigator with more than 40 years of industry experience, it was my job to analyze and understand why excellent flight crews flying perfectly good aircraft failed to bring their passengers safely home. Again and again it was clear to me and my colleagues that the central point of this book is one that has escaped an industry that prides itself on safety. Angle of Attack technology is available, relatively inexpensive and easy to train to. It is used on most military aircraft and many business aircraft. General aviation pilots can and do opt for it all over the world. They use AOA because it saves lives.

This long-overdue book is destined to start an important conversation within my industry. Thanks to their diligent research, Rapoport and Malmquist have documented why it is in the airlines' own self-interest to incorporate Angle of Attack technology.

There is no reason for further delays. This one simple change will benefit flight crews and passengers everywhere. I hope you will join me in pressing the airline industry to make this long-overdue reform.

Curt Lewis

Introduction: Approach To Stall

After thousands of commercial jet flights to the far corners of the Earth, Captain Shem Malmquist, was ready to confront challenges that regularly test the skills of flight crews around the world. As a training pilot and accident investigator, he understood the kinds of surprises that could instantly transform a routine flight into a crisis where he had seconds to recover from an unexpected event. From takeoffs on icy runways to landings in the midst of pop-up thunderstorms, this aviator had trained for nearly every circumstance imaginable. With a perfect record after more than 40 years of flying, problems passengers fear were routine for him. He was well versed on how to safely handle hidden dangers like clear air turbulence or the best way to respond to an on-board fire.

For more than 30 years Malmquist had trained for a myriad of hazards on simulators, in the classroom and on numerous check rides. Regularly examined and reexamined, he was well prepared for the surprise challenges a veteran flight crew might see once in a lifetime. Nonetheless, today was something completely different. He was headed to the airport and would learn to fly an Airbus A330 carrying 228 passengers and crew into the worst kind of emergency imaginable.

His flight departed in the early evening and flew perfectly to a cruising altitude of 35,000 feet. Then, with no warning, the plane's automatic pilot shut down. He pulled back on the controls and the big jet entered a high-altitude aerodynamic stall. Still he held the nose of the airplane high and the big jet

1

went deeper into the stall and began to plummet towards the earth. It was time to recover. Following special training well beyond what most pilots receive, he put the nose down 20° and dove 10,000 feet. A minute later, after gaining sufficient airspeed, he pulled the nose up and recovered from the stall.

With his spring 2016 mission accomplished to the satisfaction of his simulator instructor at the Federal Aviation Administration's flight research center in Oklahoma City, Malmquist became one of the first line pilots in America to learn how to recover from an event that has brought down three commercial airliners since 2009. Every American airline is now required to teach all pilots the same vital lessons. Under the Federal Aviation Administration's final Federal Aviation Regulation (FAR) 60 Rule on flight simulators in conjunction with new recommendations for upset recovery training, the air carriers have three years to make sure their flight crews know how to avoid these high-altitude aerodynamic stalls that have taken 506 lives over the past seven years.

The FAA regulation took effect the day before the June 1, 2009, anniversary of the crash of Air France 447 on a flight from Rio to Paris. Two subsequent 2014 crashes in the Java Sea and Mali have added a sense of urgency to this new challenge. With 506 people lost in these three accidents, the American airline industry is moving to reprogram their simulators to correctly model high-altitude approach to stall and stall recovery. The same rule will be implemented in Europe, Canada, Australia and many other countries, eventually costing the industry as much as $1 billion.

This book explains why some carriers, concerned about this recent series of unanticipated high-altitude stalls and subsequent losses of control (LOC), are jumping ahead of the FAA's 2019 FAR 60 deadline to quickly reprogram their simulators and complete new stall-recovery training. It also answers many important questions asked by aviation professionals and passengers alike. Air France 447 is an accident that has revolutionized aviation safety and pilot training and challenges important assumptions about the primacy of flight automation. As FAR 60 demonstrates, this catastrophe and a few other serious incidents has forced the industry to put more emphasis on stick-and-rudder training. The renewed hands-on flying emphasis affirms the belief that the number one safety system on any aircraft is a well-trained pilot.

Even if you don't fly, you can appreciate the fact that the lessons of Air France 447 have become a landmark teaching moment. As automation dominates our lives, we all need to understand its critical limitations. In science, medicine, education and industry, the human touch remains much more than an afterthought. After marching for decades toward the automated cockpit where pilots are downgraded to systems managers, the airline industry is trying to change course.

Based on many millions of hours of flight time, this decision is being carefully watched by other industries eager to learn from aviation's experience.

Government regulators, manufacturers and airlines now understand that dozens of computers are no substitute for gifted and talented aviators who thoroughly understand aerodynamics and can, on a moment's notice, hand-fly their planes without the benefit of flight automation. From the self-driving car to the hospital room where medical teams focus on their machines at the expense of patient feedback, this challenge is not going away. Join us now as the best minds in commercial aviation explain what has gone wrong and how we can work together to ensure that human beings remain central to the safety management systems that dominate our lives.

CHAPTER 1
Rio

Shortly before midnight May 28, 2009, Air France 447, an Airbus A330, left the gate at Paris Charles De Gaulle and taxied to the runway. Number one for takeoff, the flight climbed out over Île de France and headed southwest. Captain Marc Dubois regretted that one name was missing from the passenger list, a Biarritz friend he invited a few days earlier; fellow Air France pilot Arnaud Lorente.

Known for his spur-of-the-moment invitations, Marc, 58, always encouraged family and friends to join him on flights to exotic destinations. Like his father Jean-Paul, an Air France captain who had died two months earlier at the age of 89, he was a great traveling companion and a pretty good tour guide.

Having made more than 40 flights between Paris, France and Rio De Janeiro, Brazil, Lorente was easily sold on the idea of riding along with Dubois. The lure of sugar-sand beaches warmed by the trade winds, reconnecting with close friends and seaside dining at favorite restaurants was irresistible. It was hard to say no to a Dubois flight with a good chance of a first class upgrade. This captain was well known for spontaneous acts of kindness like treating his entire flight crew to orchestra seats at the Prague Opera. Alas, a previously scheduled Air France assignment to Caracas forced Lorente to send his regrets and take a rain check. With any luck he'd soon be joining his old friend on another trip as a passenger or, even better, as copilot.

If there was an Airbus A330 captain better qualified than Marc Dubois to command this twin jet as it headed out over the Bay of Biscay, above Galicia, and Lisbon before heading southwest via the Canary Islands and Cape Verde, Air France human resources would have welcomed their application. His right-hand men were two outstanding copilots: David Robert, 37 and Pierre-Cédric Bonin, 32.

Settled comfortably in coach was Bonin's wife Isabelle, a high school physics and math teacher always ready for another trip with her husband. Like her fellow passengers, she was protected by a seemingly perfect safety system that appeared to magically bubble-wrap these indefatigable flying machines. No one needed to worry about bumps in the night along the way to South America.

Ten hours later their Airbus touched down on the Galeão island runway at 140 knots and taxied to the terminal named for the godfather of bossa nova, Antonio Carlos-Jobim. Dubois, Robert and Bonin had shown their passengers, once again, why Air France was one of the world's top-20 most trusted airlines. While ground crews turned their aircraft around for the flight back to Paris, the pilots caught the shuttle to Sofitel Rio de Janeiro Copacabana. Soon they would be exploring this sultry city long favored by French tourists.

By the time the pilots returned for their flight home on the evening on May 31, they were relatively relaxed and rested. As is often the case when crossing multiple time zones, the rest is not always what the pilot might like. The body does not always cooperate to sleep on command. Captain Dubois fell victim to the jet lag and was unable to fall asleep during the usual nap long-haul pilots use to take before a night shift. Still, he had the legally required rest period and in the manner of most pilots, he did not raise any concerns. Pilots are used to just "powering through" issues such as lack of sleep, often not helped with layovers and departure times that are designed around schedules created by marketing departments rather than human factors researchers. Their preflight briefing was reassuring. Hundreds of unseen hands in management, operations, dispatch, maintenance, meteorology and air traffic control had all done their jobs. There were no dings on the plane's maintenance record. From Rio to Dakar and Paris, not one of these seasoned experts suspected that Flight 447 was destined to become a landmark in aviation history. Both the worldwide Airbus A330 fleet and these pilots enjoyed a perfect record.

Drawing on more than a century of experience, flying had become so safe that people afraid to board an airplane were ridiculed on sitcoms. Expensive fear-of-flying classes thrived on the facts. No matter how you crunched the numbers, traveling on a modern plane operated by a major airline was not dangerous. This was certainly not some bucket of bolts flown by junior birdmen to a foggy dirt strip in the Republic of Congo or Java. The chances of this flight landing safely in Paris the following morning were better than 20 million to one.

Since its inaugural flight in 1992, over 100 million passengers—more than the entire population of France—had flown around the world on nearly a million A330/340 flights. A miracle in the sky, the A330's satisfied customers included French President Nicolas Sarkozy, who had selected one as his presidential jet, buying it used from Air Caraibes for $227 million just six weeks prior to the loss of AF 447. His flying palace, which made him the envy of every leader in Europe, came complete with a meeting room for 12 and a private bedroom and bath. Air France Flight 447, of course, had no such amenities. But then, President Sarkozy's plane wasn't equipped to carry 216 passengers and a crew of 12.

A typical late-fall evening in the Southern Hemisphere, the weather was calm and warm. Stars were just starting to appear. Inside the air-conditioned terminal, the passengers waiting for the boarding announcement had no reason to worry that their routine flight was about to make aviation history.

The pre-boarding announcement came in Portuguese and French. It took 23 minutes for the passengers to get their carry-on bags and small children down the jetway, find their seats and settle in for the long flight. The boarding ramp doors closed, Air France Flight 447 rolled out onto the tarmac and took off at 7:29pm (12:29am Paris time). Under the command of Captain Dubois, the red, white and blue twinjet headed north along the Brazilian coast at dusk just as constellations began gracing the southern sky. Everyone on board looked forward to arriving in Paris in time for petit déjeuner.

CHAPTER 2
Paris

There are no small roles in the aviation drama that has transformed our world over the past century. Even a bit player can have a critical impact on a flight thousands of miles away. A non-English speaking mechanic at an El Salvador maintenance hangar can make a mistake on the repair of an American jet. Poorly translated Mandarin at a parts depot can impact a French plane in China for an engine overhaul. A Japanese engineer who makes a mistake on a lithium battery system may inadvertently contribute to a fire on an aircraft parked at Boston's Logan Airport.

Much as we take for granted the many benefits of air travel, it remains a relatively young industry still on a challenging learning curve. Important challenges are often discovered years after a new jet goes into service. Despite impressive new technology, the success of every flight depends on a network of people who may live and work thousands of miles away. Artificial intelligence is promising, but is still no substitute for the experience and the good judgment of human operators. In turn, these aviators depend on the skill of colleagues who diligently manage flight operations, maintenance, meteorology and air traffic control. Every role is carefully cast in the drama of flight where even the smallest bit player is critically important.

Air France flights set a high standard, mixing an admirable blend of technology and admirable airmanship. Pilots here and at similar well-run airlines can easily fly their entire careers without experiencing a single engine failure. They are most likely to never be forced to sweat out any sort of emergency outside of the scripted learning scenarios presented to them when training in their company's flight simulators.

Captain Marc Dubois, and co-pilot Pierre-Cédric Bonin were both sons of Air France pilots. Their fathers, Jean-Paul Dubois and Jean-Louis Bonin, had come to the airline from impressive Air Force careers that included combat in battle zones like Northern Italy and Chad. The second "relief" co-pilot, David Robert, was a graduate of France's leading aviation academy, ENAC. Together, these men had more than 20,000 accident-free hours of flight time, the equivalent of more than 40 trips to the moon.

Marc Dubois, certified to fly 17 aircraft ranging from a single-pilot puddle jumper to a continent-hopping jet, was also a popular flight instructor, and the proud owner of a difficult-to-get mountain flying certificate. In his spare time, he climbed Mt. Blanc and rebuilt his village home into an architectural showplace.

This Airbus A330 captain loved to show off the plane's glass cockpit to family, admiring students and other aviators he frequently invited along for the ride. During breaks, he broke out his iPod preloaded with favorite Mozart operas. Unwinding to *Le Nozze di Figaro* while a flight attendant was taking his order from the first-class menu, Dubois really was flying high at the ceiling of his world.

The captain's favorite plane boasted no less of an accomplished pedigree. After 15 years and nearly a million flights that had carried more passengers than the population of France, the A330/340 series was an Airbus triumph. This Toulouse-built underdog that sold only 15 planes in its first five years now claimed roughly half of the commercial market for long-distance jets.

One key to Airbus's remarkable success — sales soared

into the thousands after Airbus introduced its first fly-by-wire aircraft, the A320, in 1988 — was its development and integration into the cockpit of the automation system designed to prevent the problems that had doomed far too many flights in years past.

Unlike traditional aircraft, where pilots operated hydraulic systems manually via their cockpit controls, the new Airbus system electronically converted crew inputs into flight computer commands. These computers automatically limited the airplane from getting into too steep a bank, or flying too slowly or fast, thus eliminating problems that might be triggered by momentary lapses. This was a critical addition to flight safety.

The new approach appeared to rule out a variety of loss-of-control accidents. The system was designed to overrule pilots making mistakes due to confusion or overreaction on an emergency maneuver.

The new planes also provided for much simpler pilot response to a dangerous wind-shear encounter. Glass flight display screens had replaced the assortment of analog "steam" gauges found on older aircraft. The result was more robust information displays and simplified maintenance.

Although there were predictable glitches at first, Airbus had a hit that was a boon to the French economy and the company's European partners. Unlike the first fly-by-wire Airbus 320, the reputation of the newer A330 (and its sister A340) had not been dinged by any crashes.

The crews flying A330s were often a blend of seasoned aviators and younger pilots well on their way to the top at Air France. Like their captain, co-pilots Bonin and Robert were proficient at hand flying. Dubois was a glider and acrobatic pilot, just like Bonin who had never scored less than perfect on any of the many exams he had taken in his training career. Bonin was one of just 60 hired out of more than 1,000 Air France applicants in 2002. Robert, a highly regarded veteran on the

South Atlantic route with 39 trips behind him, also worked as an executive at the Air France operational control center, a prestigious position.

There was every reason for the passengers and crew of Flight 447 to feel as secure as if they were in their own beds. Behind the gate crews stood the technicians and engineers of the new but not entirely formalized Air France safety management system. Thus, redundancy, the scariest word in the human resources department lexicon, had a positive meaning within the airlines' bureaucracy.

Even the backup systems came with backups. Updates were performed effortlessly on flight control systems running different software. If one of the critical flight computers failed, another would easily replace it. And mechanics were always available to make last-minute hardware changes if pilots spotted any problems on their preflight walk-arounds.

Few were better trained than Captain Marc Dubois who took command of Flight 447 for the first three-and-a-half hours. He had grown up in an aviation family. His father, Capt. Jean-Paul Dubois of St. Germain En Laye and Champdeniers-Saint-Denis, fought for the Free French Air Force in northern Italy during World War II before embarking on an Air France career flying DC-4s.

Jean-Paul Dubois and Marc's mother, Helene, a former flight attendant, met at Air France. All three of their sons — Marc, Jacques and Michel — were pilots.

In many ways, Marc and his father bookended the story of Air France, arguably the world's most romantic airline. Jean-Paul Dubois had come to the national carrier after beginning his career flying the hated American P-39 Airacobra in 1944-45.

Derided as a "snake that lacked a poisonous bite," the American fighter was powered by an engine in the middle of the fuselage and attacked its prey with a 37mm cannon that fired rounds through the nose propeller hub.

Although the plane was very responsive to the pilot's

touch, it was easy for P-39 pilots to lose awareness of pitch changes. When the plane was out of ammunition, the center of gravity shifted rearward. At this point the Airacobra pilot could easily find himself at a high angle of attack, the critical angle between the aircraft flight path and the relative wind. To avoid stalling, P-39 pilots like Jean-Paul Dubois kept a close eye on their angle of attack indicators, making sure the angle of attack was safely maintained between 4-14°.

The nose-firing P-39 also often required pilots to don gas masks to survive artillery fumes filling the cockpit. Lacking a turbocharger, the plane had been abandoned by Britain's Royal Air Force as a bad joke. Unfortunately it couldn't climb high enough to be useful over Western Europe. It was incapable of reaching higher altitudes necessary to dodge enemy fire. Emergency procedures included crawling out of the cockpit onto a wing and jumping to safety, whenever possible. Many of these planes were shipped east to the Russians who learned how to fly them successfully against the Luftwaffe by taking advantage of the P-39's agility.

Despite its drawbacks, the P-39 was a great way to learn stick-and-rudder skills. It taught pilots the necessary art of hands-on flying under the worst conditions imaginable. Unlike a simulator that stripped some of the motion and emotion of predictable crises, this aircraft taught pilots how to survive a true emergency. Thanks to their hands-on training, bravery and ingenuity, these Airacobra pilots flew through and survived emergencies that would have certainly led to crashes for pilots only schooled on simulators. Muscle memories of these scary challenges help develop a light touch and educate great pilots in the same way muscle memories would aid the early jet pilots in later years. After the war, Marc's parents, Jean-Paul and Helene Dubois, raised their sons at the family's late-19th century classical French home in St. Germain En Laye. The birthplace of France's longest-reigning monarch, Sun King Louis XIV, this was also the city where Alexander Dumas wrote his beloved and immortal classics, *The Count of Monte Cristo* and *The Three Musketeers*.

Perfectly located midway between Charles De Gaulle and Orly airports, this Paris suburb was also an ideal sanctuary during long breaks between flights around the world. Visitors quickly discovered why centuries of French royalty had remained loyal to this Valhalla on the Seine.

A whitewashed tower that had once served as a carrier pigeon base was Jean-Paul's office aerie. From here he overlooked the glorious gardens gracing his two-story home. Friends of the Dubois boys were cautioned to play quietly to avoid disturbing their father the airline captain during afternoon naps before long flights around the world.

A great pairing of compensation and prestige for former military pilots, there were few better jobs in commercial aviation than flying for Air France. On board no one challenged the authority of an immaculately dressed Air France captain. Even as hand flying gave way to the automation age, veterans like Jean-Paul Dubois still were seen as aviators able to work their way out of any crisis.

His senior stature gave Jean-Paul a chance to choose the most desirable routes, with enviable layovers in the capitals of Asia, the Americas and the Middle East. In 1980, the family celebrated his mandatory retirement at the age of 60 by joining him on his final flight to Tokyo.

Happily, the Dubois flying legend would continue. Although young, Marc enjoyed teaching his brothers how to fly at a local aviation club. Jacques gave up flying to focus on his career in architecture. His first commission was the restoration of a family farmhouse on the outskirts of Champdeniers-Saint-Denis in the Poitou-Charente. Their brother Michel was equally passionate about cabinetry.

Marc, however, knew he was destined to become a captain at his father's airline.

He began the climb to achieve his dream after finishing

boarding school in famed composer Maurice Ravel's hometown, Monfort L'Amaury, by following his mother's lead and signing on as an Air France flight attendant. For six years Marc's salary helped pay for his own pilot training — it cost him €50,000 for just one of many licenses he needed after finishing ground school.

At family gatherings, Jean-Paul's sons continued to share their father's love for classical music. Cabinet-maker Michel loved playing the piano, architect Jacques was a trumpet player who performed in brass bands and pilot-in-training Marc was a passionate opera devotee who hung out with musicians at home and abroad.

In retirement, Jean Paul and Helene spent more and more time at Champdeniers-Saint-Denis, eventually relocating to this village in their 80s. They loved rural life in their restored country home where the family frequently gathered for holidays and long weekends.

This retreat was adjacent to the family estate and its fairytale castle donated to the church by Jean-Paul's sister. A local landmark, it was now a home for Alzheimer's patients. The castle was also a great photo opportunity for tourists drawn to the region famous for its half-timbered houses, tranquil canals reflecting memorable sunsets, Romanesque art, Renaissance town halls, and archaeology dating back to the Bronze Age.

At his father's funeral here in March 2009, Jacques Dubois, now a prodigious Paris architect, drew on iconic author and pilot Antoine de Saint Exupéry for the eulogy. One of France's aviation pioneers like Jean Mermoz and Helene Boucher (both of whom perished in accidents), Saint Exupery wrote the beloved children's classic, *The Little Prince*.

"Grown-ups," he said famously, "never understand anything for themselves and it is tiresome for children to be always and forever explaining things to them."

By the time of Jean-Paul's passing, Marc was flying many

of the same Air France routes favored by his father. He had worked his way up the general aviation ranks as a corporate charter pilot, a Mitsubishi pilot for a sheikh living in Spain, a demonstration pilot and flight instructor.

At the regional carrier Air Inter, he proudly flew the French Dassault Mercure and Sud Aviation Caravelle. The Mercure, a descendant of the former Mirage III, Mirage IV and Falcon jets, was known for stomach-churning dives at a hair-rising rate of descent of nearly 11,000 feet a minute (when the aircraft's very efficient speedbrakes were deployed, it would "fall out of the sky"). That maximum descent rate could bring a "regular" flight from cruise altitude down to 5,000 feet in about three minutes. This colorful airline paid him well.

A fellow Air Inter pilot, Gerard Arnoux, completed his line training with the airline's chief pilot, a man in his 60s who arrived at the airport on his Harley Davidson sporting colorful Santiags cowboy boots. This boss made it clear that pay raises were based on performance. The faster an Air Inter pilot flew, the better he was paid.

"You see that, young guy," the chief pilot told Arnoux as he gestured toward the airspeed indicator, "don't forget this instrument is calibrated in piastres. Our airline is earning billions thanks to fast legs and short turnovers. Basically I only want to see only two speeds on this instrument, 380 knots climbing, Mach .80 cruising and 380 knots down to initial approach fix."

Airbus, one of Mercure's languishing competitors, had spent its first 16 years trying to steal business from companies like Boeing, McDonnell-Douglas and Lockheed.

Along with Air France, Air Inter launched the new Airbus 320 on popular routes in 1988. A U.S. carrier, Southwest Airlines, even sent a team to study this little airline that had developed the densest network of the world in such a small country.

The genius behind this new fly-by-wire competitor was

a former French Air Force pilot named Bernard Ziegler. His flying career was launched in the French Air Force where he made a name for himself on August 29, 1961 at the controls of a low-flying F84F jet fighter. One of his aircraft's wings struck and broke a cable, hurling three tourist cable cars into a 500 foot descent between two peaks near Mount Blanc. After six passengers perished, rescue workers crawled hand-over-hand overnight on a primary support cable to reach and rescue 59 survivors trapped above a gorge. Ziegler flew the slightly damaged military jet back to base where he caught up with the news coverage that made front pages and led news broadcasts worldwide.

While Bernard continued to train, his father, Henri Ziegler, served as managing director at Air France before being named the head of Sud Aviation in 1968. The company competed head-on in the 1950s with the British Comet, a failed design that was withdrawn from service after a series of crashes. Sud Aviation's Caravelle, launched in 1955, was the first commercially successful short haul jet with 279 aircraft sold through 1973. At Sud Aviation, Ziegler led the French-British development of the supersonic Concorde. Convinced that French aviation manufacturers could not succeed on their own, he moved on to found and direct a French-German-British consortium, Airbus Industrie in 1970, a move that led one French minister to summon him to his office and call the CEO "a traitor to his country."

In early February 1973, just two years after Airbus opened its doors, major American airlines skeptical about the supersonic jet's operating costs, environmental impact and noise pollution, cancelled their Concorde orders. Undaunted, Henri Ziegler watched the first Airbus plane, the A300, take off three months later at the Paris Air Show. Struggling with a nearly empty order book, the CEO dispatched his recently hired test pilot son on a demonstration tour that began in sultry Rio de Janeiro.

Pausing for an interview with French television not far from the Copacabana, the younger Ziegler tipped his hat to the courageous French pilots who had pioneered the same route across the South Atlantic more than four decades earlier on the fabled Latécoère 28 flying boat: "Our arrival enabled us to pay tribute to the Aeropostale pioneers."

Unfortunately this South American barnstorming trip and others like it didn't lead to many orders. During Airbus's first five years a mere 15 A300s were purchased.

Henri Ziegler left the company abruptly in 1974 and by 1977 the manufacturer's Saint-Martin factory was parking unsold planes on the tarmac.

While the A300 and A310 slowly attracted major airlines, the company still lacked the sales hook necessary to loosen the industry grip of its American competitors. Sales were worse than the French Caravelle which was becoming a dud for a number of airlines who would ultimately crash 22 of these aircraft (seven percent of the fleet), including two Air France planes that went down in Morocco and Cap d'Antibes

In 1984, it was Bernard Ziegler, now Airbus's director of engineering, who persuaded the company's chief operating officer Roger Béteille to build a fly-by-wire plane. A firm opponent of the Concorde program which he predicted would fail commercially, Ziegler laid out his impressive concept in a short memo, green-lighted overnight. There was no proof of concept, no marketing studies, no expensive consultants. The company was now literally flying by the seat of its pants.

He argued for a radical flight deck change, one that would cause severe turbulence at pilot unions in France and around the world. Autopilots were standard on commercial jets, but fly-by-wire, a technology used on some advanced military aircraft and the Concorde, redefined the pilot's role.

Bernard Ziegler's dream was to improve flight safety by building planes that could, except for a few minutes during takeoff and landing, be counted on to fly themselves thanks to redundant computer controls that replaced traditional hydraulically operated control surfaces with electronics. The computers would not simply fly the plane but would also protect it from pilot error with built-in design limits.

Airline buyers were impressed by the Porsche-designed beige-and-blue flight decks that hid distractions behind fiberglass panels and sheathed landing-gear controls in leather. They scarfed up the Toulouse *foie gras* and drank premium Bordeaux at trade shows. Some boldly asked French flight attendants aboard demonstration aircraft for their phone numbers. Unfortunately, when it came time to close deals, the sales force often came back to the office empty handed.

On February 22, 1987 the A320 took off on its maiden three hour and 22 minute flight from Toulouse's Blagnet airport. The long wait was over. After eight decades France and its allies in Germany and England had created an airplane destined to win over customers from Sydney to Moscow.

Under normal flying conditions, a bank of redundant computers operating on different software systems would provide fail-safe backups for the A320. When problems arose, the computers would alert the pilots to take command as needed. But built-in protections would make sure that a tired or poorly trained pilot didn't overreact and put the flight in harm's way. Instead of asking pilots what they thought about this change, the technical director presented them with a *fait accompli*.

"Ziegler asked, what do we have available in technology that could bring a significant change to an airline from a safety point of view?" says Airbus vice-president for product safety Michel Guérard in his conference room decked out with Airbus models. While the company tried to woo pilots with news that they could take full control of the aircraft at any moment, it was obvious that the computers running the autopilot were built around what one sociologist called "a logical system that is not always totally accessible to the pilot."

The fly-by-wire flight computer systems, all operating on different software platforms, communicated between themselves, making command decisions that were not always easy for the pilots to understand or follow. And because these systems worked very quickly, it was often not possible for pilots to keep pace with the new systems that automated decision-making.

Gerard Arnoux remembers the transition with the same empathy motion picture executives must have shown when some of their silent film stars struggled to make the transition to talking pictures. Pilots had to trust the fly-by-wire technology, intervening when they were alerted to do so, the autopilot switched itself off, or the captain realized something was wrong and decided to override the autopilot. While flight crews were told their workload would be significantly reduced, some worried about anomalies that could be hard to unravel in the time allowed.

"Relations between Airbus and the pilots were difficult, tense and certainly inadequate," recalled veteran French aviation journalist Pierre Sparaco, the author of *Airbus: The True Story*. One leader of the French SNPL pilots union worried that "the A320 was built on the ruins of organized labor." Another suggested that the plane was an insult to French aviators, "a non-sensual aircraft inspiring neither the sense of touch nor hearing, only the eyes."

To Bernard Ziegler this was Luddite rubbish: "After all, the airline pilots are no more than taxi drivers." This particular debate has been virtually extinguished with the commercial success of fly-by-wire design. Ziegler's winning argument, that a properly designed aircraft can virtually eliminate the possibility of pilot error, helped transform Airbus into one of the great business success stories of the 20th century.

Unfortunately the success of fly-by-wire technology does not eliminate the market for flight insurance. "Zero risk does not exist," says Arnoux at the beginning of a frank discussion of what could have gone wrong aboard Air France 447.

One of the contributing factors to the crash of a brand-new Air Inter Airbus A320 in Mont Sainte-Odile during a snowy winter night in January 1992 was a new clash between culture and design. Unfortunately the maverick carrier had chosen not to install a Ground Proximity Warning System (GPWS) on its new fly-by-wire fleet. This was a standard fitting for most airlines, but was refused by Air Inter management and pilots as this safety device was considered "troublesome" during high-speed approaches, delivering "nuisance" alerts as the pilots routinely exceeded the boundaries for the GPWS warning parameters.

Programmed to display upwards of 500 different emergency messages that would ostensibly tell pilots how to solve any problem, the new Airbus A320 always appeared to be able to provide the answer to every challenge. It could even anticipate potential conflicts that might mislead a flight crew.

Due to the protections integral to this French design, pilot training was streamlined, saving time and money. A series of design limits would reduce the margin of error by effectively preventing pilots from stalling their aircraft. In effect, they would not be able to fly outside the plane's envelope protection. Or as Ziegler liked tell to skeptics, the aircraft could be flown by his housekeeper.

While this may have only been a joke designed to pique interest in the plane, it was clear that the regulators were impressed by this Airbus breakthrough. Relying on the company's reassuring engineering documentation, regulators at the Joint Aviation Authority (which would become the European Aviation Safety Agency) waived the requirement to demonstrate that the new jet could recover from an aerodynamic stall in the unlikely event that these protections failed. The JAA accepted the company's position that the probability was so low that such a demonstration was not necessary as "deterrent" buffeting was supposed to be "dissuasive" enough to prevent any pilot from exiting the normal flight envelope.

The U.S. FAA would not accept the waiver and required the testing in spite of Airbus advertising of the moment: "A new intelligence is born."

In 1987, says Arnoux, a number of pilots were sent to Toulouse Airbus training center in 1987 to earn their A320 rating. An instructor from the prestigious military flying academy, École de l'Air, told the airmen their days on the flight line might be coming to an end.

"Hey, guys, you are going to sit in this cockpit and learn to fly this aircraft but before long there won't be anybody in those seats but premium passengers as this aircraft is going to fly by itself soon..."

What better proof could there be that the revolutionary Airbus fly-by-wire philosophy ("fly-by-computers" would have been more like it) was aviation's greatest modern breakthrough? Unlike previous legacy aircraft designs, this airplane was sold on the premise that it handled identically at different altitudes. In training pilots no longer had to make allowances for flying at high altitude where thinner air required them to use a lighter touch than they would need at low altitude on other aircraft.

Also, all of the fly-by-wire Airbus jets created after the A320 were very similar to one another. This standardization made it quicker and easier for pilots to transition from, say, the A320 to the A340. Cost savings realized by eliminating apparently unnecessary training would translate into lower fares, a true win-win for the airlines and the traveling public.

Airbus's optimism was seconded by accident investigators at the prestigious French Bureau d'Enquêtes et d'Analyses (BEA):

"The normal law of the fly-by-wire flight control system on the A330 offers high angle of attack protection that limits it to a value that is below the stall angle of attack. When this protection works, the airplane can thus not stall even if the crew maintains a full nose-up control input to stop."[1]

Airbus gave itself a standing ovation on this historic achievement in a special issue of its FAST magazine mailed to customers and their pilots. Airline training departments were lectured on the brand-new principles of large aircraft upsets and upset recovery techniques. Vice-president for Training and Flight Operations Pierre Baud spelled out the difference between the classic Airbus 300 flown by Dubois years earlier at Air Inter and the fly-by-wire A330 Air France aircraft now headed home to Paris.

In clear language that would appeal to the bean counters at any airline cutting a purchase order for the A320 or upcoming A330/340, he pinpointed how the newer models slashed training costs.

Acknowledging the lack of protections designed to prevent a stall on older planes, Baud treated the whole subject like the introduction of a new software operating system. Customers stuck with outdated planes would still be allowed to work the old-fashioned way. "Specific training about unusual situations will be provided on 'classic' types of aircraft," he explained.

Some pilots rolled their eyes as they read there was no need to waste valuable training dollars for the same purpose on Airbus's new failsafe planes:

"Information regarding the principles of recognition and recovery from the upsets will be provided on Airbus Fly-By-Wire protected aircraft, but specific training is not necessary."

When some carriers echoed this party line and discouraged their pilots from actually hand-flying the new plane, cultural collisions were inevitable. Even after decades of Airbus success not every training department agreed entirely with the Airbus philosophy. A good example was a major American carrier's decision to hire Avianca A330 pilots and fly them to the Midwest for training.

---

1. Consider the analogy of an automobile's anti-skid system. The anti-lock system prevents someone from "locking up the wheels" even if someone were to push on the brakes "to the stop" or as hard as they could.

One of these Latin American veterans, with six years experience flying the Airbus around the world, questioned his new employer's insistence that he hand-fly an A330 in simulator sessions and on check rides. This new hire admitted that during hundreds of passenger flights he had never actually flown the plane except for a few minutes during initial takeoff and final approach.

Under questioning, the Brazilian pilot confessed he had not used his stick-and-rudder skills above a few thousand feet where thinner air could dramatically alter the aircraft's handling characteristics. The aviator confessed that he was "scared" about demonstrating his ability to hand-fly the plane. His new flight instructors quickly explained that he would have to find a way to get over his fear of flying.

This new normal, as it were, challenged the traditional value of stick-and-rudder training. Carriers like Air France didn't want to pay for this frill, particularly when their pilots were effectively prohibited from hand flying above 29,000 feet where most air journeys took place.[2]

Pilots with limited opportunities to fly hands-on during commercial flights could certainly keep their stick-and-rudder skills sharp if they wanted to pay for small aircraft training on their own time. While helpful, this supplemental training was no substitute for experiencing how a big airplane handled at high altitudes.

Although the Air France pilots union SNPL pressed for more airline-paid stick-and-rudder training time, Captain Marc Dubois, who flew small aircraft and taught classes, was not an activist.

He liked to relax by working on his courtyard home in the tiny village of Saulx-Marchais. During the 18 years he had lived in his wife Sophie's family village, he turned an old barn

---

2. Separation on transoceanic routes spacing has been reduced. Pilots are effectively required to fly on autopilot above 29,000 feet to avoid deviating from their assigned altitude and risking a collision. The sensitivity of the controls is much greater at higher altitudes where even a small input can lead to a very rapid climb or descent.

into an impressive two-story residence where the couple raised their two children. A trained carpenter and mason who used native limestone inside and out, Marc was an easy man to find, particularly when he was laying tile on his roof. Proud of his job, Marc frequently invited neighbors to accompany him on flights. One childhood friend and his Japanese spouse received repeated requests to join him on trips to Tokyo.

On May 28, 2009, just two months after his father's funeral, Marc said goodbye to his wife, left his beloved brick-and-timber home and drove to Paris Charles de Gaulle. The captain was well known in the Air France community, in some measure because of his own history as a flight attendant who had broken the wall between himself and his colleagues in the passenger cabin. On one flight he walked to the rear of the aircraft and greeted an unrelated flight attendant who shared his common last name. This kind gesture astonished colleagues who had never seen a captain in the rear galley. Relaxed and, according to his brother Jacques, a man who had never been drunk in his entire life, Marc appeared to succeed at anything he tried, from climbing the alps to building a swimming pool in his backyard. Marc also volunteered as an instructor at a local Paris flying club.

Despite his lack of interest in union politics there was one issue that did attract the captain's continuing attention. Marc told friends he didn't want to quit flying at 60 like his father was forced to do (a former Air France rule). He was eager to see Air France raise the mandatory retirement age to 65 in line with the new International Civil Aviation Organization (ICAO) recommendation adopted by the French authorities.

Dubois told friends it would be a pleasure to continue working until he was 70. Prior to 1995, the government did not impose an age limit for French pilots. This worked at his former employer, Air Inter, where a handful of pilots with valid medical certificates continued flying Caravelles or the Airbus A300 past the age of 65.

Co-pilot Pierre-Cédric Bonin, who had known he was going to be an Air France pilot from the age of five, shared the captain's love of flying. The son of a retired Air France pilot, Bonin, like his father before him, loved working for Air France.

A few days earlier, he and his wife Isabelle waved goodbye to their two young sons, left safely in the custody of his parents, and headed for Bordeaux's Merignac Airport. They had departed their hometown, a vast UNESCO world heritage site, on a commuter flight to Paris. As their plane climbed out over the vineyards of the Medoc, the Bonins looked forward to a short stay in Rio, their latest destination on aviation's version of a whistle-stop world tour. At Charles De Gaulle, he headed for the briefing room with Capt. Dubois and fellow co-pilot Robert, who had made the easy commute from the Paris suburb of Montreuil.

While Isabelle checked in, Pierre-Cédric reviewed the flight plan with his colleagues. This four-day journey with a long layover was a perfect fit for his busy life as a husband and father who also enjoyed running, aikido, and skiing on both snow and water.

Like online blind daters, these aviators connected through a scheduling computer. His fellow pilots eagerly bid for this desirable route pioneered by French pilots ferrying mailbags stacked up to their shoulders.

Pierre-Cédric Bonin had also taken his 59-year-old father and mentor Jean-Louis, an Air France Regional Air Captain, on short breaks. A few months earlier they had spent New Year's Eve together in New York's chilly Times Square. Father and son traveled well thanks to their many shared interests that included flying, sports, car racing and foreign cultures.

A passionate student of the arts, Bonin loved to visit galleries and historic cathedrals, as well as photographing world-class architecture. Isabelle, a teacher at Bordeaux's Lycée Gustave Eiffel, joined her husband on his long journeys when a substitute could be arranged. This was a blessing for their parents, who enjoyed extended time with their two young grandsons.

Their enviable life together had begun a decade earlier when Isabelle agreed to tutor this ambitious math student. They married at a romantic seaside cathedral, Cap Ferret's Notre Dame des Flots.

Illuminated by the sunlight streaming in through the oceanfront cathedral's stained glass, they said their vows and then celebrated with family and friends at this sugar-sand resort south of Bordeaux. Jean-Luis Bonin, who sailed to Brittany and Spain from his berth in adjacent Bassin d'Arcachon, frequently took his son's family on local sailing outings that included trips past Pilat, Europe's highest sand dune.

Because slightly less than perfect vision in his right eye made him ineligible for a coveted spot in the Air Force, Bonin completed his math studies and then, with his father's help, spent €60,000 for flight training at a local airport. They frequently flew together over the Cap Ferret coast in both fixed-wing aircraft and gliders.

An exceptionally talented pilot who always scored perfectly on his exams, Bonin had dreamed of being a pilot since he was a little boy. His passion was fueled by his wanderlust, a determination to see remote places others could only see in their dreams. The new hire took additional pilot training courses at Amaury de la Grange flight school in Melville. Type rated for the Airbus 320 in 2004, he qualified for the Airbus 330/340 series a year later.

Bonin, the plane's youngest pilot, had gone through upset recovery training before hiring on. He knew what it felt like to stall on a smaller aircraft and how to get out of it.

For years Bonin went beyond theoretical training in the simulator where some airborne environments could not always be reproduced. His solo flying experience was a benchmark for old-school pilots who believed nothing beat the self-reliance that came from flying by hand. With his experience in both the traditional and glass-cockpit worlds notably on A320 (318/319/321) the medium- and short-haul Air France workhorses, Bonin was clearly flight deck ready for the A330.

For Bonin, Dubois and Robert, the key to their successful careers was impressive knowledge of aeronautics and extensive hands-on flying experience. At a time when their airline was beginning to hire and train new pilots with no previous flying experience, these men all had impressive resumes.

The proficiency of flight crews like this one on a long international flight was taken for granted by most passengers. Unseen and often unheard except for brief departure and arrival announcement, pilots are nearly invisible to the billions of passengers boarding planes each year. Aviation futurists even talk about eliminating their jobs entirely and selling cockpit seats to premium customers.

Many passengers believe incorrectly that a pilots' job is less demanding today than it was 30 years ago thanks to technological upgrades that require less calculating and interpretation of "boiler gauge" flight instruments. It is true that instead of making math computations on paper with the aid of thick aircraft manuals and charts, pilots rely on computers to make lightning-fast calculations. The results are integrated on a single screen. Decisions are made so quickly that sometimes it is hard for the pilots to know exactly what the automated systems are doing.

This promising technology led directly to reducing cockpit crews from four to three and even two-man crews on short- to medium-distance flights. As long as the system works and operates within limits predicted by designers, the pilot's job is considered "routine." The treachery begins when critical technology, those systems that provide information or operate the aircraft, fail, which can happen if the limits predicted by the designers are exceeded or if algorithms are incorrect. Only the most important 10% of these designs are actually tested by air-framers or their subcontractor's engineers. It would take too much time and money to go through every single problem.

Aircraft designers, consciously or not, have relied on the fact that a well-trained pilot can fill "gaps" they missed to provide an adequate margin of safety. Equally worrisome are features that create a "wall" between pilot perception and reality. Emergency situations beyond the designers' vision create sudden upsets that demand a quick recovery. What might have looked like a good design to save work and reduce error can contribute to an accident. In the real world, things do not always happen as they are imagined by engineers, programmers or procedure designers.

Short of an accident, it can take the industry decades to make overdue reforms. Grounding a fleet to modify aircraft is an expensive proposition, especially when some airline insurance contracts only reimburse this cost for a mere three days.

Modern engineering design has addressed the major causes of past accidents by further "boxing in" the pilots. In the research laboratory humans have been seen as error-prone creatures that must be controlled and protected from themselves. This logic was based on the assumption that when the systems are running right only humans can be the source of a problem. Some critics argue that irresponsible pilots are responsible for as much as 80 per cent of all airline crashes. This view ignores the fact that pilots prevent many potential crashes. Good piloting is one of the reasons why there was only one jet hull loss for every 2.86 million flights in 2016.

From the 1970s through 1990s when many automation designs in current use were invented, many scientists tried to blame most air carrier accidents on pilots. In recent years some perceptive and unbiased researchers began questioning this unproven theory. They realized, correctly, that only a human being can fill the gaps when things do not go as anticipated in the drawing room. Naively optimistic designers expect a human to pick up the pieces when their machine makes a life threatening error. If a pilot fails to correct an unexpected and untrained-for machine error, the industry all too often shifts the blame. Suddenly everything is the fault of dead pilots who "made a human error" or "lost situational awareness." They are truly guilty until proven innocent.

Ironically, as flying gets safer, pilots face a new set of challenges. No matter where they went to flight school, how long they spent in the Air Force, how many hours they have flown or how recently they checked out in a simulator, a safe flight depends on a crew's ability to fly well beyond the scope of their training. It is left to the pilots to "fill the gap" between designer simulations and unfortunate events the engineers didn't see coming. Because nearly all of these designers and systems engineers are not commercial airline pilots, they may inadvertently create new and unexpected problems.

Fortunately, aircraft test pilots can test these new designs in the real world of flight. They can pinpoint unanticipated problems that will help the manufacturer make necessary modifications. The wrinkle is that test pilots are more skilled than the typical pilot. By handling aircraft anomalies subconsciously, they may not note or flag challenges that could be a problem for less-experienced pilots.

Of course, not every pilot recommendation on new designs is taken seriously because of cost considerations, marketing pressures, or acceptance of standard industry operating procedures. A case in point was a B-787 test pilot's concerns regarding the design of the auto-throttle system that was later a factor in the crash of an Asiana B-777 (that had the same design) in San Francisco. Pilots often are not aware of the design assumptions made by the engineers. This translates to a training program deficiency if the pilot's understanding, competency and performance could be enhanced by inclusion of that information in the training.

A 1993 B-747 Air France landing overshoot (runway overrun) in Tahiti was also a consequence of a mismatch between what the pilots expected the system to do and the way it was designed. The pilots assumed that the system was in normal landing mode.

Unbeknownst to them, the flight controls had actually moved into a "go-around" mode. The pilots fought to keep the auto-throttles from applying full thrust. When one of the four throttles slipped out of the pilot's hand during landing, the aircraft overshot the runway and ended up nose-down in the lagoon.

Since system failures are rare, pilots aren't always allowed to rehearse for worst-case scenarios. They must be able to identify and correct unprecedented problems when their flight instruments fail. That means that when they no longer have access to approximately 80 computers, the pilots must instantly stand in for both hardware and software systems that suddenly fail to accurately communicate. This kind of improvisation is hard work.

Flight crews must also be prepared for the unpredictable, and correct compound system errors rarely confronted during their routine training. When one of their colleagues makes a mistake in the cockpit, they must quickly identify the error and correct it on the spot. Like a figure-skating pair in the midst of a full axel, they have no time left to discuss making any adjustment.

At Air France, the modern miracle of relaxed and comfortable flight was a tribute to the brave aviators who pioneered this once-dangerous route for Compagnie Générale Aéropostale. Mishaps and accidents were once so common that ships were often scheduled to follow in the sea lane beneath the flight path in order to pick up survivors along the way — if there were any. On one 1930 flight, legendary French aviator Jean Mermoz was forced to ditch his Latécoère 28 flying boat due to mechanical difficulties. The captain and his co-pilot were rescued a day later by a ship trailing the plane's South Atlantic route. But on December 6, 1936, Mermoz, the three other crew members and their plane "La Croix du Sud" disappeared 380NM off the African coast en route to Natal after a last mayday saying they were cutting the rear right engine.

Many of these pioneer tragedies were dim memories surviving only in the pages of history books. Thanks to "normal law" protections, Air France 447 flew with computer protections safeguarding the plane from flying too fast or slow, or banking, climbing or descending too steeply. While automation did not reduce the pilots' workload, it did shift their focus toward what Airbus called "system management."

As pilots became familiar with fly-by-wire technology, they began asking themselves who was in charge. The pilots were taught how to manage the computers, but often it felt like the computers were managing the flight crew. Design limits meant that the pilots did not always have the final say. Management responsibilities shifted depending on how the plane was doing. There was also the disturbing possibility that there could be gaps when neither the computers nor the pilots were in control. This potential anarchy was certainly not what Airbus intended.

CHAPTER 3

The South Atlantic, June 1, 2009[3]

Well rested after their two days in Brazil, Dubois, Robert and Bonin are still required to take their assigned naps on the rigidly scripted flight home. Rest, even enforced rest, is welcomed on a night flight that required the crew to be awake well past their normal bedtimes. At the prescribed time, co-pilot Robert heads to the bunk behind the cockpit first while his colleagues guide the aircraft to its initial cruise altitude.

Despite all the work ahead, these aviators are delighted to be flying again after their time off in Brazil. Behind them in the passenger cabin, surfers are seated alongside families winding up Latin American holidays. Sharing the wine and *hors d'oeuvres* behind the cockpit are Michelin and Coca-Cola executives, political leaders from half a dozen countries, newlyweds, and enough musicians and singers to create an ensemble that would thrill the classical music buff up front, Captain Dubois.

Among the passengers is Pascal Linguet, credit manager for France's largest electrical components manufacturer, CGE Distribution. The only unaccompanied member of CGE's all-expenses-paid incentive award trip to Brazil, the 48-year-old

---

3. Chapters 3 and 4 are written from the perspective of the pilots and what they likely knew during the crisis. It benefits from details unknown to the flight crew at the time of these events. The pilots could only react to what they knew at the time and did not have the benefit of what investigators learned years later.

Linguet is also the oldest member of the 19-member CGE tour group.

After landing in Paris Linguet will head back to his home in Rilhac-Rancon, a commune on the outskirts of the porcelain center of Limoges, about 200 miles south of the capital. There his wife, Marie-Noëlle, and his two sons await his return. Together, Linguet and his wife had visited New York, Ireland, Venice, and the best of France. But when Linguet invited her to join him and his colleagues each traveling with a spouse, partner or friend, she declined and stayed home with their children.

Like many of his fellow employees, Linguet is a seasoned traveler, at home on a plane built by Airbus. But not everyone in the CGE group is relaxed about the trip. Twenty-three-year-old Laetitia Alazar is completing her first plane trip. Afraid of flying, she reluctantly decided to accept her ticket from a colleague who could not make the journey. Alongside her for the journey home is a reassuring friend, Aurelia Pasquet.

Seven political figures are on board including Luigi Zortea, mayor of Canal San Bovo, Italy; Chen Chiping, vice mayor of China's Liaoning province; Daniel Bencat, former mayor of Kozarovec, Slovakia; and Marcelo Parente, cabinet chief to Rio's mayor. Three municipal counselors from the French village of Ermenonville are also among the passengers. One is Anne Grimout, an Air France chief steward who is taking advantage of her employee discount to buy two seats for her friends, Nathalie Marroig and Marie-Josée Treillou.

Among the parents boarding with children are Christine Schnabl and her five-year-old son Philipe, heading back to Sweden to visit family. Taking advantage of airline frequent flyer points, her Brazilian husband Fernando and their daughter Celine left for Paris several hours earlier on another carrier.

Many performing artists have seats, including dancer Eithne Walls, who had appeared in Riverdance while studying to become a doctor; Fatma Ceren Necipologu, a Turkish harpist; Silvio Barbato, conductor of the Teatro Municipal de Rio de Janeiro; and Juilian de Aquino, a Brazilian singer heading to Germany to start rehearsals for the stage musical *Wicked*.

Numerous business executives and engineers booked on the flight included Canadian Coca Cola executive Brad Clemes, headed back to his home in Brussels, Luiz Roberto Anastacio, president of Michelin South America and two colleagues headed to meetings at the French headquarters of the company that makes tires for the entire Airbus fleet.

While they are in a good mood, the cordial flight crew is all business. Indeed, their cockpit is in every sense their flying office, complete with pullout worktables and a panoramic view of the illuminated coastal cities of South America.

In Recife, Dakar, the Canary Islands, Spain and southern France, this plane will be handled by a dozen control centers working seamlessly to make sure they are in constant communication all the way home.

Although the pilots don't know it, this aircraft, F-GZCP, is scheduled for service after landing in Paris. Crews are set to replace all three airspeed-monitoring pitot tubes mounted on the bottom of the aircraft.

Originally devised in the 18th century by French inventor Henri Pitot to calculate the velocity of water in the Seine, pitot tubes have been the primary airspeed measurement device since they were first installed on a DeHavilland plane in 1915. A hole in the front of the tube measures the dynamic air pressure hitting the moving aircraft. Holes on the side measure the ambient or static air pressure.

The difference between these two figures yields the airspeed — critical information integrated into the plane's Air Data and Inertial Reference Unit (ADIRU) linked to the flight control computers. This information is central to every phase of flight operation from takeoff to touchdown.

As a good corporate citizen, Air France is making this

A330/340 modification voluntarily under a program carefully worked out with Airbus, the French pitot manufacturer Thales, and the European Aviation Safety Agency.

By the time the plane reaches Recife and begins its Atlantic crossing, most of the passengers are asleep. Shortly before Robert's return to the cabin, Bonin and Dubois begin analyzing the flight path via their on-board weather radar.

"We're going past the equator. Did you feel the bump?" asks a deadpan Bonin. "Ah, no," says Dubois, not realizing his co-pilot was pulling his leg.

"Ah, well," replies Bonin. "There you are."

No longer in direct contact with the rest of the world, Air France 447 isn't even a blip on a controller's radar screen. Because an electronically transmitted Air France flight plan sent to the Dakar, Senegal center covering this remote region contains incorrect information, the normal electronic communication system is not able to hook up (much like having the wrong cell phone number prevents a call from going through). Communications via a 1940's vintage high-frequency network is all that is available.

For now no one can see or hear this aircraft hundreds of miles beyond the range of coastal radar. It heads across the Atlantic, electronically confirming its position to the company every 15 minutes via silently transmitted signals.

Out here in the middle of the ocean there is no visible light above or below. The Airbus moves across the pitch-black sky shrouded in clouds blocking starlight and the moon. Wind hitting the aircraft is the only outside sound Capt. Marc Dubois and co-pilot Pierre-Cédric Bonin can hear. Lights have been dimmed in the cabin to help passengers sleep.

Going by the book, all three pilots are scheduled for a mandatory three- to four-hour rest break. Unfortunately, there is no getting used to this schedule that requires flying at all hours across multiple time zones. Their circadian rhythm is a perpetual casualty on these long journeys. Still, they attempt to sleep on a regular schedule.

To stay alert, the pilots turn up the cockpit lighting to full brightness. This helps ward off the inherent fatigue linked with these long trips.

Captain Dubois and First Officer Bonin fly for three hours while co-pilot David Robert tries to rest. Technically, this journey is Bonin's turn to fly, but other than the takeoff and landing most of the trip is on autopilot. Bonin's job is to enter the autopilot commands and ensure they are followed. He also "hand flies" when the autopilot is off, generally below 10,000 feet, and oftentimes only in the few moments just after takeoff and just prior to landing. Dubois acts as the pilot monitoring, working the radios and backing up Bonin, even though he remains in command as the captain.

Dubois and Bonin review the emergency divert airport options for the oceanic portion of the flight. These airports are alternates in the event of an engine failure or other emergency. The weather is supposed to be reviewed, as are the notices updating runway and equipment conditions. The pilots send their request to the Air France operational control center (OCC) suggesting airport choices.

The OCC sends an electronic response recommending a different set of alternatives. Dubois and Bonin accept this decision rather than get into a debate. The pilots keep their alternate plan handy, knowing that the Captain can make the final decision in an emergency.

Flying above the cloud tops would be great if the plane were a little lighter. Up above they might catch the moonlight that could help them see and avoid looming storms. They may also spot a few flashes of lightning that will pinpoint convective cells and help them find smoother air.

Nonetheless, both pilots remain cautious about exceeding their assigned cruise altitude. The airplane is fuel heavy and further limited by higher-than-expected temperatures reducing lift.

The inability of their engines to produce sufficient thrust, plus limits on what the wings can do, restricts the crew's ability to safely climb in thin air. They must hold the plane at 35,000 feet, realizing that a climb could be a mistake, putting the plane into rougher air with tighter margins. Dubois and Bonin have the passengers to consider, as well as flight attendants who must travel the aisles with little protection against a sudden jolt.

Of course, this airplane has the latest on-board weather radar. Unfortunately, interpretation of that radar is as much art as science. It should all be science, but the industry has managed to get by with pilots passing down various tricks of the trade. This "good enough" approach, a kind of aviation folklore, is justified by the fact that ruggedly built planes virtually always survive bad weather at cruise altitude.

It might surprise passengers to know there is little concern about the enroute weather. For Dubois and Bonin, like most pilots, the weather ahead is more of a nuisance than a concern. During cruise, planes end up inside thunderstorms more often than the airlines admit. Mistakes caused by inadequate radar instruction can be compounded by the lack of good weather training (the latter ideally taught by aviation meteorologists).

Meanwhile, considering dense traffic, it is sometimes difficult to arrange for alternative routing while in cruise. This should have been taken care of in advance by the OCC, in case of expected severe weather. The OCC can be reluctant to lengthen the flight, lose time delaying the next leg to be flown by the aircraft and spend more fuel. In truth, they are not really in the position to micromanage the flight in this manner. While they might be able to, and generally will, plan the flights around large areas of bad weather, choosing a path through thunderstorms is quite challenging considering how dynamic the situation can be. What is left to crews is circumnavigating thunderstorms the best they can. But some young first officers and even new captains don't dare to challenge controller instructions as they should.

Pilots, dispatchers and flight controllers are often at a disadvantage in a cost-conscious industry when it comes to avoiding weather. Meteorology is a vast field unto itself and few pilots, dispatchers or air traffic controllers get more than a rudimentary introduction to it. This may partially explain why study after study has proven that too many crews take unnecessary risks in bad weather, especially when it comes to operating in the vicinity of thunderstorms. Fortunately, these turbulent events seldom lead to catastrophe. It usually takes an accident for the industry to recognize this kind of problem and deal with it.

Dubois and Bonin start to experience St. Elmo's fire, which is essentially electrical buildup from friction that leads to harmless sparks arcing across the windshield. This break in the inky blackness outside lasts momentarily. Dubois says "it's snowing."

After dimming the cockpit lights, Bonin turns on the exterior lights to confirm that the plane is entering more cloud cover. Taking another look at the flight display, Bonin calculates that the plane is light enough for a small climb even though this new altitude would send their aircraft in the "wrong direction" for their heading. Both he and Dubois know a request would likely be turned down. They also realize there is a chance that the bumps will be worse with the climb and they could also be stuck at a higher altitude.

Air traffic controllers, working these planes via balky high-frequency (HF) radios, have other good reasons for not authorizing these changes. Pilots often have trouble understanding a ground controller over the whines and whistles of a system virtually unchanged since the 1940s. If a change is needed, it can be difficult to reach the pilots because the system relies on first sending a signal to activate a "chime" in the cockpit.

The pilots respond by calling and establishing communication which can be hard to understand through static in the best of conditions. The fact that neither the Air France pilots nor the ground controllers are native English speakers complicates conversations. They can easily be tripped up by unfamiliar English dialects.

Another difficulty is the fact that the ground operator talking on the HF radios is not the actual controller, but rather a third party relaying messages between the actual controller and the pilots. These "radio" operators add another potential layer of miscommunication. In addition, the controllers must separate airplanes without the benefit of radar. Instead, they track reported positions, times and altitudes, making hand calculations to prevent a potential collision. This is coupled with the problem of the modern digital data communication equipment remaining off line. This was triggered by the error in the Flight 447 flight plan sent earlier by the airline to Senegal air traffic control computers covering much of the South Atlantic sector.

Although neither pilot can see the horizon at this point, Captain Dubois is not worried about the weather as it was just as usual, a little bit "bumpy" in the inter-tropical convergence zone. Like all experienced pilots, he had seen and handled worse. By now it is time for Captain Dubois to take his required rest as planned by the three crew members (usually the order is decided during the preflight and the precise timing is calculated by the pilots before taking the first leave). It might surprise some non-pilots that he chooses to rest now with potential weather ahead, but in truth not much is showing on the radar and if he delays his rest he might not get any at all as there is the potential for more storms and turbulence later as well. Delaying his rest could actually increase the risk of him not being fully alert during the more risky approach and landing portion of the flight.

He pushes the button to chime the crew rest area located directly behind the cockpit, a set of narrow bunks sometimes referred to by pilots as the "coffin." A knock is heard on the wall signaling that co-pilot Robert is awake. Before taking his turn to retire for a rest, Dubois reconfirms that Bonin is fully qualified to serve as the acting captain. Robert comes forward to take the captain's seat. Familiar with this kind of weather, especially in the South Atlantic, he has flown this route more than Dubois.

The captain asks Robert how he slept. "So so," says the co-pilot, confirming that the first nap can be a challenge if the flight departs before a pilot tires.

Bonin updates Robert on the lack of a high-frequency radio link, the fact that they are too heavy to make a significant climb, and the forecast turbulence ahead. With everything in order, and satisfied with this short briefing, Dubois heads back to prepare for his rest, leaving Robert and Bonin up front, knowing that the flight is in good hands.

Why wouldn't it be?! Air France, like many other airlines, has opted for one commander and up to three copilots. The first officers are fully qualified to replace the captain during the enroute portion of the flight. The weather was, after all, very routine for this route.

They bid their captain good night, and turn to their jobs.

Traveling at eight or nine miles a minute, avoiding weather is mostly a "tactical" job for pilots on a dozen planes passing through this region tonight. While operations and dispatchers rely on broad weather forecasts derived from satellites, they are not able to see cloud-top heights that can have a major impact on planes at cruise, particularly when these cells top 50,000 feet.

Conditions change so rapidly that with the exception of major storm systems, such as a hurricane, most pilots take a "wait-and-see" approach. They use their on-board radar to avoid the tallest storms. This approach has, on balance, served the airline industry well for decades.

Just before 2am the copilots take a few moments to review the "Notices to Airman." These published advisories cover changes to airport procedures, maintenance and out-of-service equipment, as well as potential concerns with enroute navigational aids and related issues that might impact flight safety and planning.

Like doctors reading their medical journals, the pilots are determined to stay up-to-date. The pilots also discuss how much longer their flight will remain in the intertropical convergence zone. When turbulence increases slightly, they review the recommended maximum altitude determined by the flight's weight and outside temperature. After checking his radar at 2:06am, Bonin calls the flight attendants and suggests they take their seats, "It will be a little rougher than it was before."

As the pilots continue discussing the weather, they confirm that the autopilot remains connected to the flight management system. The Airbus remains secure in a protective envelope. While the automation keeps an eye on the airplane, the crew makes sure the computers are doing their job.

This cross-check routine on any flight includes a look at the flight mode annunciators (FMA), navigation and flight instruments, as well as a look at the flight director, an instrument that helps pilots ensure that their flight remains on the programmed course. The flight director normally reflects the same commands that are sent to the autopilot.

Given their experience, no one is surprised or worried. Switching to a 60-mile view on the radar screen, Robert points to a storm cell and suggests deviating to the left. Bonin does so and the pilots also switch on the engine anti-ice, providing extra protection even though the conditions technically do not require it. Robert turns the radar "gain" up to make the storms more prominent on screen. This will help them continue to pick their way around the worst of the storms.

At best, weather avoidance is a mix of knowledge and experience. This is more of an art, due to the lack of formal training provided by the airlines, and many unscientific "folk theories" passed down by well-meaning pilots. It's difficult to pinpoint every storm based solely on radar returns. Pilots are always on guard for those rare times when they might get slammed around.

Handicapped by incomplete training in meteorology, they keep an eye on the radar and listen to reports from air traffic controllers and nearby pilots.

While the forecasting system over water is far from perfect, pilots do their best to fly around convective storms, always attuned to subtle changes in smell, sound, temperature, or motion. Sound is especially important. Each component has a unique tone, from the engines to the air conditioning system. When they sound different, the pilot tries to sort out the cause. A staccato sound can indicate hail, while a buzz may signal an impending system failure.

The same is true for odors which can warn of a fire, hydraulic fluid leak or a chemical spill. It is important to bring these changes to the other pilots' attention, to make sure they aren't missing a signal.

"What's that smell now?" asks Bonin.

"It's ozone," says Robert, who knows about this common phenomenon in the inter-tropical convergence zone.

"It's ozone, that's it, we're alright," agrees Bonin.[4]

Seconds later the pilots hear a new sound they identify as rain hitting the windshield. Preparing for worse turbulence, Bonin selects the slightly lower airspeed recommended for a rough ride. He asks Robert to turn on engine ignition to make sure the engines can automatically relight in the event of a flameout.

Suddenly an unfamiliar alarm sounds. Their autopilot has just disconnected.

---

4. Storms in the tropics are often a bit different than other regions. The weather is usually worse at lower altitudes. The upper portion is not particularly turbulent but activity below can send the ozone upwards.

CHAPTER FOUR

Latitude 2.98°N/Longitude 30.59°W: the Last 264 Seconds[5]

Losing their trusted autopilot with no warning is startling and it prompts Bonin to take control of the aircraft while Robert immediately sends a chime to call the captain. Bonin instinctively reacts to loss of altitude displayed on the altimeter as well as on the rate of descent showing 400 feet a minute. He pulls back on his side stick controller, which looks like a big joystick. The aircraft warning system aurally calls "stall" twice, perhaps due to pulling back a bit too hard as a consequence of being startled.

For the first time, the pilots question their trusted instruments. "What is that?" asks Robert.

False warnings can happen and pilots are accustomed to confirming the validity of an alert on their flight display before reacting. Unfortunately, key parameters are unavailable and their trusted flight director displays have gone blank. The Electronic Centralized Aircraft Monitor (ECAM) is not

---

5. Chapters 3 and 4 are mostly written from the perspective of the pilots and what they likely knew during the crisis. It benefits from details unknown to the flight crew at the time of these events. The pilots could only react to what they knew at the time and did not have the benefit of what investigators learned years later. There are portions that are speculative. We cannot know what the pilots were actually thinking, nor the actual perceptions of the passengers and flight attendants. The portions regarding the pilots likely perceptions are based on author Malmquist's actual experience as a senior international captain coupled with his extensive safety and accident investigative work. This is supplemented by the opinions of other experts, including NASA researchers, multiple articles and books written on the topic and, of course, the official report itself.

displaying any warning related to this unexpected situation.

Is this alarm correct? At the moment the airplane feels like it is flying fine. Before they have time to react, a serious new problem appears, one neither pilot has seen outside a low-altitude simulator exercise.

"We've lost the [expletive] speeds," says Bonin, concerned that airspeed is no longer displayed on their screen.

Pilots learn early in their training that the range of safe speeds at cruise altitudes can be narrow. Fly too slow and the plane will stall. Flying too fast can cause an overspeed. Without airspeed information, the acting captain doesn't know if the aircraft is overspeeding or underspeeding.

These speed boundaries become the highest priority. If the plane were overspeeding Bonin would have to cut the thrust and perhaps raise the nose. But if he guesses wrong and the plane is actually underspeeding, he could trigger a stall. Without matching secondary indications confirming the earlier momentary stall alarm, it's hard to pinpoint the right response. Equally important, many pilots are under the false impression that loss of airspeed indications can lead to a bogus stall warning. At this point there is no reason to think there is a risk of stalling.

The Airbus alerting system includes a provision that looks at all three airspeed indications supplied by the external tubes. When the airspeeds differ, a warning is triggered. Absent this, a pilot may not know whether all or some of the airspeed information furnished by the pitot tubes is accurate. The pilot, of course, can disregard the airspeed information if he or she suspects all the pitots have failed.

There is good reason for pilots to be suspicious of dubious airspeed readings. Over the years, insects, tape, ice and snow have blocked air intakes leading to crashes of civilian and military aircraft. Electronic malfunctions have also sent incorrect airspeed information to flight control computers, which have then inadvertently sent planes into rapid ascents or sudden dives.

One of the worst incidents took place near Perth, Australia, on October 7, 2008, when a Qantas Airbus A330 dived suddenly as it automatically tried to gain speed and avoid a hypothetical stall signaled by a faulty Air Data Inertial Reference Unit computer. In that event, it was the inertial part of the unit which appeared to have failed for unexplained reasons. Thirty-six passengers were injured.

More frequently, water and ice are key factors behind pitot tube failure leading to incorrect airspeed indication. When water enters a pitot tube, a heating system prevents freezing. This same system is designed to melt snow or ice that clogs the intakes. But if ice blocks the tube or clogs an intake, the pitot can act like an altimeter, providing dangerously inaccurate airspeed readings that rise and fall as the plane climbs or descends. This can mislead the pilot and create an overspeed or underspeed situation.

Failing to recognize a pitot problem can trigger a crisis for pilots and air traffic controllers. In 1996 a Boeing 757 Aeroperu jet was brought down by incorrect airspeed information after maintenance crews failed to remove protective tape covering the pitot tubes. Even a preflight visual inspection by the flight crew did not catch the error.

When the flight crew radioed in to air traffic control for altitude information, they were given what proved to be fatal data based on a transponder signal that relied on the plane's own inaccurate airspeed information.

Flight 447's airspeeds have failed. Normally one computer goes bad, or perhaps a bug gets stuck in one of the pitot tubes. This is a much more serious problem because the warning system does not immediately signal a major anomaly. It is possible that this was due to the airspeeds failing in unison. Perhaps the system is trying to confirm that it is a valid problem before alerting the pilots.

Per design, there should have been two different possible warnings in such a situation. One occurs if the Air Data parts of the ADIRU fail together at the same time and the warning should be "NAV ADR 1+2+3 FAULT." The other would be if the Air Data differs between the inputs to show a difference in indicated airspeed of 15 to 25 knots. That is the situation ultimately encountered by Air France 447. In that case the warning per design should have been: "NAV ADR DISAGREE SPEED CROSSCHECK." The designers never imagined that all three pitots would essentially agree on the same incorrect airspeed coupled with a failure of the warning system. In this case, a critical triple backup system has completely failed. All of this is beyond the scope of Air France training and does not appear in any flight manual. Because they are considered highly unlikely, rare events like this one are not trained for.

Known and studied icing conditions are mitigated by properly heating the tubes. Unfortunately the phenomenon of high-altitude impact ice was rare and poorly understood. Only aviation meteorologists, who rarely train pilots, dispatchers or air traffic controllers, fully understood the potentially catastrophic risks of this special icing condition. Air France 447 had run into a condition beyond the designers' imagination. Now everything depended on human resilience — the pilots — to avert catastrophe.

Unfortunately no airline flight crews were trained on how to handle the situation in which these pilots found themselves.

Reading from the system display screen Robert calls out "alternate law protections" and below it "MAX SPEED........330/.82." This means the plane no longer handles like a fly-by-wire Airbus in normal law. The dramatic shift is a great leap backward for the crew to a much less sophisticated airplane, one not designed to be flown in the traditional basic mode. To the crew's surprise the airplane handles much differently.

Given a test in a classroom, most would understand the major differences on how the plane handles under "normal law" and "alternate law." They would know that under alternate law the Airbus's flight control system no longer had the protections against stalls or overspeeding found in "normal law."

Tonight, the pilots of Air France 447 are not in a classroom, they are hundreds of miles from land. It's unrealistic to expect them to recall all the subtle nuances of degraded flight controls briefly taught years earlier in initial training. This daunting challenge has never been revisited in simulator or hands-on training. Also, none of the pilots had ever been told about an accident or near accident related to alternate law flight in an extraordinary inter-tropical convergence zone storm. They know nothing about weather conditions that might dramatically impact their instruments.

The prominent next line on their display screen adds to their confusion and becomes an important turning point in this emerging drama. They are told in no uncertain terms that maximum speeds for the airplane are now reduced. From the pilot perspective this is critical. The computer is clearly warning Bonin and Robert that it will not protect their plane against overspeed. In the pilot's mind the emphasis is clear, it must be important! Lacking is a similar emphasis for flying too slow.

Key parameters the pilots must have to do their job have either disappeared or are incorrect.

Robert rings the chime again for the captain to come forward. He does not hear the expected confirming knock on the wall.

Reading from the system displays, Robert confirms that the auto-throttle has disengaged.

For the first time in their careers, the pilots now have an unanticipated opportunity to learn how to go back to basics and hand-fly at cruise altitude. In the past pilots would often hand-fly airplanes at cruise altitude, gaining experience naturally while doing their job. Fly-by-wire added another layer. While certainly easier to fly when the system was working, the transition to a degraded state added a major challenge.

The problem is similar to stopping a car in slick conditions with anti-lock brakes. Unfortunately, a person who grew up only driving cars equipped with anti-lock brakes might not know what to do when that system failed. With no experience on older cars they might have forgotten that someone once warned them to simply "pump the brakes."

The pilot's job was easier when the system worked the way the designers intended in normal law. Unfortunately a new challenge had been created for the degraded alternate law flight mode.

This was the critical fact missing from the famous article in the Airbus magazine on the advantages of fly-by-wire. In arguing against stall avoidance and upset recovery training for pilots flying their new planes, the company appeared to have missed a key point. Losing the normal law system meant that advanced aircraft presented tricky challenges at cruise altitude. Depending what systems are lost, it might fly entirely like a conventionally controlled airplane (direct law) where the pilot would have to adjust inputs to compensate for any surprises. In the case of Air France 447, the plane went to alternate law where the pitch control felt the same as normal law (but lacked the protection features that prevented stall or overspeed), however, the roll control was in direct law. At this point the advantages of fly-by-wire control systems envelope protection systems are lost and the plane handles like a traditional legacy aircraft in roll mode, and this is quite different than the normal law and requires a light touch to prevent overcontrolling. In normal law just neutralizing the side stick stops the roll, but now the natural aerodynamic and inertial properties dominate and it is a bit tricky for the uninitiated.

The switch to "traditional flying" is accompanied by several unpleasant surprises. In this degraded flight mode, a fly-by-wire aircraft can be less stable than a legacy plane. That is why the Airbus flight crew operating manual recommends to descend 4,000 feet below the optimum flight level, which was FL350 for Air France 447. The problem is that this sophisticated plane is a bit harder to handle in roll when it is not operating in normal law. While the pitch control would feel the same, the amount of concentration for roll will impact the pilot's ability to maintain an altitude. This is coupled with the fact that it takes a very small change in pitch to cause a very rapid climb or descent just due to the high speeds involved in cruise flight. A one degree pitch change can mean 800 feet a minute climb or descent or more and the roll control feels much more sensitive as previously described. An action that would be limited under fly-by-wire controls is magnified in direct law. Without normal law protections, the flight crew needs to use a light touch on their side stick controllers.

Unaware of this critical issue, the training departments at Air France and other airlines made a mistake. They failed to realize that even pilots like the crew of Air France 447, who knew and understood hand flying on older planes, needed to practice stick-and-rudder training at high altitude with both fully functioning controls and with degraded flight controls on this fly-by-wire aircraft. Without this experience they had no feel for the handling characteristics of their Airbus at cruise altitude, particularly in degraded modes.

The designers were also at a disadvantage because the high-altitude ice crystal phenomenon was not understood at the time they designed the systems for the Airbus. The potential size of the ice crystals was significantly underestimated. Despite this latent problem, the A330 flew for ten years without airline recognition of the potential problem. The trouble began when the aircraft was fitted with the Thales C16195AA pitot probes, which first entered service in 1998 although the first incident on the A330/340 Air France fleet was not until September 2004.

In September, 2008, the pilot of a Paris-bound Air Caraibes A330 flight from Martinique tried to climb over rough air and hit extreme turbulence. According to a blistering 13-page memo to Airbus from the small carrier's chief safety officer, Hugues Houang, the pilot followed the recommended turbulence procedure by reducing airspeed. The pitots iced up, leading to loss of airspeed indication, quickly moving the plane into alternate law.

Unfortunately, the crew had difficulty following the unreliable speed indication emergency checklist. Contradictory instructions regarding stall warnings in heavy turbulence challenged the crew, which was able to troubleshoot the problem. After discussing this issue with Airbus engineers, Houang wrote that the company agreed to modify their checklists.

Air Caraibes quickly decided to switch pitots on their four A330s (including the aircraft later sold to President Sarkozy) to the Thales BA model. While Air France also began difficult discussions with Airbus about the crystal ice/pitot issue, the airline waited until late 2008 to generally notify pilots about the problem through a note from the flight safety officer.

As reports of more high-altitude pitot icing problems continued to come in, Air France decided to install the BA tubes in the spring of 2009. At the airline's urging, the delivery schedule was expedited, and replacements arrived a few days before the A330 operating as Air France 447 left for Rio.

The pitot icing requirements are linked to icing standards used for engine intakes. The airline industry began experiencing unexplained icing-related engine malfunctions toward the end of the 20th century. In 1999 the FAA's Ice Protection Harmonization Working Group began working on an NTSB recommendation to amend icing requirements. Unfortunately, nobody in this air worthiness group, including European Aviation Safety Agency staff, recognized that the same problem also threatened pitot performance.

The FAA's first new requirements covering crystal icing were issued by the FAA in 2014, 20 years after scientists first recognized the hidden dangers of this weather anomaly. The regulatory community's lack of urgency surrounding the unique dangers of crystal ice minimized industry concern. The fact that ice crystal conditions at high altitude could potentially defeat the backed-up airspeed monitoring system was never anticipated.

Industry experts based their incorrect assumptions on the lack of a history of significant problems. Pilots had flown legacy aircraft hands-on with no problem through these conditions, or at least without significant problems, and the reporting systems were less robust if any problems had occurred. Hand flying was relatively common in legacy aircraft prior to the 1990s, and these traditional aviators learned through experience that airplanes are much more sensitive to control at high altitudes and high speeds than at lower altitudes and lower speeds. The pilots who hand-flew these big jets developed muscle memory on how to handle the controls with tender loving care. They made only the smallest corrections at altitude because a big one might create a stall buffet or a large and unexpected climb or descent. Pilots got in the habit of watching their instruments, making small changes and then waiting to see the results before proceeding.

By the early 21st century, when regulations started limiting pilots from hand flying at cruise, most pilots still had previous stick-and-rudder experience at high altitudes. Absent a known problem or a regulatory requirement, there was no incentive to add training to compensate for the fact that younger pilots like Robert and Bonin were effectively prohibited from stick-and-rudder flying advanced jets above 29,000 feet.

Backed up by the argument that fly-by-wire aircraft would handle the same at high altitude as at lower altitudes, airlines had no incentive to add this important training to a packed schedule under constant cost-cutting pressure, nor even a reason to believe it was necessary. Newer fly-by-wire pilots never learned that light touch so vital to maintaining controlled flight during high-speed, high-altitude cruise.

However, now, the failure of their company (and the

industry) to prepare them for this moment created an unexpected crisis on a plane designed to fly under a well-designed but now partially functional flight-control system.

The aircraft is climbing, but neither pilot seems to notice, likely because it is taking a lot of effort to keep the plane stabilized as the wings rock side to side. This phase lasts about 30 seconds. The flight director, a system that provides essential guidance, is still blank.

When hand flying, most pilots use the flight director full time to stay on course and at the desired aircraft pitch attitude. They spend very little, if any, time flying without it. The flight director is designed to command the ideal pitch and bank angle to fly the desired path selected by the pilot. Losing this critical resource in mid-flight and under storm conditions makes a flight more challenging.

"Watch your speed, watch your speed!" calls Robert, who is concerned that the plane is accelerating.

"OK, I'm going back down," responds Bonin.

"According to all three you're going up so go back down," says Robert. "Okay," responds Bonin.

The flight director suddenly pops back on and commands an aircraft nose pitch-up. The flight director is very compelling and hard to ignore. It jibes with the display warning to be careful of overspeeding, which many pilots learn in early ground training can lead to losing control due to what is known as "Mach tuck."[6]

Following the flight director's guidance, Bonin pitches the nose up and climbs.

Once again, the plane approaches the stall threshold.

The warning system starts calling out "stall stall," followed by a "cricket" sound.

It has been 30 seconds since the autopilot disconnected.

Bonin is struggling to control the hard-to-handle plane,

---

6. In the early days of jet airplanes, pilots who flew too fast would find themselves in a situation where the supersonic shock wave moved the pressure such that the airplane pitched downwards uncontrollably.

now rolling back and forth.

The airplane is pitched up at a much steeper angle than normal cruise, similar to the climb that occurs a bit after takeoff. At this point it is very difficult for the flight attendants or pilots to move about the cabin.

Some of the automation continues working, but it's hard to know how well it's performing and why key components like the flight director continue going off and on.

The plane begins to shudder as it continues rocking.

Now, even the more experienced flight attendants are worried. Chimes sounding from the back may be the passengers ringing call buttons as flight attendants call one another.

Robert continues trying to get Captain Dubois to come forward, but it appears he is not in the crew rest area. Could he be in the lavatory where the chime would not be audible? When a flight attendant calls the cockpit, the pilots do not respond.

The airplane appears to be still climbing, but can the altimeters be trusted? They are driven by some of the same sources as the airspeed. Might they also be corrupted? Why is the airplane not responding?

Bonin calls for maximum thrust but there is not much more available in this thin air. The airplane is still rolling back and forth and sideways, a great concern to the pilots. The flight directors are popping into and out of view. When visible they are commanding another pitch-up.

By now, the stall warning is sounding fairly continuously but this noise has become just a nuisance sound in the background as the pilots frantically try to trouble-shoot the problem. The confusion many pilots experience with airspeed indications and stall warning may be contributing to the uncertainty. Could the stall warning be a false alarm due to the lack of correct airspeed readings?[7]

---

7. In a study conducted by Captain Malmquist it was found that a majority of pilots incorrectly believed that the stall warning could be triggered by a faulty airspeed system.

The aircraft has climbed to almost 38,000 feet and begins, for some unexplained reason, to fall.

Robert and Bonin can feel the descent—similar to a runaway elevator. For the passengers, the turbulence is like nothing they have seen. Some try to sleep and wait, others are scared. The seat belt sign is on, but there is no explanation from the pilots over the intercom.

"But we've got the engines, what's happening?" asks Robert, referring to the fact that the plane is at full power. "Do you understand what's happening or not?"

The flight directors still command a pitch-up.

It has been just over a minute since the autopilot disconnected.

"I don't have control of the airplane anymore now" responds Bonin. "What is going on?"

Adding to the confusion is the disconnect between the aircraft monitoring system and its stall-warning system. Compounding this problem is Air France's decision to not install optional angle-of-attack indicators commonly found on military aircraft and on some of the first Airbus A320s ordered by the company and the French regional carrier Air Inter in the late 1980s.

Angle-of-attack indicators would clearly warn the pilots that their aircraft is unexpectedly entering a stall. Without them or training on this emergency situation, the flight crew fails to realize that the aircraft is entering an aerodynamic stall. As the angle of attack reaches an extremely high 45 degrees, low airspeed shuts off the stall warning system. This problem is triggered by the fact that there is not enough forward airflow and the system cuts off the stall warning. By design, if the airspeeds fall below 60 knots it is assumed that there is not sufficient airflow for the angle of attack vanes to be considered reliable. This is counterintuitive for most pilots who expect the stall warning to stop as the nose is lowered (reducing the angle of attack) and for the warning to come on when the nose is raised (increasing angle of attack). Here the stall warning *stops* as the angle of attack is increased and vice versa!

This on-again, off-again alert confirms the pilots' impression that the stall warning system may have broken down. Neither pilot knows if they can trust the intermittent alarms. By now the situation is well beyond any recovery maneuver the pilots have been trained for.

Robert tries his hand at the controls.

"I have the impression we have the speeds," says Bonin. The two co-pilots continue struggling with the controls.

The aircraft is exceeding the normal three degree pitch and rocking excessively.

This goes on for a few more seconds when Captain Dubois returns to the cockpit.

The high deck attitude combined with the rolling may have made it more difficult for him to come forward since Robert chimed for his return to the cockpit a minute earlier.

Did he even hear it, or is he checking on the shaking and rolling? "What are you doing?" asks Captain Dubois as he comes forward.

"What's happening, I don't know what's happening?" blurts out Robert, now clearly agitated.

The stall warning, which was present just as Dubois entered the cockpit, goes silent.

Everyone stands confused. As the plane continues falling rapidly, Robert pulls the power back a bit, probably trying to reduce the possibility of overspeeding.

The aural stall warning then resumes but the pilots are focused on the oscillations rolling the aircraft from side to side. They are determined to avoid loss of control.

Behind them, in the passenger cabin, the flight attendants are nervous, looking to each other for reassurance. They know these are experienced pilots flying a safe airplane on a first-tier airline, even if the weather is terrible.

The stall warnings stop again, but it makes no difference as the pilots have tuned them out entirely. Bonin is now focused on another critical issue.

"I don't have vertical speed information. I have no more displays." In the back the flight attendants hear an unfamiliar whistling sound.

Although Flight 447's nose remains pointed up at around 10°, the shaking plane continues falling at a very steep angle. The shuddering and rocking now has the attention of everyone on the airplane. Even the sleepiest passenger is awake.

"I have the impression that we have some crazy speed what do you think?" says Bonin in an attempt to summarize what he is seeing and hearing.

The flight directors he has been trying to follow with limited success are still popping in and out.

It has been two minutes since the autopilot disconnected. Bonin reaches to extend the speed brakes, a handle on the pedestal that extends panels on the upper surface of the wings. Pilots often use speedbrakes to help slow the aircraft down, was he thinking they were going too fast?

"No, above all, don't extend," says Robert perhaps because speedbrakes are also often utilized to increase the rate of descent which is already high in this case.

"...Okay," says Bonin. "So we're still going down."

"We're pulling, what do you think about it? What do you think we need to do?" Robert asks Capt. Dubois.

"I don't know," says Dubois.

Because pilots are trained to focus on problem solving, they remain relatively calm given the confusion. In this case there is no reason for them to think they won't recover, and years of experience has taught them that they will. They just want to know how and when. After all, they are flying an Airbus certified on the basis of engineering data showing that it could not depart the protective flight envelope.

Bonin takes back the controls, again trying to hold the plane upright and prevent it from rolling over. The stall warning starts again but is still ignored as a nuisance.

Despite Bonin's attempts, the airplane is continually rolling off into a steep bank. "The wings to flat horizon," commands Dubois, telling Bonin to right the airplane.

Dubois is clearly concerned that too steep a bank could lead to a further loss of control. Bonin tries to comply but it is a challenge. Is something wrong with the controls?

In an exchange showing the confusion and conflicting indications Robert says, "Speed? You're climbing," trying to sort out the confusing indications.

A second later he says "You're going down down down." Meanwhile, the flight directors command another pitch-up.

The stall warning stops for a few seconds and Bonin announces that he has selected maximum thrust from the engines.

"What alti, what do we have here?" he asks trying to make sense of the unclear altitude display.

"It's impossible!" says Dubois. Nothing is adding up, the displays are indicating a situation that should not be possible. The only explanation is that they are either caught in something completely outside their experience or the instruments are wrong.

It has now just been two and a half minutes since the autopilot disconnected. Bonin again asks, "What alti do we have?"

"What do you mean on altitude?" asks Robert. "Yeah, I'm going down, no?" says Bonin.

"You're going down, yes," calls Dubois as the plane banks. "Get the wings level!" he orders.

"Get the wings horizontal," echoes Robert.

"That's what I am trying to do. I'm at the limit with the roll," responds Bonin.

What is wrong with the controls? Why won't they respond? The fight displays match nothing they have experienced in training. The airplane is rolling but not responding to their commands. The flight controls are failing to hold the aircraft pitch, which continues wobbling up and down.

Robert gives it a try and after a moment says, "I've got nothing there." Three minutes have passed since the autopilot disconnected.

"How come we're continuing to go down right now?" exclaims Bonin.

As the plane continues descending at 10,000 feet per minute, Robert, thinking they may be having a software problem, asks Dubois to try to reset the control computers.

The captain responds that it won't help, but tries anyway. It takes a few moments for the system to reset itself.

Bonin continues struggling to keep the airplane upright. Dubois is mostly monitoring, calling out deviations that he sees: "Careful with the rudder bar there."

Sadly, there is not much to say, the indications are just not adding up to a coherent fix. The flight directors continue commanding a pitch-up.

It has now been about three and a half minutes since the autopilot disconnected.

A pilot never wants to have a descent rate that will result in hitting the ground in less than a minute—but Flight 447 is now well inside the "one minute to live" boundary.

Passing through around 8,000 feet, Robert says "Climb, climb, climb!" Bonin responds that he is trying.

"No no no, don't climb," counter-orders Dubois.

It is not clear what he is thinking. Does the combination of a high descent rate and nose-up attitude seem incorrect? He does not say.

"So go down," echoes Robert and then adds, "Give me the controls." "Go ahead, you have the controls," says Bonin. The flight director is still commanding a pitch-up.

A moment later Dubois warns, "Watch out, you're pitching up."

"Well we need to, we are at four thousand feet," says Bonin.

Dubois realizes they have no alternative because the plane is too low and descending way too fast. There are no other options left.

"Go on, pull!" says Dubois.

It has just been four minutes and five seconds since the autopilot disconnected. "Let's go, pull up, pull up" says Bonin, perhaps talking to the airplane at this point, pleading with it to climb.

"We're going to crash, this can't be true, but what's happening?"

"Ten degrees pitch attitude," says Dubois, resigned to hit the water at the best possible angle and hopefully minimize the damage.

CHAPTER 5

"I Have To Fly"

As the A330 went down, its Aircraft Integrated Data System and Centralized Fault Display System transmitted a series of malfunctions and failures via satellite over the jet's Aircraft Communications and Reporting Systems (ACARS) to company headquarters at Charles de Gaulle Airport in Roissy north of Paris. This document, which would become known as the plane's last will and testament, triggered no alarms at the airline's French maintenance base. Staff assumed that the ACARS messages were signaling equipment failures that needed to be remedied upon the aircraft's arrival in Paris. They saw no reason to notify operations that Flight 447 might be lost at sea.

Because the oceanic flight was not being actively monitored on a radar screen, controllers in Dakar, Senegal responsible for the plane at this point in its journey, did not see it crash. They were not expecting the aircraft because Air France operations had accidentally omitted Dakar in a routine email message with 447's flight plan to control centers on the trans-Atlantic route.[8] Even after the Senegal center was notified by Brazilian controllers that the flight was en route, a communication mix-up led to confusion about the plane's whereabouts.

More than two hours after the plane crashed, controllers in the Canary Islands, who had received the original Air France

---

8. Author's interview with Col. Xavier Mulot, Roissy-En-France.

447 flight plan, called Dakar for a position report. The Senegal control center tried and failed to contact the plane via high frequency radio. Other pilots in the region also had no word from the flight.

At 6:18am (Paris time) another Air France jet messaged headquarters that it was unable to contact Flight 447. Minutes later the company sent an ACARS message from Paris to the missing plane. A little after 10am (Paris time), not long after maintenance began putting a crew together to fix the problems catalogued by ACARS after Flight 447 arrived in Paris, Air France initiated emergency search and rescue tracking.

By 11am the airline had put a crisis center into place, and the airline's CEO, Pierre-Henri Gourgeon, received a devastating call from Gilbert Rovetto, the company's senior vice president for operations. Gourgeon learned that controllers at air traffic centers downline from Atlantico confirmed they had no contact with the missing flight.

"That meant it was very likely we had lost an aircraft," said Gourgeon. Across the airfield Colonel Xavier Mulot, head of research at the Interior Ministry's Air Transport Police, hastily convened a meeting with representatives from the nation's aviation authority, the DGAC, and its accident investigation unit, the BEA, as well as the federal prosecutor's office[9].

President Nicolas Sarkozy was briefed at the meeting before being driven to de Gaulle Airport to console more than 70 relatives waiting for word in a briefing room. As airline officials shared the tragic news, Paris was at the end of a three-day holiday weekend. Pentecost Monday had begun with perfect weather, an ideal day for a bike ride in the Bois de Boulogne or a Bateaux Mouche excursion on the Seine.

But as next of kin notification began, the tranquility of a holiday gave way to a grim reality. Within the Air France community, cell phones began to ring and text messages suddenly popped up around the world. There was word that

9. Ibid.

military aircraft had left Dakar to search for the missing jetliner.

In busy sidewalk cafés, talk quickly shifted from Rafael Nadal's loss the day before in the French Open to rumors about a crash. At 1:30pm the story went live on Paris television, radio and the web. Journalists were stunned. "How, in the era of Mars landings and stock prices on cell phones carried into the Himalayas, does an aircraft with two-hundred-twenty-eight people, eight of them children, go missing?" wrote the *Christian Science Monitor*'s Robert Marquand.

Clergy was summoned to assist the families, along with counselors and staff who began notifying next of kin. Reporters continued to break in to regular programming to somberly provide the latest updates. Hopes for a miracle were dashed the following morning, when the Brazilian Air Force spotted two debris fields 620 miles northeast of the coastline. Ships sped toward the wreckage. Images of the recovered tail fin, striped with the red-white-and-blue colors of Air France (and the French flag) appeared in news stories around the world.

In 32 countries, mourners wept. President Nicolas Sarkozy joined 10,000 mourners at Notre Dame Cathedral for a June 3 ecumenical service. During his eulogy at Paris's Notre Dame Cathedral's interfaith memorial for the victims of Air France 447, Aeroport Charles De Gaulle chaplain Rabbi Haïm Korsia spoke of the "brotherhood that unites all, believers or not. We must love because they loved, believing as they believed, hope as they hoped. We are the temple of their doom."

Evoking the memories of other fallen French aviators like Aéropostale pioneers Antoine de Saint-Exupéry and Jean Mermoz, thousands of Jews, Muslims, Catholics, Christians and even atheists read in French, English, Portuguese and Arabic from the Book of Lamentations of Jeremiah and the Gospel of Luke and the Koran. After a choir sang the 42nd Psalm, Monsignor Patrick Jacquin urged participants to take home a candle to honor the memories of all those lost.

"Our mission was to bring our passengers home safely,

and we failed," CEO Gourgeon said afterward. "Everyone in the company was thinking: 'This is not Air France.' It was a very emotional moment."

Around the world, memorials in churches, synagogues, and mosques were accompanied by smaller gatherings on the great surfing beaches of Brazil and villages of County Down, Ireland. From Catalonia to Korea, thousands mourned their lost loved ones and cherished friends. Heartfelt eulogies were delivered in Turkish, Swedish, Russian, Icelandic, Filipino, Mandarin and Cantonese, and many other languages. Small communities in France, where many of the country's 73 victims lived, were devastated. Others, such as Captain Dubois's friend and fellow Air France pilot Arnaud Lorente, grieved privately. Sitting in his Biarritz home he read and reread "the message he sent me where he insisted that we leave together."

One of the most touching memorials for the victims of Air France 447 was a poetic oceanfront ceremony for Brazilian orthodontist Jose Rommel Souza and the love of his life, Isis Pinet. A brilliant doctor who spoke four languages and always kept a close eye on surf reports, Souza had been on holiday in Brazil with Pinet, a Moody's financial analyst from Paris. Friends believe they may have married during their visit to Brazil, because she appeared on the passenger list with his surname. Apparently the couple was returning to France to visit her parents.

Well-known for his remarkable surfing skills with the pipeline set, Souza had friends around the world. "He was a fantastic surfer and an inspiration to keep going at it even if you're having a bad day surfing," said his friend Rupert Gaunt.

In an interview with *Surfer Magazine*'s Taylor Soppe, Gaunt recalled the legendary story of Souza's ride on an Uluwatu, Bali pipeline wave that quadrupled overhead.

Souza caught it perfectly and surfed for an astonishing kilometer and a half. "He rode the wave so far he had to get a motorbike back from Padang Beach."

On June 13 and 14, friends in New York and Rio organized memorial paddle-outs. "He was one of the finest surfers in any lineup—from Porthleven [England] to [Hawaii's] second reef pipe, and in his passing we have lost a true warrior," said his surfing buddy, Jimmy Brady. "We formed a little circle and we did it quietly. And we did a little thank-you and a goodbye and put them out of their worries just outside the Atlantic. It's always special when you're in the water anyway, and to be in the water to say goodbye to someone, that way is even better. We take solace in the fact that they were together in the last moments and that he was returned to the water."

The catastrophe that ended so many lives transformed a few others—those who were scheduled to fly on Air France 447 but, for various reasons, did not get on board and so experienced personal miracles they would carry through life. Among them were Claude Jafiol and his wife Amina, who had been in Rio for a seminar and decided to return home ahead of schedule. Their efforts to get on sold-out Air France 447 failed, and they lived.

Andrej Apinc, a sailor from Slovenia, arrived at the airport early because his cab driver was rushing to attend a soccer match. He cancelled his reservation after learning that no seat had sufficient legroom for him to stretch out a bad knee. Fortunately, an earlier 4pm flight had seats with extra legroom, and he was able to switch flights.

One of the two Dutch passengers booked on the flight, Stefan van Oss, decided to cancel at the last minute after a friend called unexpectedly and told him not to board the plane. He came back from Brazil on a later flight. In a parallel tragedy, Johanna Ganthaler, who missed Air France 447, flew home with her husband Kurt and then perished several weeks later in an Italian car crash.

During the summer and fall there were packed memorials for the flight crew. David Robert was honored at the Montreuil city hall on June 16, the eve of his 38th birthday. Air France management and many uniformed pilots grieved with Marc Dubois's family at his Saulx Marchais funeral. Pierre-Cédric and Isabelle Bonin were memorialized at the Cap Ferret church where they had married.

More than 10,000 turned out for a ceremony at Charles de Gaulle and a second event at Le Bourget. Stunning lucite memorials adorned with images of soaring birds honored all the victims at Paris's Père La Chaise cemetery and on Rio's seaside Penhasco Dois Irmãos Park. Sculptor Fernando Chancel has carved 228 swallows on a glass stele at the Brazilian memorial where gardeners lovingly care for 228 plants. The words "in memoriam" appeared in 28 languages. There were also two changes on Air France's daily flight schedule from Rio's Galeão—Antonio Carlos Jobim International Airport to Paris Charles de Gaulle. Flight 447 now operated as Flight 443 on a Boeing 747.

Devastated by the loss of their son and daughter-in-law, Jean-Louis Bonin and his wife now shared custody of their orphaned grandsons with Isabelle's parents. He also took early retirement from Air France's Regional Air. Marc Dubois's teenage niece Elisa began studying the news accounts and decided to continue the family's flying tradition. She persuaded her father Jacques to resume flying after a long hiatus and they began piloting small planes together. "I have to fly," she told friends and dreamed of becoming her family's next Air France pilot.

Both Jean-Louis Bonin and Jacques Dubois became active in the Victims of Air France 447 Family Association, working closely with Air France, the BEA, and the DGAC, and Paris court investigators. This group coordinated their work with families around the world, especially relatives of the 56 Brazilians and 26 Germans lost. While they were treated well by the Air France team, some victim's families began hearing unfounded conspiracy theories. One snarky rumor making the rounds was the accusation that the Sarkozy government, the

DGAC, Air France, and Airbus were quietly sabotaging the Flight 447 sea search to protect French interests.

In fact, all parties eagerly sought the plane's recovery. Sarkozy, who had just spent $217 million French taxpayer dollars on the presidential A330, was determined to find out what went wrong. The only way to understand and properly document the crash was to find the aircraft remains and the two critical flight recorders. Without them, it was impossible to restore full confidence in both the French airline and the manufacturer. In aviation, "blood priority" meant identifying anomalies before they caused another accident like TWA 800 that contributed to the downfall of a great airline.

The future of air safety depended on better safety management systems built around the industry's catechism. Accidents were seen as departures from the carefully orchestrated norm. The holes had to line up like layers of Swiss cheese to defeat an otherwise secure industry. Employee mistakes, a counterfeit part, smoldering lithium batteries, a sloppy runway ground controller, a pilot falling asleep, poor security: these were the kinds of problems that led to tragedy. But as the experts began poring over weather soundings over the South Atlantic on the night of June 1, 2009, studied EASA's slow response to hidden airspeed sensor failures, analyzed tracking problems that handicapped recovery efforts, parsed confusing messages from satellites and the lack of emergency locator beacon signals, no one could answer the tough question posed by the *Christian Science Monitor*. The families of those lost remained in a state of confusion.

The victims' families were asking the same question. Surely one of the many computers aboard Flight 447 would have the ability to send an accurate position report. This turned out to be a false hope based on the illusion that all flights are continuously tracked. While the remains of 50 victims, including Captain Dubois, were being picked out of the Atlantic along with the emblematic Air France tailfin in early June, most of the aircraft, its passengers and crew were lost 13,000 feet below the surface.

As the French BEA launched the first of four searches, aided by world-class oceanographers from 13 countries, the agency did its best to analyze a series of messages transmitted by the plane over satellite during its final minutes. Without the aircraft and its flight and data recorders it was impossible to understand this tragedy or effectively prevent a similar disaster. Because this was the first loss of an A330, it was critical to apply lessons learned to training while also making appropriate modifications to hardware and software.

As the BEA search continued, a manslaughter investigation was underway in the French Court of Appeals, First Chamber. Technical experts at the Air France 447 Family Association and two pilots unions did their own due diligence, while EASA, the French DGAC, its American counterpart the FAA, the National Transportation Safety Board, NASA, the U.S. Coast Guard, the Brazilian Navy, Airbus, Air France, and aviation schools around the world all kept a close watch on the BEA's frustrating sea search.

The failure of search teams to pick up the sound of Flight 447's underwater pingers from the deep underscored Rabbi Korsia's remarks at the Notre Dame memorial for those lost. Because there was no hope for their deliverance, people of faith and nonbelievers alike "must hope as they had hoped."

While the crash investigation ramped up, industry apologists were quick to cite statistics proving that flying remained the safest way to travel. Like all air accidents, this one created an opportunity to reassure the skittish that air travel had no equal. Actually those statistics failed to cover the fact that flying in Western Europe, the Americas, or Australia, was roughly 20 times safer than flying in certain parts of India, East Asia, or Africa. When factors such as the quality of training, the locations and total support structure are considered, it becomes clear that pilots around the world are fairly equally capable. However, it is the framework in which they operate that leads to differences. The industry's Achilles heel was a risky sense of complacency leading to training cuts around the world.

The positive impact of the BEA's early investigation was already apparent. Key issues raised by Air France 447 were beginning to impact the syllabuses of flight instructors everywhere.

Even without the recovery of the cockpit voice or flight recorders, preliminary data from the BEA prompted immediate replacement of the controversial Thales AA pitot-static airspeed monitoring system worldwide. Regulators told airlines to switch to pitots manufactured by American competitor Goodrich or the Thales BA pitots that had been waiting for Air France 447 after it had landed in Paris. For the first time Air France pilots learned that 32 aircraft, including ten company planes (not including Air France 447), had encountered high-altitude pitot icing in tropical regions over the past few years. Ice clogging the intakes of these narrow tubes corrupted airspeed data and shut down the autopilots on these long-range Airbus planes.

There were also larger unanswered questions on stall recovery procedures, hands-on training at high altitude, less dependence on automation, a new look at the need for standby angle-of-attack indicators (an option offered by Airbus and Boeing), and possible changes on the ECAM warning system that had apparently failed to magically protect the pilots on Flight 447. This was only the beginning of an investigation that would become Europe's biggest aviation manslaughter case in a new mass disaster court.

CHAPTER 6

The World Cup of Search and Rescue

A nyone who has dropped a cell phone out of a plane into the Swiss Alps at night understands the search for Air France 447. Go ahead and bury those mountains thousands of feet below the surface of the South Atlantic and you'll understand the challenge facing French and Brazilian teams launching the hunt for this missing plane.

Minutes count. When a plane ditches, it's critical to begin hunting for survivors. As delays turn into hours and days, everything becomes trickier for the search teams. Floating debris can quickly be swept away from the crash site. Because emergency locator beacons and underwater pingers have time-limited batteries, the crash location must be quickly pinpointed. This problem is compounded by the fact that underwater signals coming from the deep can attenuate before reaching the surface.

For all these reasons a quick call to the United States Coast Guard is a wise move crossing geopolitical boundaries. A search-and-rescue superpower, these military experts can rapidly deploy the planes and tracking equipment critical to recovery.

Blessed with the best planes, satellite connections and data processing technology, the Coast Guard can quickly determine where to begin.

This explains precisely why Arthur Allen, who oversees many searches from the Coast Guard's New London, Connecticut headquarters, was sorting through numerous messages on Air France 447 on the morning of June 1, 2009. Surprised that none had come from his counterparts at the BEA, he phoned France to offer his agency's invaluable services.

Without a signal from an emergency locator beacon or any wreckage visible from French Air Force jets, it was essential to track the missing plane's drift.

"Normally the Coast Guard would immediately drop a group of self-locating data marker buoys (SLDMB) in the vicinity of the crash to help track oceanic currents," says Allen. "That's always the number-one priority, pinning down the direction survivors and the plane are drifting. Unfortunately the French weren't directing resources. The Brazilian Navy was in charge here and they didn't request our services. This was the World Cup of search and rescue. There is a lot of national pride on all sides.

"When we are notified that someone is missing, the initial information is pretty sparse. Assuming we are not in direct contact with the person in trouble, we go to our best estimate of where they are. Typically there is a delay built into that. For example there may be a notification lag. You go fishing for the day and your wife doesn't get worried until two hours after dark. Then she has to work up the courage to the call the Coast Guard. Those delays are built in. Even with the Air France crash there was a delay."

This problem began prior to takeoff. Air France operations failed to correctly transmit the plane's flight plan data to Dakar, Senegal controllers who should have been handling the aircraft at the time it disappeared. This explains why the normally reliable Automatic Dependent Surveillance (ADS) system failed to connect the plane with the African air traffic control center. Neither the airline nor Dakar controllers were initially aware that the plane was lost early on the morning of

June 1. The lack of a mayday call and the failure of Air France maintenance to immediately understand the tragic significance of satellite messages detailing the plane's multiple systems failures, also contributed to a nearly six-hour delay on news of the crash.

"This plane went down in a place where the information available was very sparse," says Allen. "You need global models and the models are very limited. We have to project where the wreckage and debris will be by the time we get there. That's part of drift analysis.

"Our self-locating data marker buoys are air deployable. Usually we are looking for a person in a life raft, a small boat or a sea kayak. After a big event like this we would have normally dropped our buoys from a C-130. They are GPS-trackable and drift in the upper one meter of water in the ocean.

"The Brazilian Navy was in charge here. If they had dropped the buoys immediately they would have known what the currents were during the essential first five days when they were not finding wreckage or bodies. The big challenge was understanding currents during that period.

"If the buoys had been placed in a timely manner and were reasonably distributed you can assume we would have had information from day two to day six when the first wreckage was discovered by a passing ship. If the Brazilians had brought us in at the beginning, the impact zone might have been narrowed, making it easier to find the wreckage and bodies.

"The first debris and victims were found on June 6. By now we had a six-day drift. What we tend to do is a reverse drift analysis. We take the point where they are found and then do a backwards drift to see where they started. Unfortunately that is a long time to drift backwards. The cloud of uncertainty gets bigger and bigger. It doesn't tell you much about where the jet impacted."

All of this put the BEA, respected for its excellent oceanic recovery work, on the defensive. With pressure from the airline and Airbus, regulatory agencies, victims' families and attorneys, BEA leaders were becoming minor media celebrities recognizable on television screens in bars, living rooms and airport departure lounges around the world. A Paris investigative magistrate, Sylvie Zimmerman, was dispatching aviation gendarmes to uncover why the plane and its passengers were still missing. Without the critical voice and flight data recorders it would be difficult for the French court to prosecute a manslaughter case. The BEA would also be unable to fully analyze the accident and make recommendations aimed at preventing a similar tragedy.

Olivier Ferrante, head of the BEA's safety analysis division, was an ideal choice to head the French search. A pilot and graduate of ENAC, France's National Civil Aviation School, he was also secretary of the European Network of Civil Aviation Safety Investigation Authorities. In addition to working in oceans around the world to pinpoint French crashes, Ferrante assisted other governments trying to find downed jets such as the Swissair MD-11 that crashed in September 1998 off Halifax, Nova Scotia.

The remote location of the Air France 447 crash added to the complexity of this challenging underwater search. Headquartered in a Le Bourget neighborhood that has more in common with Beirut than the heart of Paris, the BEA is across the street from the airport where Charles Lindbergh landed on his pioneering nonstop transatlantic flight in the summer of 1927.

After a scary Long Island takeoff, flying through snow and rough weather, Lindbergh arrived unprepared for the welcoming French mob that surrounded The Spirit of St. Louis on the apron. In much the same way that French aviation enthusiasts had mobbed the Wright brothers after their first Flyer demonstrations in Le Mans decades earlier, Lindbergh was greeted like a rock star. Police had to perform a Moses like parting of the crowd to get the lucky hero safely inside the terminal.

Just one small part of the vast story chronicled at Musée de l'Air et de l'Espace, adjacent to the Le Bourget, Lindbergh's big reception hints at the French passion for aviation. While school groups and aviation buffs from around the world climbed onto the museum's Concorde and 747, the BEA labored in a fenced two-story building that looks like an old Lycée waiting for a new coat of paint. While it may be far from Paris's grand boulevards, the BEA's considerable reputation attracts some of the best talent in the world of aviation accident investigation. Nations like Libya and Indonesia consult with these French experts on their own mysterious accidents.

From the disappearance of Amelia Earhart's plane on a trans-Pacific journey in July 1937, to the crash of Air France 447, the aviation world has never come up with a perfect way to find planes lost at sea. Although the technology continues to improve, every search can be a challenge, even when a plane crashes in waist-deep water. Cost constraints add another degree of difficulty along with confusion over the considerable difference between deep- and shallow-water searches.

Although some recoveries can take years, most aircraft are located fairly quickly. Exceptions are rare. Underwater archaeologists and amateur historians are still looking for a Northwest DC-4 that crashed in Lake Michigan thunderstorm June 23, 1950 on a Minneapolis–New York run. The aircraft and remains of 58 passengers on board are still lost in 200 feet of water near South Haven, Michigan, despite a lengthy search partially bankrolled by thriller author Clive Cussler. Also missing are a Varig 707 that crashed in 1979 just 30 minutes after departing Tokyo, a low-on-fuel Faucett Airlines Boeing 727 which ditched off Newfoundland in 1990, and an Ethiopian Airlines Boeing 767 that went down for the same reason near Moroni, Comoros Island in 1996.

Of the previous 27 aircraft that crashed at sea since 1980, most were lost after takeoff or while landing. Only nine went down en route. Typically the cockpit voice and flight data recorders were found within a month. As the Flight 447 search continued, recovery costs ballooned for Air France, Airbus and the French treasury. A key problem was F-GZCP's remote location — over 600 miles offshore. While that might not sound like a major obstacle in an age of satellite surveillance and high-speed military aircraft, the logistics were daunting.

Typically sea crashes take place within 25 miles of shore, helping recovery crews commence operations close to the point of impact. If the plane is close to land, reconnaissance teams can begin tracking the pingers on the flight and cockpit recorders before they are embedded in mud or an oceanic mountain range. During the first hours, surveillance aircraft typically spot floating wreckage and transponders may continue working.

Even shallow bodies of water can delay the search team. In November 1996 it took Florida Everglades recovery crews fifteen days to find a ValuJet cockpit voice recorder in alligator-infested waters just two feet deep. Prior to Air France 447, the most remote sea crash was a November 1987 South African Airways 747 crash in the Indian Ocean. The accident, caused by an on-board fire, 125 miles west of Mauritius, took the lives of 159 passengers. Twenty-five other commercial aircraft lost at sea over the past three decades all went down within 12 hours (by ship) from the nearest port. Twenty-four of these planes crashed within 25 miles of shore and many were less than 10 miles away. Of the 27 plane crashes studied by the BEA, only five of the 52 underwater locator beacons on board failed to function

Most of these 27 maritime aircraft recovery operations between 1980 and 2009 took place at depths of less than 200 meters. Only eight were over 1,000 meters deep.

"The best place to lose a plane is in shallow water with a flat bottom close to the coast," says Ferrante. For example, when an Egyptian charter operated by Flash Airlines crashed January 3, 2004, in the Red Sea enroute to Paris with 134 French passengers on board, the recovery operation went quickly. Working in the transparent waters off Sharm-el-Sheikh, search crews found the flight data and cockpit voice recorders less than two weeks later. Critical data read out in Egypt was central to the investigation.

A more difficult August 2007 search took place in the Pacific after an Air Moorea plane on a fifteen-minute hop to Papeete crashed taking the lives of all 14 aboard. This time the search zone was 800 meters deep.

"We had guys there with the right sonar equipment who pinpointed the pinger from the flight recorders," says Ferrante. "But we had to charter a vessel from New Caledonia five or six days away."

Although the plane drifted, the experts were able to recover the cockpit voice recorder in three weeks. The flight data recorder was never found, a rare event that has only happened twice on crashes since 1980.

After the disappearance of Air France 447, two Brazilian tugboats were joined by a French ship dispatched from the Gulf of Guinea and an American Naval vessel. While they were en route, Brazilian authorities were forced to retract premature announcements that they had pinpointed the jet's debris field and a related oil slick on June 2.

This mistake, based on erroneous airborne surveillance, highlighted the confusion created by the enormous amount of garbage floating in the Atlantic. The first confirmed Air France 447 victims and wreckage were spotted on June 6 by a merchant vessel, the Ursula. French AWACs military jets flew to the site and the following day the Brazilian Navy began retrieving the remains of Captain Dubois and 49 deceased passengers. Divers hauled out pieces of the aircraft including the tail fin, which quickly became this disaster's iconic photo. As the recovery efforts continued, the BEA was now finally able to begin its drift analysis to pinpoint the crash site.

"Unfortunately this debris field discovery was very

late," says Ferrante. "During the five days it took to find the wreckage, it drifted more than 100 miles. In the first search phase we had 40 days to focus on acoustic transmissions. There are two search methods. Both have advantages and disadvantages. Near the shore you can detect the pingers by using a hand-held hydrophone that works like a wand.

"For a deeper search you need to tow the hydrophone along the bottom with kilometers of cables and winches. This equipment was supplied by a U.S. Navy team. You need to tow at three to four knots per hour, overlapping the search area. With this approach you can cover $10km^2$ per hour.

"The other approach is a side-scan sonar, a radar-like tool, to survey the seabed. This device sends an acoustic ping and reflections show acoustic images of the seabed. The radar can be towed or mounted on autonomous underwater vehicles also known as remote submarines."

Ferrante and his colleagues quickly began chartering survey vehicles and submarines at their Paris office. In August 2009, the BEA commenced a second search with a small armada at its disposal. Brazil contributed five frigates, Black Hawk helicopters, a Hercules C-130 military transport and search planes. French helicopters ferried crew and equipment between the ships and Fernando Noronha Island, 338 miles east of Brazil. They were joined by a sonar-scanning equipped nuclear submarine. Three French robotic submarines were also dispatched from the Cape Verde islands aboard the Pourquoi Pas? (Why Not?).

Thanks to sonar, Ferrante's team was able to create a topographic map of the seabed. "You can image the seabed to obtain a better idea of the geology of the area," he says. "You get a better idea of the sediment and geology, if it's rocky terrain, if it's sedimentary. This kind of knowledge shapes the recovery effort. "

Understanding how the wreckage slipped away required the combined efforts of eleven research organizations around the world. Their hypothesis became the basis for a third search in April and May 2010.

"This time," says Ferrante, "we had two groups working on parallel tracks. We modeled the possible crash zone on a reverse-drift analysis. If you know when and where you collected debris as well as the current at the time of impact, you can backtrack to the right location. We created this reverse-drift computation or simulation with the best specialists from France, the United States, Russia and the United Kingdom. The second working group brought in search equipment including two robotic submarines equipped to lift wreckage to the surface, as well as a towed sonar-scanning device.

"On flat sedimentary terrain you can pinpoint a small barrel. The problem is that our 40-nautical-mile search circle on top of the mid-Atlantic ridge is highly technical.

Working at 700 meters on top of a cliff that drops off to more than 4,000 meters is challenging. It is much harder working on the side of mountainous terrain like the Alps. Building images on a steep slope is complicated.

"When there is an accident on a mountain in the United States, it is difficult to quickly find the plane. It's the same problem underwater. Consider a 2009 accident in the Comoros Islands waters. That was challenging even though the wreckage was only 1,200 feet deep on a relatively flat surface. In that case it took sixty days to find the flight and cockpit recorders with a remote submarine."

Searching at the rate of 30 square miles a day with a matched pair of robotic vehicles, the investigators moved ahead optimistically. A false May 2010 story claiming the plane had been found became international news.

"We were all so confident in the third phase," says Ferrante. "We had so many experts and it was clear we would be successful. All of us were very disappointed not to find the wreckage and the flight recorders at the end of May."

During the summer of 2010, the BEA and its colleagues

around the world reanalyzed all the data. "It was a huge amount of work," says Ferrante. "Time pressure was not a good thing for the BEA. We live in a society where everything must be fast, everything must be quick."

"A safety investigation is complicated," adds BEA spokesperson Martine Del Bono, now a recognizable face on French television news.

"If we want to improve air safety and prevent future accidents, we must take our time to be sure that the safety recommendations are the right ones. It is a big system and when you change an element everything can change. You can jeopardize the system if you go quickly.

"Accidents are spectacular. But when you determine the causes of accidents, it is not spectacular. It's complex. You need time to untie the knots..... If you don't find the facts quickly, people speculate. You have emotional reactions. Thirty-two countries are involved in this accident. There are so many people impacted from different cultures. These people need to know how their loved ones died... It was difficult for people to believe that you cannot find the plane.

"We are always facing a chain of events. It is never one thing that causes an aviation accident. That is a little confusing to the public."

Great leadership is essential. When the $12 million fourth phase investigation, paid for by Air France and Airbus, began in late March 2011, many of the experts who had worked on the previous searches voiced confidence in Woods Hole Oceanographic Institute's David Gallo and Mike Purcell. For the first time, an American team was directing the recovery in collaboration with their French colleagues.

In their report to the BEA reviewing the failure of the first three Air France 447 searches, Virginia-based Metron consultants Lawrence Stone, Colleen Keller, Thomas Kratzke and Johan Strumpfer concluded that the lack of positive radar tracking or satellite surveillance of the aircraft, the depth of the

Atlantic and slow initial recovery of floating debris stymied the search. After the Ursula crew began recovery on June 6, it took another week to bring in tugs equipped to tow hydrophones along the mountainous seabed. The Metron analysis concluded that operating at depths up to 4,000 meters was a problem for two reasons.

Due to a design limitation, the emergency locator beacon attached to the black boxes only had enough battery life to transmit a pinger signal for 30 to 40 days. Another difficulty was the pinger's signal frequency was set for transmission in relatively shallow waters.

In addition to the delay in dropping drift buoys, a deep-sea search led by Phoenix International's Michael Kutzleb was held up. The BEA instructed this American team to wait half a day until a French submarine finished listening for the pingers with its "golden ears."

These problems and the lack of reliable drift data made the hydrophone search problematic. "Our success rate in finding an aircraft is over 95 percent," says Kutzleb. "The fact that this one was in remote mountainous bottom terrain along the mid-Atlantic ridge made our work difficult. We couldn't get a good feel for where things were. We've never been in a situation quite like this with circular currents and eddy currents.

"On most of the other aircraft searches we had an idea of what happened before we went out. I would have to call this one mysterious. If you searched the primary area and didn't find the plane you either missed it or it's not there. Then you need to go back and reexamine the most fundamental assumption and look at every scenario. From a search-and-rescue perspective, this was the worst accident we have been involved with, the worst confluence of coincidences."

"Air France was looking at 10,000 square kilometers," says Metron consultant Johann Strumpfer. "That is larger than many countries. No area that size has ever been so thoroughly searched. The area is really a whirlpool. The currents are inherently confused and inconsistent. And the average non-technical person does not understand that height increases uncertainty. When you descend from a higher altitude, the size of the search radius increases because the plane can fly much farther.

"Knowing a plane's position a few minutes before it hits the water provides critical search information. But without a positive radar track on the flight's descent pattern it is hard to know how far the plane flew before it hit the water. It would have been much easier to find Air France 447 if its last reported position had been at an altitude of 2,000 feet instead of 35,000 feet.

"As you ascend," says Strumpfer, "the size of the search area increases by the square of the radius. It's a basic nonlinear math calculation."

The worst-case scenario is to have no information beyond the fact that the aircraft disappeared at cruise altitude. For Strumpfer, who reexamined all the data from the first three searches, it was clear that "something in our data was wrong. Despite the fact that the BEA did phenomenally good research, there was still considerable uncertainty."

As one of the leaders of aviation's most difficult oceanic recovery efforts — the search for South African Airways Flight 295 — Strumpfer believes the key to a good search is to move quickly. "The return on effectiveness is highest at the beginning. It's kind of like losing your keys. There's a 50% probability of finding them in the first five minutes because you are looking in the most likely locations. In the next 15 minutes you only gain another 25%. The longer you look, the harder it gets."

The South African Airways Indian Ocean crash makes his point. It had many similarities to the Air France disappearance. Although the plane went down in another submerged (4,400 meter) mountain area far from shore, the search-and-rescue team had three important advantages.

The 747 tragedy, caused by an on-board fire in the cargo

hold, took place near three small islands where radio beacons were set up to help with the drift analysis. Positive flight-path information gave the experts a last altitude position at 14,000 feet. Three passenger watches found in the first wreckage confirmed that the plane was in the air for another two minutes and 46 seconds before hitting the water.

This forensic detail, which correctly identified the search zone, is one of the reasons why it is critical for Coast Guard teams to reach the crash site quickly. The unfortunate delays that held up the Air France 447 recovery effort remained a stumbling block for the best experts in the world.

"We have done hundreds of these sea searches since 1975," says Phoenix International's Kutzleb. "This is the worst confluence of coincidences we're been involved with.

In late March 2011, the fourth search for submerged Air France 447 began along the treacherous South Atlantic ridge, 680 miles east of the Brazilian coast. Nearly two years after the plane disappeared, theoretical explanations gave little comfort to the victims' families or impatient critics of the investigation.

The search began days after French investigating magistrate Sylvie Zimmerman met with the chief executives of Airbus and Air France, Tom Enders and Pierre-Henri Gourgeon, to notify them both companies were being investigated for involuntary manslaughter. The prospect of conducting another lengthy criminal trial, months after a verdict in the lengthy Air France Concorde crash case at Pontoise, raised an intriguing legal question. How would an Air France 447 investigation proceed if the flight and data recorders were never recovered?

Disagreeing with Zimmerman's decision, Enders told the media, "Airbus maintains that the focus should be on finding the cause of this accident and making sure it can never happen again."

Air France's Gourgeon agreed, "We do not recognize any good reason to justify this and it is up to us to demonstrate that."

He added that his airline's failure to replace the suspect speed sensors "would not have changed the case."

In an earlier meeting with families, a dismayed Judge Zimmerman reported that an international commission investigating the case had not received the Senegal air traffic control tapes from Dakar for the night of May 31/June 1, 2009. The magistrate's court was also studying the European Aviation Safety Agency's failure to issue an airworthiness directive in the spring of 2009 after a surprising spike in abnormal speed indication incidents on the A330/340 fleet due to pitot failure.

"There are at least a thousand other possibilities," said the International Federation of Airline Pilots Association's Paul McCarthy in early 2011. "We don't even know if it was an internal or external event. It is just as likely that it was pitot icing as it was a Klingon Cruiser that came by and shot the thing out of the sky. We just can't say what happened. It could have even been a structural failure, perhaps a crack on the wingbox that caused the wing to come off in the vicinity of a thunderstorm. It's happened.

"No one can say if the pilot missed his radar and flew under an overhang and was hammered with hail. It could have been an electrical fire like TWA 800 or a structural failure like American Airlines 587 at Kennedy. The best chance to find the black boxes was when the pingers were operating for a month after a crash. Now we have to find the wreckage at 13,000 feet and then locate a small box. With no locator beacon I'd say the chances are between none and zilch. It's an awfully big haystack."

While waiting for word from the search teams, France's defense ministry kept a tight watch on scattered wreckage of the aircraft held in a Toulouse warehouse. These remains recovered in the summer of 2009 were potential exhibits in Judge Zimmerman's chambers. Working in her behalf, the French gendarmerie's air transport division commanded by Colonel Xavier Mulot continued its own worldwide investigation.

All these possibilities were on the personal radar of John Clemes, a leader of Entraide Solidarité Air France 447, one of three family associations representing relatives of the 228 crash victims. At his Juno Finance office, a short walk from the Élysée Palace, he spoke emotionally of the day he lost his brother Brad, a Coca-Cola sales executive on his way home to his wife and children in Brussels. After numerous meetings with both BEA and Air France, and finishing the latest BEA interim reports, he had many good questions. Until Brad died, John, a frequent Air France passenger, knew little about what was going on up front in the cockpit.

The diligent prodding of John Clemes and 61 other French families who lost loved ones in this tragedy was turning up promising leads. Their association, working with family groups around the world, had successfully pushed the French government to keep the expensive search alive.

"It is very difficult for anyone to be happy that the answer hasn't been found," he says at his busy seventh arrondissement office.

"Clearly there were lots of mistakes and problems. The interactions between the controllers were amazing. They were so nonchalant for so long. I can't believe that a big jet is missing for four or five hours and the controllers are saying 'maybe it will show up.' Look at their conversations:

'Are you sure it's coming? We haven't seen it. You sure about the plane?'"

For Clemes, it's impossible to make sense of this slow response.

"This goes on for hours. There was one brief moment when they thought another plane flying behind 447 was the missing aircraft. These big jets have identities. The people who come out looking pretty good were the French controllers in Brest who raised the alarm and actually tried to get something done. They were on the phone to Charles De Gaulle two minutes after it was due in the Brest sector. There was one point where

Brest called the Cinq Mars La Pile Regional Control Center to suggest launching a search. They are told 'Sorry, it's not our responsibility.'

"Here you have guys who have understood the plane is missing. They ring up a catastrophe center and ask them to announce a catastrophe about this obviously missing plane and the center says it can't raise the alarm until the time it is due in their area. Brest managed to raise the alarm on their own.[10]

"It took eleven hours to start searching for the plane," says Clemes. "Nothing was found for six days. Had there been any survivors, they wouldn't have had a chance. It took a long time to find any of them. The BEA and the French government admitted that this was unacceptable.

"The BEA has been tasked with doing a deep-sea search to find a plane and that is not their primary business. Their business is analyzing the debris from a plane that scatters over a field. Their job is not to organize a sea search in the most difficult area of the world. They have made a number of mistakes that they admit. It has taken longer and cost more than if you had an agency that knew what it was doing.

"When you lose a big plane in the 21st century and can't locate it, a lot of people find that hard to believe. You have a huge number of families who actually believe the authorities have the plane and all this is a deliberate cover-up. I don't think that's the case. But when you add the fact that you don't communicate well, some people are convinced they are lying or incompetent."

Like fellow members of the family association, Clemes discovered that working successfully with the French scientific bureaucracy required persistence.

"At first we had a history of transparency problems with

---

10. Unlike air traffic control centers in Dakar and the Canary Islands, the Brest Center responded immediately to the plane's failure to appear on radar or check in. Several hours later staff here was informed that Air France 447 was missing. The controller working this sector broke into tears and was temporarily relieved by a colleague.

the BEA. They did their thing and after four or five months their reaction was 'hang on we will let you know in good time.' We didn't appreciate it and starting putting pressure on them. It has been difficult. Now they meet with the families and inform us regularly and they have been exhibiting a great deal of patience.

"True to their national character, the families of the 58 Brazilians lost on the plane are much more emotional. The German families, who lost 28 people, are engineering oriented. The one thing we can agree on is the fact that Air France has treated us well.

"The airline flew everyone to Rio for a ceremony in November 2009. On June 1, 2010, they flew us there for the one-year anniversary. They were generous in the days following the accident. Of course there were some families that refused to fly Air France for the ceremony. They were brought over on another airline.

"Generally what seems to motivate most of us is finding out what happened and preventing a similar accident. Basically you get compensation for noneconomic and economic damages. The economic damages are mathematical. What did the person earn? What would he have made? You replace lost income based on life expectancy of the person. No one really wants to go to court. It's bad for the airline and costly and time consuming for the families.

"Reviewing details from the minimal wreckage so far raises many questions. No one knows why three of the cabin crew seats were empty, why the oxygen masks never came down or why the pilot never called for an emergency landing. It also appears that some of the passengers were not wearing their seat belts."

Like other relatives of the victims, Clemes continues to pepper the authorities with questions. One of his frustrations was lack of communication with Airbus.

"We have been asking the judge for a flight simulation of

the crash. We heard Airbus agreed in the spring of 2010 and then announced they weren't able to do it."

At the end of his workday, Clemes turns from the interim BEA report to ask a difficult question. In the midst of all the uncertainty surrounding this tragedy, he cannot understand Air France's failure to make easy decisions that might have saved the plane. On his desk is a 2007 article on Airbus's optional Back Up Speed Scale system (BUSS). It's a quick solution for pilots confronted with unreliable airspeed due to frozen pitots or any other computer problem.

"Look at this," he says, pointing toward the work of Airbus Flight Operations Engineer Joelie Barthe. "This system gives you the capacity to adjust and stay level when you have a computer failure and are dealing with unreliable airspeed."

Barthe's deathless prose makes BUSS sound like a must for every Airbus pilot: "If you lose the autopilot, you still know what the attitude and thrust is. BUSS is designed to 'decrease the crew workload in the case of unreliable speed.'"

Because the BUSS calculations are based on a reliable angle of attack sensor, not the occasionally unreliable pitots, icing problems do not hamper this instrument. As a result, the captain can switch from autopilot to manual mode without worrying about the possibility of accidentally entering an aerodynamic stall.

Barthe concludes that BUSS is a work of genius, not to mention a security blanket for Airbus pilots flying by wire on a dark and stormy South Atlantic night:

"The primary flight display speed scale is immediately replaced by the back-up speed scale and GPS altitude which allows the pilot to fly at a safe speed, i.e. above stall speeds by adjusting thrust and pitch." Back-Up Speed Scale System, which is triggered when all three of the Air Data Inertial Reference Units (ADIRU's) are offline, is currently not designed for use above 25,000 feet.

This article, published 18 months before the crash of Air

France 447, mentions that BUSS is standard on the Airbus 380 jumbo jet and an option on other fly-by-wire planes. As he shuts down his computer and gathers up the BEA reports at the end of a long working day, Clemes has a suggestion.

"BUSS is certainly something that could have helped the Flight 447 crew that night. I don't understand why this system wasn't on all Air France planes. It should be standard on every Airbus."

By now the search for Air France 447 was news in Papeete and Philadelphia, Bogota and Bangalore. Passengers who didn't know the difference between an elevator and a horizontal stabilizer were now having dinner party conversations about why the plane's pitot tube heaters failed to immediately melt that uninvited convective ice.

Pilots wanted to know why the second and third pitots, which essentially served as backups, didn't provide correct airspeed information to the pilots. It was difficult to understand that all three pitots were essentially sending the same incorrect information after they froze.

At the online Professional Pilots Rumor Network (PPRuNe) Air France 447 chatroom, the latest theories were debated by thousands of aeronautical experts at computer workstations and on laptops, tablets and smart phones. There was even a significant media debate about how long Captain Marc Dubois had slept the night before his flight home. Rumors had become urban myths and the many theories, including some built around conspiracies, threatened to exceed the number of passengers on board.

CHAPTER 7

Maryanne and Ginger's Big Day

For 22 months satellites, reconnaissance aircraft, Air Force helicopters, commercial jets, freighters, nuclear submarines, research vessels, tugs, support ships and autonomous underwater vehicles tried to pinpoint the final resting place of Air France 447. Using radar, sonar, video and still cameras, underwater imaging and even binoculars, French, Brazilian, American, Norwegian, and Dutch search teams had worked tirelessly in a remote corner of the Atlantic. Costs soared over $50 million dollars with no end in sight.

Eleven elite maritime research organizations, including France's IFREMER, the Leibniz Institute of Marine Science and Russia's Institute of Numerical Mathematics had lent their top scientists to this effort.

A heavily illustrated analysis of the previous sea searches published in the Brazilian paper Zero Hora had become a poster in leading oceanographic laboratories around the world. A series of BBC specials and feature-length coverage in *The New York Times, Le Figaro* and *Der Spiegel* fascinated readers with *grande reportage* on the flight. Like the "unsinkable" Titanic, this aircraft, once considered un-stallable, had become the subject of master's theses at aviation law schools, as well as the subject of NASA special reports and academic conferences. Training pilots even lectured their students about the "mistakes" that had led to this tragedy.

The failure of many of the world's leading oceanographic experts to find the plane on three previous searches prompted Airbus and Air France to finance the fourth expedition. Promising new reverse-drift analysis work done independently at Wood Hole was one of the reasons Gallo and Purcell were given command of the new BEA search. At least if this hunt failed critics couldn't blame it on the French.

Woods Hole Autonomous Underwater Vehicle (AUV) co-inventor and senior engineer Mike Purcell took command of the fourth search. At the heart of the new hunt were Maryanne and Ginger, twin yellow submarines just 14 feet long. They were named for actresses Tina Louise and Dawn Wells, who starred in the early '60s hit American TV series, *Gilligan's Island*. As the Woods Hole-designed AUVs began exploring remote sea beds at depths up to 12,800 feet, governments, families, and scientists around the world waited hopefully for good news. The world's largest sea search had become a *cause célèbre* and a chance for the Woods Hole Institute team to make its most celebrated find since pinpointing the wreck of the Titanic. Only six of these remarkable submarines, capable of exploring a mile wide path, operated in the world's oceans.

Under the command of Woods Hole's Purcell, operators brought the subs up from the deep to download the results of their sonar search. As soon as the data was secure, the subs headed back down for another look.

After months of preparation, 14-foot-long AUVs Maryanne and Ginger were shipped by container to Seattle where they were loaded on the M/V Alucia. These $2.5 million torpedo-shaped underwater vehicles had a unique capability to search the deep end of the ocean, easily descending along mountainous ridge lines and surveying flat terrain with side-scan sonar that "mowed" 1,400-meter-wide paths. Under development on Cape Cod for many years, the first Remus AUVs had gone into service in 2001. The Waite Institute purchased two of these vehicles and made them available to Woods Hole. Built by neighboring Hydroid, a division of Konigsburg Industries, they were used to map the site of the Titanic remains, search for the wreck of Amelia Earhart's plane, and localize coral in the Gulf Stream.

Although the BEA put out feelers to Woods Hole about the possibility of joining the first search in 2009, no deal was struck. "We were not considered an option," explains Purcell. "BEA had done a lot of work with Phoenix International, and there was no reason not to use them. They had a contract with the U.S. Navy to supervise the salvage. Phoenix had recovered more planes than anyone else from the sea floor. But they don't use our technology. Doing this kind of thing with an AUV was not common."

Unfortunately, the BEA-directed efforts of Phoenix International, the French and Brazilian navies and other contractors proved unsuccessful on the first two searches. In the spring of 2010, Maryanne, Ginger, and Geomar's Abyss were invited to join Phoenix International on the BEA's failed third search. A starting point on the fourth recovery effort was knowledge that aircraft lost at sea are typically found within eight miles of their last known position. Could acoustic surveys using a towed pinger locator in the vicinity of the crash have missed the plane? Perhaps the pingers had broken or their batteries had failed.

The new three-month hunt began in late March 2011 along the treacherous south Atlantic ridge, 680 miles east of the Brazilian coast. The twin underwater vehicles were scheduled to begin a series of dives from the new search team's host ship, the futuristic M/V Alucia.

Formerly the R/V Nadir, operated by France's Institute for Exploration of the Sea (IFREMER), the Alucia was reconfigured for expeditions and movie shoots. A cross between a luxury yacht and scientific laboratory, the 183-foot-long ship was a geek's dream. The research and exploration vehicle was built by Deep Ocean Quest, the first company to make abyss-rated submersibles available to the general public.

In 2007, founder Mike McDowell had been one of six divers on the Mir deep submergence vehicle that reached the abyssal plain 14,500 feet below the North Pole. For $59,000 each, Deep Ocean Quest had taken 150 wealthy explorers 12,500 feet under the sea for two hours to visit the Titanic wreck. Another 25 customers paid $45,000 to descend 15,700 feet to the Bismarck, a World War II German battleship 600 miles west of Brest, France.

Being chosen over more experienced and better-known recovery ship operators was a coup for Deep Ocean. "A long time ago," said McDowell, "nautical charts labeled unexplored regions with the phrase, 'Here be Dragons.' That's what M/V Alucia is all about. We want to visit the dragons."

The company's expedition leader, Rob McCallum, who circumnavigated Antarctica in 2001, was prepared for any contingency on the retrofitted ship's first commercial search.

"It's a 24-hour-a-day mission, and once we get there we will be working around the clock," he told Seattle reporters while preparing to depart Puget Sound. Now on the seventh day of his latest deep-end-of-the-ocean expedition that would continue until July 2011, Captain Heyden headed to the mission control suite. His crew would brief him on the latest data gleaned from the 17,000-square-kilometer (6,600 sq. mi.) search zone.

Deep Ocean Quest's corporate mission, "Bringing the Abyss to Life" neatly summarized the challenge now facing the BEA, the French judiciary and, of course, Woods Hole.

In Suape, Brazil, Captain Heyden picked up a third AOV, Geomar's Abyss along with the Woods Hole team, BEA search leaders, Airbus, and investigators from the French Air Transport gendarmerie. Dockside as the 33 members of the search team prepared to depart on the Alucia, BEA Director Jean-Paul Troadec went live on Brazilian television:

"Last time, our strategy targeted a relatively limited area, located in the northwest region of the perimeter, where we know the crash occurred. This time, we are going to survey the entire area inside the circle. This was not previously done. This is a really peculiar situation. There are very few instances in which accidents occurred and we were not able to either explain their causes or retrieve flight recorders."

For Ferrante, inexperience was part of the problem. Although it had been more than a century since the Wright Brothers took off at Kitty Hawk, he considers aviation a relatively young science. Compared to the maritime world, he explains during a late-night conversation after putting his young daughters to bed at home in Paris, the aviation industry can be victimized by inexperience:

"You have to keep in mind that an airplane is not designed to be in the water.

"The emphasis is always on keeping planes safe in the air. It is extremely rare for a plane to crash in the water far from the shore. Typically planes that crash in the ocean, go down close to the airport, which makes the search easier because you have radar contact, witnesses, faster access to the site, better knowledge of currents and search-and-rescue teams that can quickly collect crucial evidence.

"But in this case we had nothing: no witnesses and no radar coverage. Debris was found and recovered five to six days after the accident and the location was very remote and very deep. The underwater locator beacons may have been damaged on impact. When a plane is over 3,000 meters deep, you have only two towed hydrophones in the world, both owned by the U.S. Navy, that can sweep vast underwater areas. It is an expensive and cumbersome device to operate.

"We did use them, but damage to the pingers probably prevented picking up the signal. A much better solution would have been to install a lower frequency device that has a longer range that can be heard by all military search-and-rescue teams. All civil aircraft in the world have these pingers, but only two hydrophones can go that deep to find them. It's a mismatch."

Why wasn't this A330 or any other transoceanic commercial jet equipped with lower-frequency underwater locator beacons already in use on French and British military planes? The extra cost was negligible for the longer-range pingers with a 90-day battery life that could have probably sent a detectable signal.

"We all know," says Ferrante, "that accidents are what happen to others. They are not related to the core business of aviation. Changing the frequency of the emergency locator beacon is not very sexy."

The failure of the pinger search did not prevent the BEA from finding Air France 447 by other means. "It is hard to understand why they didn't do a side-scan sonar or AUV search for the plane within ten miles of the original track of the plane," says Dick Limeburner, senior research specialist in Woods Hole's Physical Oceanography Office. "Sonar was first used on the second sea search during the summer of 2009.

"The ship Porquoi Pas? deployed a towed side-scan sonar system to look at a 300-nautical-mile square a little south and east of the last known position. I think if they had done this search from the aircraft's last known position they might have found it.

"This area hadn't been done before and there was reverse drift. This priority zone was a hole in the search plan. Black box recovery has worked well in the past for crashes near the shore.

"Unfortunately, everything was different about this accident. They went out there with the attitude that we will do what we did before because it worked in the past. They counted on being able to find it, and that didn't happen."

The third search, which relied on the collective view of a distinguished international scientific team, got off to a bad start. After conducting a reverse-drift analysis, these experts concluded the plane was most likely in the northwest corner of the search zone. The failure of this abortive effort was compounded by a decision in early May 2010 to move the search two hours' sailing time to the south. This call was made after a brand-new French Navy review of data gathered in the summer of 2009 identified potential acoustic signatures from an emergency locator beacon.

Unfortunately, these hopeful leads from the nuclear submarine Emeraude were just one more disappointment for the search teams and the victims' families. By now worldwide coverage of the failed search for Air France 447 generated a small avalanche of unsophisticated advice from would-be experts. Even psychics were offering their best thinking. One wandered into the wood-paneled headquarters of Woods Hole Oceanographic Institute and knocked on the door of special projects director David Gallo.

Looking at a detailed map of the search zone, she pointed to the sector where the lost plane simply had to be. At the same time a Woods Hole-trained expert, Changseng Chen, was reviewing work he and the international experts hired by BEA did on the third search. Now at University of Massachusetts Dartmouth campus in New Bedford, Massachusetts, he created a new reverse-drift analysis in collaboration with his own team and Woods Hole's Limeburner. Because the BEA did not want to pay for another drift analysis, this essential American work proceeded on the scientists' own initiative.

On the first anniversary of the crash, nine new drift buoys were dropped at the crash site with the BEA's cooperation. Arranged in three rows, they were tracked by Chen's team with an eye toward creating a new reverse-drift analysis based on currents corresponding to the time of the original tragedy.

Chen's independent team was able to rerun the reverse-drift data and come up with a new model that suggested another solution for the puzzled international scientific community. In late 2010 and early 2011 these American academics became convinced that some of the satellite data and other components of the earlier work was not complete. They concluded that this research failed to take into account local conditions in the equatorial South Atlantic where currents sometimes collided to create whirlpool-like conditions. In the midst of the oceanic equivalent of tornado alley, the crash search zone was unpredictable and at times counterintuitive. Their influential report, highly regarded by experts at Air France, Airbus, and the BEA, underscored the case for a fourth search led by Woods Hole.

"We were looking in a notoriously remote area where there were no direct observations of the ocean or atmosphere," explains Limeburner. "In this intertropical convergence zone the trade winds of the northern and southern hemisphere come together. You have equatorial currents going west toward Brazil and other currents going east toward Africa."

"This follow-on work was very useful to us," says Purcell as he prepared to take operational command of the fourth search aided by BEA experts. "What Chen learned from his detailed analysis of the new floating buoys was that the international models used for the phase three search were poor."

The decision to go with Woods Hole and the Remus AUVs was a big disappointment to competitors. Although Purcell and Gallo were confident about finding Air France 447, some at the BEA were still smarting over time lost a year earlier on the third search when the AUV Abyss went AWOL. The prospect of losing this key $2.5 million asset central to the recovery effort was stressful to Ferrante. Fortunately, a day later a position report transmitted by the off-course sub's Iridium satellite communications system allowed the support ship Seabed Worker to find the missing AUV, 50 nautical miles to the north.

Experience gained on 91 missions conducted during phase three gave the Woods Hole team a head start on their new search along the dark ocean floor sandwiched between vast mountain ranges.

"On the third search we were out there for twenty-five

days and found an oil barrel," says Purcell at his office in Woods Hole steps away from tourists just off the boat from Martha's Vineyard. "It was pretty rough. We learned a lot about operating a vehicle in severe terrain along the mid-Atlantic ridge. Exploring steep underwater terrain, the AUVs can run into a mountain or cliff. This stops the mission, and we then use a drop weight to float it back to the surface. Another problem is the inability of the vehicle to swim down a slope as quickly as it's falling off. That means it has to go back and swim up the slope."

The new team worked outward from the last point of contact four minutes before the plane disappeared. No one knew if the plane had broken up on an underwater mountain ridge or landed on the seabed nearly 13,000 feet below the surface. Despite all these uncertainties, Airbus executives in Toulouse were confident that the new team would find their airplane.

The AUVs were dispatched on 24-hour missions sending out acoustic pings that imaged natural and manmade objects. At times, a single pixel can stand out in a way that makes it possible to identify objects more than 4,000 meters below the surface. An experienced crew is able to pick out metal objects that typically have sharp or square edges. Surfacing only long enough to download data gleaned by their side-scan sonar mowing sectors 1,400 meters wide, the subs were well on their way to exploring a region the size of Paris.

Like mountaineers rappelling down cliffs, Maryanne and Ginger illuminated the Atlantic depths well beyond the reach of dive teams. As soon as these AUVs surfaced, sonar images and photos were downloaded from hard drives. Within hours the search vehicles were sent back down for another look.

Back at BEA headquarters in Le Bourget, Ferrante and his colleagues waited for updates on the three-month-long search of this poorly understood oceanic region.

Finding the plane was only the first step. Without the

critical cockpit voice and flight data recorders, accurately reconstructing the accident would be unlikely. Even if these orange boxes were retrieved, it was possible that the plane's impact, intense water pressure at 12,000 feet below the surface, and corrosion could lead to a loss of data.

On the afternoon of Saturday, April 2, after a week of searching, Woods Hole consultant Greg Kurras was discussing how the team would identify targets with Purcell, fellow consultant Andy Sherrell, and senior engineering assistant Greg Packard. Looking at Maryanne's latest acoustic images, he pointed to well-lit pixels with sharp edges on his screen:

"What about this?"

The entire team crowded around his desk for a closer look.

"That's a good target," said Purcell who quickly called an Airbus representative in to the Alucia's processing room. He confirmed that the outlined image found 3,980 meters below the surface looked like it could be Air France 447. Instead of sharing their good news with the entire crew, the Woods Hole scientists imposed a blackout. After nearly two years, the American leader knew this was not a good time to go public.

Although Kurras was 95% sure they had just found the missing plane, no one grabbed for a phone.

"There had been so many bad press leaks," says Purcell. "There was no celebrating. We wanted to keep this quiet and confirm it." Maryanne was sent back down for a closer look, followed by Ginger later that night. Hovering 10 meters above the sea floor, Ginger began swimming lanes 20 meters wide, firing off 15,000 photos illuminated by a strobe flash. Finally BEA representative Jean Claude Vital woke Olivier Ferrante in Paris along with investigator in charge Alain Bouillard and the agency's director Jean-Paul Troadec.

Ferrante was skeptical and cautious, "We had false news before, promising dives locating targets that were only geology. I wanted to be very careful although I knew it was something solid."

A rough storm Sunday morning slowed the recovery of Maryanne at 11am local time. Two and half hours later she was brought to the surface, followed by Ginger. By 5pm the American scientists began putting their extraordinary photos on their secure FTP website. In France, the BEA's Troadec, Bouillard, Ferrante and their colleagues enthusiastically studied the aircraft photos. From her Paris home, the BEA's Martine Del Bono sent out a press release that instantly became the world's number-one news story:

"The BEA reports that the team led by Woods Hole Oceanographic Institute on board the vessel Alucia has located pieces of an aircraft in the course of an underwater search operation conducted over the last 24 hours. These pieces have been identified by the BEA safety investigators as parts of commercial airliner Airbus 330-203, AF flight 447, just 6.5 miles north of the jet's last known position."

Within hours, Ginger's first grainy photos of the plane, pieces of the landing gear, one of the GE engines and sections of the hull, were published and broadcast worldwide. Stunning reports a few hours later that a Navy SEAL team had shot and killed Osama Bin Laden at his hideout in Pakistan didn't diminish worldwide interest in the plane's recovery.

Grateful families around the world were notified that their loved ones had been found. The BEA would do its best to bring these victims back home to their families for funerals. Among those recovered were copilots David Robert and Pierre-Cédric Bonin, along with his wife Isabelle.

A few families resisted recovery of their loved ones, but the French government's decision was non-negotiable. This case was also a homicide investigation, and the air transport gendarmerie was on board the Alucia to make sure the victims were treated with the same dignity accorded any potential manslaughter victim. As the Woods Hole and Alucia crews made their plans to return home more than 10 weeks ahead of schedule, a salvage ship, the Île de Sein, sailed from Dakar to the crash site. Crew began recovering evidence that would become part of the felony prosecution moving forward in France.

Sold to a private yacht owner while the search was still going on, the Alucia had earned its place in maritime history as a designated hitter batting 1000. In its first and only recovery mission, the ship had been a perfect base for the Woods Hole team. After a week of follow-up at the crash site, the Alucia sailed off to its new life of luxury. In Le Bourget, 85,000 pictures taken by the AUVs were assembled into a photo mosaic. This new work was aimed at locating the orange Honeywell voice and flight data recorders on the near-freezing ocean bottom under pressure comparable to a small elephant standing on top of a postage stamp.

As the Alucia returned to Suape, Woods Hole Special Projects Director David Gallo praised his team and their AUVs. He was astonished to learn the oceanographers pinpointed the aircraft in search sector J30, the same location predicted by the psychic who had wandered into his office months before Purcell's team left for Brazil.

CHAPTER 8

The BEA Report

From the Wright Brothers, to Francis Gary Powers' U-2 spy flight over the Soviet Union, to the advent of the supersonic Concorde, pilots have always faced unseen demons, be they weather, mechanical breakdowns, or enemy fire. The challenges they confront every day could easily fill a book.

Accident investigators face a different challenge. It is their job to determine what went wrong and how to make sure it doesn't happen again. They are dedicated to the proposition that diligent research will prevent future crashes.

Alas, important and long-overdue reforms proposed by independent agencies such as France's estimable BEA are routinely met with industry skepticism. Airlines, manufacturers, regulators and politicians worry about making expensive changes with no proven benefit. This is the ultimate irony in air safety. Blood priority means, all too often, that overdue changes happen after lives are lost. Adding to the confusion is the vast disparity between the world's airlines.

At the international level, badly needed reforms are balanced against the fact that some impoverished carriers don't have the resources to pay for them. For these companies, typically located in the Third World, raising fares to pay for better pilot training or new safety systems runs the risk of pushing them down the runway to bankruptcy.

105

When a design problem is recognized, the aircraft manufacturers will recommend a change or modification. Fleets are rarely grounded for such recommendations unless they rise to a critical safety level and the regulatory agencies issue a directive. One problem is that in countries like France, insurance only compensates airlines for revenue lost due to aircraft grounded for three days. Beginning on the fourth day, the carriers have to pick up the entire tab for cancelled flights.

Another problem is potential unintended consequences. Modifications are exhaustively studied to make sure they don't create new problems in other systems. Transport aircraft are extremely complex and what might seem like a good idea can create unexpected challenges. In the long run, the airlines and manufacturers often find it easier to reprogram their software than to initiate new training programs.

There are few better examples of how the accident investigation process should work than the BEA's final report on Air France 447, which was released on July 5, 2012 at a Paris press conference. This worldwide news event helped bring closure for the grieving families and friends of the people lost. It also challenged the aviation industry to make affordable reforms with readily available technology.

The BEA's three-year analysis of Air France 447 was an instant aviation landmark contradicting the dangerous assumption that accidents are nearly always the result of human error. Drawing on the insights of some of the best accident and search-and-recovery analysts in the world, it offered a promising critique applauded by the air safety community.

This comprehensive study went beyond the specifics of the crash to carefully analyze the human factors central to air safety. In much the same way that a 1996 American Airlines crash into a Columbian mountain triggered installation of enhanced ground-proximity warning systems, Air France 447 has created an important opportunity to make flying safer. The

BEA's scientists challenged outdated assumptions based on obsolete technology grounded in hopelessly out-of-date test data.

Eight years later most of the BEA's well-documented arguments for better hands-on training, surveillance, and emergency warning systems have yet to be implemented by commercial aviation and the regulatory community. In many ways this inertia is as big a story as the crash itself. Failure to make overdue reforms contributed to at least two more accidents in 2014. Perhaps the most obvious takeaway from the 22-month search – the failure to quickly implement off-the-shelf tracking technology on every commercial jet – meant that another big jet could disappear with little hope of recovery. That's exactly what happened to a Malaysia Air flight in March 2014.

This problem has been compounded by the industry's decision to double-down on its commitment to automation at the expense of traditional stick-and-rudder foundational training and experience. Unlike the three pilots on Air France 447, far too many of the modestly paid new hires signing on at many airlines are gaining the vast majority of their experience on the ground. While there are important exceptions at forward-thinking carriers, too many airlines depend almost entirely on computers to fly their planes. Their focus is on making sure pilots utilize automation as much as possible. Inadequate training has led to far too many accidents in Asia and other regions. Clearly, failure to focus on good airmanship has failed in some of the world's fastest growing aviation markets. For example, since 2001 there have been 40 fatal aviation accidents in Indonesia. One carrier – Trigana Air – has had 19 accidents. Fifty-nine of that nation's 63 air carriers have been banned from landing at European airports.

The BEA report shows that thorough training is critical for flight crews that may only have seconds to react to an emergency. Even when the autopilot is on, pilots must ensure dozens of computers are not making mistakes or leading the aircraft into danger. Just as a driver must monitor a car's cruise control and adjust it accordingly for unexpected hazards, the pilot is frequently called on to make spur-of-the-moment corrections. The catch is that in the air this applies to all three dimensions plus time.

The autopilot can be programmed to follow a heading or a route programmed into the aircraft's flight management system (FMS) which usually is following GPS or inertial guidance. It can also track an electronic beam from a ground station (signals from an Instrument Landing System, known more commonly as an "ILS" or a VHF Omni-Directional Range more commonly referred to as a VOR). A ground system emits a vertical beam for the pilot or autopilot to follow to a landing without outside visual reference. In addition, the autopilot can be set to climb or descend at a certain rate, following altitudes programmed into the FMS, or to hold an altitude. Meanwhile, the auto-throttle system will maintain the programmed or selected speed.

Inevitably problems arise. In the same way cruise control will hold programmed speed as a car travels onto unexpected black ice or toward a truck that has stopped short in fog, the autopilot holds the programmed course in the face of unanticipated hazards. It does not think for itself or operate outside boundaries set by human programmers who fail to visualize extraordinary challenges.

In addition, an autopilot can mask certain problems. Suppose that, in our automotive example, a brake is dragging. The cruise control automatically accelerates to maintain the programmed speed without letting the driver know there is a problem. He might only figure it out after the brakes begin smoking, or taking the black ice example from earlier, the cruise control will not disengage as it encounters the ice but instead may increase the wheel speed in an attempt to hold the car's speed constant as it loses traction.

The same thing can happen on a plane. In one case, a Boeing 747 was at cruise altitude when an engine failed. The throttles on the other three engines compensated to hold the airplane level. Unfortunately, there was insufficient thrust on the remaining engines to maintain airspeed. The plane slowed to the point that the autopilot could not hold altitude or course. At that point the captain disconnected the autopilot, triggering a rapid roll and dive. The pilots struggled to make a recovery. Without their decisive intervention, the plane could have been lost.

Unexpected problems begin on the ground when designers make the mistake of assuming flight computers are failsafe as long as these machines rule out human error. This naiveté underscores one of aviation's biggest challenges. Outstanding international researchers such as Sidney Dekker, Erik Hollnagel, and Nancy Leveson argue convincingly that modern aviation safety systems are overly dependent on human resilience. Expecting pilots to prevent accidents triggered by faulty design or computers having a bad day is the wrong way to run an airline. When trusted computers and aircraft systems fail to perform as expected, recovery is dependent on the reliability of pilots who have the training and experience to quickly fix the problem. If they fail to do so, the accident is chalked up to "pilot error."

Assuming that the problem is "pilot error" opens up a Pandora's box of "solutions" that mask other major concerns. Some airlines appear to believe a pilot can have too much knowledge or experience. This is true at some of the world's top carriers where applicants are chosen "from the middle" in the belief that the highest-rated candidates may foolishly try to outsmart their computers. These companies argue that "following the rules" is more important than airmanship.

The BEA's exhaustive analysis undercuts this point of view in several important ways. In some situations there are simply no rules to follow. Unexpected scenarios exceed arbitrary design limits. Too many pilots are being trained on a "need-to-know" basis and warned about the danger of trying to interfere with computer logic. Pilots who try to gain badly needed experience hand-flying their aircraft at high altitudes can be written up, even punished, by their supervisors at many airlines.

At some major carriers, pilots are taking the copilot seat on passenger flights after just half a dozen check rides. This approach does a good job of helping airlines cut costs and keep fares down. At the same time, it may diminish pilot skills critical to the industry's current safety record. Another problem is the industry's decision to break with the tradition of hiring airline pilots who arrive with many years of prior jet experience on military, regional, charter, freight, or corporate aircraft.

Regulatory agencies, in this case the French DGAC (Directorate General for Civil Aviation) and the European regulator, EASA, are not obligated to implement the BEA's recommendations. In addition, the International Civil Aviation Organization (ICAO) has a lengthy and cumbersome process that can push overdue changes back a decade or longer. Of course, airlines are always free to go above and beyond required standards, particularly when it comes to training. For example, some companies like Lufthansa have unilaterally added satellite tracking of convective storms to their aircraft.

Unfortunately, this kind of noteworthy example seldom receives the favorable attention it deserves.

Separation of accident investigation groups such as the BEA or the U.S. National Transportation Safety Board from enforcement or research branches such as the DGAC, also leads to clashes. For example, the FAA is mandated to protect the safety of the traveling public and promote the aviation industry. This balancing act is a numbers game, relying on statistical analysis of accident probability. That means a reform can languish on the NTSB's "most wanted list" of safety improvements because the FAA's number crunchers can't justify the financial cost of changing the status quo.

A classic example is the FAA's failure to mandate long-overdue child safety restraints for children under age two. The agency fears this action would prompt parents to travel by car. This of course ignores the fact that parents often do not have this option on longer journeys, especially transoceanic flights. As a result, a parent who can be arrested for traveling to the airport in a car without a safety restraint system for their young child is free to fly with the same child unbelted on a journey to Tokyo.

Consumers Union, the NTSB and flight attendants' unions have spent decades trying to end this preposterous loophole which has continued many decades after seat belts became mandatory in cars.

Funding critical research and implementing new regulations are related concerns. The FAA spends just 1.6% of its budget ($158.79 million in 2014) on research engineering and design. Another issue, points out Dennis Filler, Director of the William J. Hughes Technical Center Office, is that the FAA R&D is on a "five-year cycle while industry advances on a one-year cycle." Again and again the industry has seen, as in the case of Air France 447, that failure to implement safety-related improvements in a timely manner can make a critical difference.

Further complicating this problem is the fact that accident investigation agencies such as the BEA cannot conduct research necessary to document their case. Instead of being authorized to independently study what is going right at the airlines, it is limited to researching accidents. While reconstructing crashes is certainly beneficial, it also makes sense to build on the success of carriers that have excellent training programs.

This balanced approach would encourage airlines to work in a positive, proactive manner that benefits everyone.

Once an investigation is completed, it is up to regulatory agencies, such as the French DGAC and FAA, to pay for studies documenting the need for overdue changes. Far too often these recommendations are turned down to save money. Regrettably, many of the obsolete standard operating procedures endorsed by the regulatory agencies, the manufacturers, and the airlines prior to the Air France 447 accident remain in place today.

One problem is distinguishing between what the pilots knew going into a crisis and what investigators learned in hindsight. After a crash, some critics think pilots should have instantly known, at the time of the accident, what an international team of experts uncovered thanks to tens of thousands of hours of research. The BEA's experts had more than three years to figure out what went wrong during the final 264 seconds of Air France 447. Adding to the confusion is the fact that many critics of the flight crew have never even read the BEA report.

There is a dangerous tendency to assume no one else could make the same mistakes or be victimized by a similar set of circumstances. Stepping back to the flight crew's reality during the crisis, we'd find they made rational decisions based on what they knew at that time.

CHAPTER 9
Changes That Can't Wait

The BEA's critical recommendations focus on an analysis of Flight 447's final 228 seconds. Collectively they create an impressive opportunity for the industry to address new challenges and hidden dangers. While automation delivers important new safeguards, it also creates new responsibilities for pilots who must understand how to take over from their computers in a heartbeat. What has the BEA's three-year analysis uncovered? Which of the accident investigation agency's important recommendations are being implemented? Why are others yet to be implemented? The answers to these questions offer a panoramic view of contemporary aviation safety management.

Pitot Tubes and High-Altitude Crystal Ice Study
On April 27, 2009, more than a month before Air France 447, the airline accelerated the replacement of pitot tubes on the A330/340 series. That decision was based on many reports of crystal ice encounters during convective storms.

Unfortunately, the pitot exchange on the aircraft operating as Air France 447 was scheduled hours after the plane went down. By June 11, 2009, the airline had completed the switch from Thales AA probes to an upgraded BA probe on all Airbus 330/340 aircraft. Over the next eight months the airline replaced the Thales BA probes with upgraded pitots from Goodrich. In addition, the European Air Safety Agency (EASA) mandated upgrading of the pitot tubes and limited the use of the "BA" probe to just one position.

To its credit, the French agency recommended new research into the special high-altitude icing conditions sometimes found in the vicinity of convective storms. The BEA was concerned that the entire industry could be flying on obsolete standards that were not "well-adapted to flight at high altitude." These icing standards were based on tests conducted in the 1940s when aircraft were incapable of flying to the high altitudes that are standard today.

The crystal ice problem that clogged all three pitots on Air France 447 and threatened many similar aircraft is a high-altitude phenomenon. Industry assumptions based on these outdated and obsolete studies have turned out to be incorrect.

In 2010, EASA issued a rulemaking study on "Large Airplane Certification Specifications in Super-cooled Large Drop, Mixed-phase and Ice Crystal Icing Conditions." The following year the agency issued new certification standards addressing many of the issues raised by Air France 447.

Better Tracking

After Air France 447 sank, an underwater locator beacon (ULB) activated and began emitting a sonar signal. Acoustic signals are used due to the very limited range of radio wave transmissions in water. Being electromagnetic waves, radio waves rapidly attenuate in water, just like light. Virtually all visible light is gone at a depth of 200 meters (656 feet) and by 1,000 meters (3,280 feet) the ocean becomes black as night even at noon on a cloudless tropical day. Radio waves are similarly limited, with the exception of very low frequencies transmitted with significant power by some military transmitters. These very low-frequency radios are typically used by submarines, and by the Russians for navigation.

Current aircraft ULBs typically transmit an acoustic pulse

at 37.5 kHz, which is better suited for shallow water and was never intended to locate an object in the deeper parts of the ocean. The BEA recommended adding a second ULB capable of transmitting over longer distances with less attenuation on a lower frequency between 8.5 and 9.5 kHz. Oceanographers agree it would have been much easier to locate the missing aircraft if this system had been in place on Air France 447. Clearly this lower-frequency ULB would have aided search teams still hunting for Malaysia Air 370.

Crew Resource Management

The BEA carefully analyzed Crew Resource Management on flights longer than eight hours with more than two pilots. The agency concluded that Captain Dubois failed to clearly indicate which copilot was in charge during his rest period. The investigation also questioned the timing of his break and recommended that captains explicitly delegate authority when leaving the cockpit. In March 2010, Air France modified procedures to ensure that the designated relief co-pilot, second in command while the captain is gone, take the left seat. The pilot temporarily in command remains in the right seat, his normal position when working under the captain's authority.

The BEA report also followed up on the lead of top-tier airlines that have reevaluated the decision-making process. The agency renewed a call to encourage co-pilots to recommend decisions before the captain makes their final call. This approach encourages co-pilots to think independently and speak their mind first, not simply defer to their boss.

Angle of Attack Indicators

To the delight of pilots' unions, the National Transportation Safety Board, and academic experts around the world, the BEA aggressively recommended angle-of-attack indicators on all aircraft. As previously explained, the wing's angle of attack is at the core of how airplanes fly. Airspeed can be an indirect representation of angle of attack, but in unusual situations such as the last minutes of Air France 447, it can also be misleading. A direct angle-of-attack indication, coupled with pilot training on how to use it, provides a rapid and intuitive understanding of what is happening. Many have argued that the addition of an angle-of-attack gauge would have prevented this accident.

Well-trained pilots, who use angle-of-attack indicators on military aircraft and other non-commercial planes, find this instrument reliable and effective. Pilots who have used them on virtually all military aircraft and many business jets consider the angle-of-attack indicator a welcome addition.

The addition of an angle-of-attack indicator would give more information to pilots making critical decisions. The device requires a small vane similar to one used to detect wind direction. The measure of that direction versus the direction the airplane's nose is pointing should be the angle of attack. If the vane is too close to the wing the change in lift-producing airflow around the wing can cause an erroneous angle-of-attack indication. An angle-of-attack gauge relying on information off the airflow outside the airplane can also be inaccurate during a turn. This is why the angle-of-attack vane is located near the airplane nose, far from the wing's disruption of airflow.

While there is always a chance that the angle of attack indicator could give an erroneous reading, there are effective ways to work around these challenges. Angle-of-attack gauges have been an available option for many years, and the addition is a fairly simple matter on those aircraft with electronic flight displays. While an option on many designs, most airlines have chosen not to buy them. Much of this resistance comes from concerns about relatively low training costs and unintended consequences.

Video Image Recording
Among the BEA's most controversial recommendations was adding video image recording of the instrument panels. When

a pilot pushes a button, and that button does not activate the associated system, it's hard to know where the fault lies. Was it the result of a sticky switch or slightly dirty contact? Did the pilot forget to hit the switch or touch the wrong switch? In the case of Air France 447, it's apparent that the flight director was displaying misleading indications. Image recording would help document what went wrong.

Understandably, pilots' unions do not want to risk flight crew images being leaked to the public. Over the years this recommendation has come up again and again. It is always rejected due to political opposition and cost. Accident investigators want it, pilots don't, and the airlines are not willing to pay for it.

Recording Flight Parameters
Much less controversial is the BEA's call for recording flight parameters displayed on both sides of the instrument panel. On Air France 447, only the left side readings were recorded, which makes it impossible to know if the copilot in the right seat was seeing identical information. If the pilots were, in fact, viewing different data on their respective flight displays this would have added to their confusion.

Transmitting Location Data Via Satellite Uplink and Emergency Locator Transmitter
The BEA formed a working group to study the addition of systems triggering satellite tracking information as soon as an aircraft emergency was declared. Based on this research, the agency recommended that basic flight data (position, speed, altitude and heading) be transmitted via datalink at regular intervals. The BEA also endorsed studying deployable data recorders that would eject and float following an accident.

Collectively these changes would help search teams do a better job tracking downed transoceanic aircraft. In some cases they might be able to recover passengers successfully evacuated from a ditched plane. The International Civil Aviation Organization has endorsed a number of these changes which will begin taking effect in 2020. Some airlines have already begun implementing these recommendations ahead of the ICAO deadline due to concerns raised by both Air France 447 and the 2014 disappearance of Malaysia Air 370. Others, limited by budget constraints, are taking their time.

Search-and-Rescue Procedures
Due to search and rescue (SAR) failures between Senegal and Brazil, the BEA wisely recommended a new procedure with a single point of contact. It also endorsed standardization for SAR operators to ensure a unified approach to training and approval. In addition, the agency advocated creating a single point of contact for each ICAO member state. It recommended replacing HF radio communication that failed Air France 447 with state-of-the-art satellite uplink data communication. The agency wants to expand datalink communications (CPDLC and ADS-C) to all remote regions of the world. This approach would supplement and, in some cases, supplant current HF radio communication.

Pilot Training
Perhaps the most time-sensitive lesson learned in Air France 447 was the urgent need for better pilot training at the airlines. The BEA emphasized that despite their 20,000 flight hours on all kinds of aircraft, Dubois, Robert, and Bonin never received the training they needed to save their plane. Only a few well-trained test pilots could have recovered from the aerodynamic stall that took down this Airbus 330.

The central lesson of this tragedy was the airline's failure to train pilots on how to recover after their computer systems failed. Lacking the necessary instruction, they did not understand what had gone wrong or how to deal with it. With pinpoint accuracy, the BEA explained why pilots must have the resilience necessary to handle instrument failure. Until all pilots receive this kind of training, random accidents like Air France 447 are a foregone conclusion.

The BEA spelled out that pilots need to understand the vast and consequential difference between flight control software modes such as normal and alternate law. In order to stay safely within the "flight envelope," they needed to know when protections were on and off. The flight crew also had to understand that an aircraft's handling characteristics change dramatically when it moves from normal to alternate law. Because planes have different handling characteristics and fly at different altitudes, hands-on training in a wide variety of unpredictable scenarios is needed. A one-size-fits-all approach to simulator training, coupled with leaving pilots in the dark on these extraordinary situations, can set flight crews up for failure.

These recommendations remain critical today. As we can see years after Air France 447, many in the industry have failed to add this long-overdue training. Notable exceptions at a few good carriers only hint at a solution overlooked by most of the industry. To be fair, much of the data needed to properly implement this was simply not available, and there is a real danger of a pilot learning the wrong thing from an incorrectly modeled simulator. The question remains: why was the data to correctly model simulators not previously available?

Loss of airspeed indications due to high-altitude ice crystals could also have been better anticipated. Consider this warning on high-altitude crystal ice delivered more than three years before Air France 447 at a scientific meeting in a paper. Boeing's Jeanne G. Mason, J. Walter Strapp of Environment Canada and Philip Chow of Honeywell reported that between 1990 and 2003 pilots attributed a disturbing series of engine power loss events to... "coincident heavy rain encounter. The report of rain threw off investigators and these events were not correctly attributed to ice particle icing (crystal ice). These events are only now being recognized as due to ice particles..."

The BEA also pinpointed another shortcoming—the need for more aerodynamic training including theoretical knowledge. To its credit, the agency also recommended that training include "startle" scenarios, as well as an emphasis on improved crew coordination (crew resource management). Another key focus was learning how to react to surprise events. Current airline training is heavily "scripted," tipping off pilots to expected challenges. This gives pilots a chance to rehearse and think through their responses, something they may not be able to do in a real emergency.

Although pilots might have no problem recovering from an anticipated stall or mechanical failure, a surprise event, like unreliable airspeed, may trip them up. In simulators they are "expecting" emergencies, and even in the best training where attempts are made to "surprise" the pilots, students anticipate that something will go wrong. This does not necessarily prepare them for the all-important "startle effect." In such a case they must respond immediately to protect the flight. Sometimes the correct response is no response.

Instructors

Improving and standardizing instruction/evaluation criteria is another key BEA recommendation. At many airlines, instructors are chosen based on their ability to handle day-to-day duties, fly the airplane from the co-pilot's seat, run the simulator, etc. Specific training to ensure that instructors have a solid knowledge base is often left out under the assumption that they have already mastered the curriculum.

Simulators

The BEA made several recommendations to improve flight simulator training and guide pilots on how to handle "situations with a highly charged emotional factor."

Simulator fidelity remains an important ongoing issue.

Ground-based simulators lack a full range of aircraft motion and are unable to replicate many forces encountered in flight. In the Air France 447 accident, the pilots were faced with g-forces that went below 1g. They would have felt light in their seats and experienced a significant falling sensation. A ground-based simulator can't make that happen.

Further, flight simulators are only able to replicate what they are programmed to demonstrate. Famously, the crash of an American Airlines Airbus A300 on departure from JFK International Airport was attributed, in part, to a procedure taught in an incorrectly modeled flight simulator.

The BEA also voiced concern that some flight simulations are based on zero data.

A good example is the lack of any flight data, beyond approach to a stall at high altitudes, being supplied by Boeing and Airbus. Supplied data packages were inadequate. Without the required data, attempts to simulate performance beyond approach to stall is unreliable and potentially misleading to pilots.

It's impossible to derive reliable data for simulation from a single "beyond stall" excursion. Required tests into this treacherous regime are hazardous even for experienced test pilots. Due to the extremely complex nature of the disrupted airflow in the post-stall and deep-stall regimes, our understanding of the aerodynamics is not complete enough to reliably model this flight condition. Since this event cannot be modeled, the question remains: how much risk can a company reasonably ask its test pilots to take? In the spring of 2016, the FAA required simulators to replicate flight into the stall regime, but implementation was a challenge.

Unfortunately many aircraft manufacturers refused to provide government regulators with proprietary data for their aircraft. This has forced simulator companies to go to third parties for data required to comply with the new FAA regulation. While the stall model is fairly generic and probably not a completely accurate model for any specific aircraft, it can give pilots some idea of what to expect.

The European Aviation Safety Agency never required the Airbus model flown by Dubois, Robert, and Bonin to be certified for recovery from a stall when operating in alternate law. While the FAA did require such demonstrations, their flight simulators did not have the data necessary to train pilots on how to avoid an aerodynamic stall.

Absent this data, the airlines were exempt from this badly needed training. By accident, the pilots of Air France 447 became the untrained and unqualified test pilots for this unexpected aerodynamic stall.

Without simulator data beyond approach to a stall, it has been difficult to train pilots on high-altitude stall recovery. There is no way to ensure computer models have not missed subtle factors that might make it challenging for pilots to recover. Even after this data becomes available, there is understandable concern that a pilot might be misled by "flying" a simulator with limited ability to replicate the sensations of a real stall. This problem underscores one of the crucial limiting factors in aerodynamic stall recovery training. Some pilots could be misled by their simulator instruction unless it is combined with training flights.

The training emphasis should be on aerodynamic stall avoidance. Failing to do so can be a death sentence, unless the aircraft is flown by specially trained and very experienced test pilots.

The BEA's recommendation for additional hands-on training in manual flight, including high-altitude approach to stall and stall recovery, is a work in progress at regulatory agencies. To date, this critically needed training has only been implemented at a few good airlines.

Flight Directors
Momentary disappearance of the flight directors triggered a

series of emergencies for the Flight 447 crew. First the plane entered a slight climb. When the flight directors reappeared they directed a pitch-up to maintain the in-progress ascent. In essence the system maintained the climb, leaving the pilots to adjust the flight path as needed. By maintaining the instantaneous rate of climb present at the time it was engaged, the flight director quickly misled the crew into an aerodynamic stall. The BEA recommends a review of flight director logic, as well as a redesign that would let the crew re-engage manually after this instrument has turned itself off and suddenly reappeared.

Alert System and Angle-of-Attack Warnings

The Airbus alerting system was another key area of concern for the BEA. When the air data system lost pitot pressure due to convective ice, it triggered a cascading array of confusing alerts that were difficult to interpret. Instead of sounding continuously, they switched on and off.

The stall warning on the Airbus 330 consists of a combination of an aural warning, the illumination of a master warning light, and an alert on the flight display's speed tape (the airspeed indicator). As Air France 447 clearly demonstrated, this approach requires considerable training and a level of understanding that can challenge experienced flight crews. The sometimes confusing alert system can actually add to the workload of pilots facing an emergency. The master warning light can be triggered by a number of different factors, so it may not bring attention to the most critical item, in this case the stall. The design of warning systems is a field unto itself. There are many trade-offs with each choice. Utilizing the master warning for a stall may actually serve to make it less salient as it is also used for so many other systems. Other warnings such as systems that vibrate the control stick or column are more difficult to ignore.

Two additional problems can lead to considerable confusion in the cockpit.

Training at some airlines has failed to clarify the critical difference between stall warnings at low altitude and high altitude. A related complication is the fact that the master warning can be activated by many system failures not associated with a stall.

It is literally a "Master Warning," aimed at focusing pilot attention on their displays where they can quickly address critical system problems. Because the master warning is frequently not indicating a dramatic problem, many pilots habitually cancel it without a second thought.

Once the angle of attack reached the values associated with lower-altitude warnings on Air France 447, both the stall warning and master warning returned. Not surprisingly, the pilots immediately canceled the master warning. All the pilots had to go on from that point was an aural warning. Numerous studies have shown that humans under stress can tune out auditory inputs. Clearly an aural warning is not good enough, but multiple warnings can also cause problems.

To better understand this alert issue, consider why it is easier to stall a plane at high altitude than low altitude. A safe angle of attack at low altitude could be dangerous at high altitudes when flying near the speed of sound in thinner air. This problem is caused by the fact that air changes as it approaches the speed of sound (Mach 1). The accelerating air can create shock waves leading to the creation of the turbulent airflow of a stall. The speed of sound, in turn, is a function of temperature. The air-data system takes in the indicated airspeed and the temperature and converts them to a Mach number. The stall-warning system factors in this important difference. The catch is that three redundant computer systems are entirely dependent on correct airspeed input derived from the external pitots.

On the Airbus A330, the Mach adjustment is limited to the highest reading of the three systems. When these speeds are lost on all three systems, the aircraft reverts to the low-speed limitations found at lower altitudes. This means the alarm system is no longer adjusted to flight at cruise altitude. The stall protection system is now dependent on incorrect data. At this point, only properly trained pilots can solve this problem.

Additionally, the BEA noted that the stall warning is blocked at airspeeds below 60 knots. Design logic dictates that a very low airspeed will not be sufficient to properly align the angle of attack vanes. This problem could lead to erroneous and false readings. In addition, research shows that false warnings rapidly mislead pilots into ignoring subsequent warnings of a real stall. While airspeed of 60 knots on an A330 is obviously a stalled condition, pilots, as seen on Air France 447, can be confused by momentary (seemingly) false warnings, i.e. stall alarms switching on and off.

To reiterate, at high altitudes and high speeds approaching the speed of sound, the warning system is correctly adjusted to trigger a stall warning at a lower angle of attack. The catch is that the computer system can only work when it knows the plane's correct airspeed. If it doesn't, due to frozen pitot tubes that block reliable airspeed indication, the consequences may be devastating.

During much of the time after Air France 447 entered a full aerodynamic stall, the stall warning was off. Unfortunately, a corrupted airspeed reading caused by frozen pitots triggered the scenario. The lack of warning from the computer system, further complicated by the complete lack of a visual stall warning that could have been provided by installation of angle-of-attack indicators, made the problem much harder to sort out.

Further, an important stall cue—the natural aerodynamic buffet created by a stalling wing—was mixing with real turbulence. Distinguishing where one stops and the other begins can challenge a pilot even when she knows the aircraft is stalled. Failure to train for this anomaly in an Airbus A330 simulator made it hard for the pilots to understand the approaching crisis. Unfortunately, the simulators did not have the data to replicate this scenario properly. The addition of an angle-of-attack indicator could help if pilots were properly trained. This device could provide vital information, and reduce the chance that a pilot might be misled. We'll talk more about this problem in a subsequent chapter. It underlies one of the most critical challenges facing the future of commercial aviation.

To be fair to Airbus, Boeing's architecture was found inferior in a study of the various approaches to alerting systems. After studying the problem, the BEA recommended replacing the complex, hard-to-understand Airbus warning system with a more streamlined approach that combined aural warnings with visual warnings.

Timely Airline Incident Reporting to Flight Crews

The BEA was concerned that warnings from dozens of flights encountering unreliable airspeed issues prior to Air France 447 were not shared with Air France pilots. Perhaps the most dramatic case, an August 2008 Madagascar-bound Air France flight that was almost a dress rehearsal for what happened to Dubois, Robert, and Bonin, was never revealed to the airline's pilots. The agency recommended that EASA follow up with mandatory operational and human factors analysis of these events and share them with the industry.

The agency also encouraged the DGAC to improve the quality of incident reports written by crews and make sure they are shared with every manufacturer and airline.

This approach is similar to the one used in the United States where an airline incident reporting system shares warnings with the entire aviation community. The American system would be more effective if the information was "pushed" to the pilots. Currently they often have to seek it out themselves. Safety would also be enhanced if flight crews were trained on key problems revealed by these incidents.

EASA Regulation of the DGAC

The BEA noted that the oversight of Air France by the DGAC

regulators failed to bring to light all of these ongoing problems. The BEA recommended that the DGAC improve its oversight, recruitment, and training of its inspectors.

Drift Buoys
The BEA recommended adding drift buoys to reconnaissance aircraft and using them to immediately capture the speed and direction of the current to accelerate aircraft recovery in deep water.

Industry Response to the BEA's Recommendations
How did the BEA's recommendations fare with the industry? The airline industry moves slowly and cautiously, and rightly so. The industry has been burned by implementing new technology and procedures too quickly without fully assessing possible unintended consequences. As a result, industry failed to make the comprehensive aircraft upgrades and quickly add the hands-on training recommended by the BEA. In fact, some airlines are moving in a different direction.

According to Flight Safety Information, at Virgin Atlantic, a new cadre of beginners — including ski instructors and lab technicians with zero flight experience — are being trained to become jet copilots. Some applicants report that at one major European airline pilot-training program, applicants with more than 85 flight hours are turned down because they have too much air time. Those with less than 85 hours are qualified to fly for major European carriers after comprehensive ground school and simulator training but only half a dozen check rides on a commercial jet. In other words, nearly all of their flight training is on simulators and a few small aircraft, not the big passenger jets they will fly once licensed to fly only this one aircraft. While the statistics have not shown any increase in risk with these programs, which are fully accredited by government regulations, this approach could emerge as a latent issue that might make a difference in the future.

Some Multi-Pilot License (MPL) programs train almost entirely on simulators, giving pilots actual twin-engine jet experience on a handful of flights before they are licensed to fly as a first officer. These newbies can only fly one aircraft type for one airline. During their time off they are not even licensed to fly a small Cessna to a nearby town for lunch. On the surface this may not seem to be a bad thing. An advantage lost is that by flying a variety of aircraft types a person learns a broader muscle memory, which can be beneficial on any type of aircraft if flight controls become degraded.

Still, an increasing shortage of skilled pilots is a driving force and these training schools, which charge aspiring pilots as much as $125,000, appear to be preferred by some airlines who are finding themselves short of qualified pilots. The European Cockpit Association has also voiced concern over so-called "pay-to-fly" programs where candidates are not necessarily guaranteed jobs in the event that the sponsoring carrier does not have jobs available due to downsizing.

An additional concern is fleet modernization that would cut back on the aircraft that these trainees are qualifying for. Of course, the other solution to the demand problem — increasing pilot wages and improving work rules to make the career more inviting — is less popular with airline management. A key factor for the air carriers is that it may take more time to attract and train new pilots with incentives than it would with these expensive MPL training programs.

The approach is widely criticized by aviation schools and training pilots in the United States. It underscores the dangerous assumption of some airlines that pilots should become hostages to their computers and avoid flying their own planes, except during takeoff and landing. As they must pay back their expensive training by flying one plane for one airline, they are essentially stuck in relatively low-paying jobs for as long as six years. The industry's determination to replace experienced pilots with newcomers initially licensed to a single jet, is widely criticized by aviation schools and training pilots in the United States.

Ironically, as British psychologist Lisanne Bainbridge pointed out, "the designer who tries to eliminate the operator still leaves the operator to do the tasks which the designer cannot think how to automate." Why can't an aircraft designer anticipate the challenges that might bring down modern aircraft? Isn't that their job?

The answer to this question, amply documented by the BEA's account of Air France 447, begins with these facts: Manufacturers want to build airplanes that can be flown just as easily by a 25-year-old newcomer as a veteran military or commercial pilot with decades of experience. Lack of previous flying experience is no longer an obstacle to joining an airline. No matter how many computers are on board in the electronics bay, despite all the built-in "protections," the warning screens, alarm systems, collision-avoidance systems, autoland features, and other enhancements, these planes continue to be victims of unanticipated anomalies such as convective ice-producing storms.

When computers fail, aircraft can't fly themselves. These exceptional problems force pilots to throw out their checklist (as was the case with US Air 1549 over the Hudson River) and rely entirely on airmanship to do what no computer system can do.

Why can't computers quickly land a plane safely in the Hudson River or work their way out of an aerodynamic stall over the Atlantic? The answer is that autopilots were never designed to handle these unforeseen challenges. Only a versatile pilot can be trained to come up with a creative solution beyond the ability of her autopilot which can turn itself off with no warning. Computers designed for routine operations cannot cope with once-in-a-lifetime situations and those emergencies still require an experienced and skillful airline pilot to fill those big gaps.

Of course, investigative agencies such as the BEA and the NTSB have the luxury of making recommendations pertinent to a single accident without considering secondary risk factors, the airline industry's equivalent of collateral damage.

For example, most pilots can't legally do much "hand-flying" above 29,000 feet because the industry needs to cram more flights into air lanes with reduced vertical separation. Tighter spacing prevents flight delays and allows airplanes to fly more direct routes. This saves money for the airlines and keeps airfares down.

Training continues being cut back at many airlines due, in part, to reliance on historical data and concepts. In the past, pilots were able to get their experience flying on the line. The shift to reduced-separation flying and the emphasis on the smoothness and efficiency of automation is dependent on better autopilots and software upgrades. It appears that there is not a training issue here—until there is another accident.

After Air France 447, the airline did break out of the industry pattern. It initiated broader training including high-altitude flight in alternate law, approach to stall, landing without airspeed indication and new weather training. Airbus also endorsed new manual airplane training and a better unreliable-airspeed scenario. A parallel FAA advisory circular and regulation endorsed these steps, and agency leaders made a strong case for additional hands-on training.

The constraints of simulator training were also revisited. Originally created by engineers in the spirit of compromise, flight simulators cannot replicate the range of motion experienced in a plane moving at over 500 miles an hour. There is a limit to their acceleration and g forces, which means simulators can only give pilots a sense of how a plane handles in a particular maneuver. There were no human-factors specialists participating in the original simulator designs. This explains why new pilots may not have a good feel for their cockpit after finishing simulator training. That critical experience only comes with actual flight. Current research is aimed at designing new motion-drive algorithms that might add more realism to the simulator experience.

Other reasonable BEA recommendations, such as wider use of drift buoys following a crash, are limited by budget constraints in many countries. None of the French agency's recommendations on adding a second ULB frequency, deployable recorders, or adding telemetry downlinks to track planes missing in the ocean have been implemented.

Interestingly, BEA did not capture another possible explanation for Bonin's control inputs. During much of this time Bonin is holding the controls full back. While this may seem surprising the Airbus flight controls are designed to put the wings at an ideal angle of attack, enabling perfect recovery from windshear and other problems The problem is that this feature is not available with the degraded flight control situation they were facing. Was Bonin trying this trained response to the unexpected situation? We will never know.

Many of the BEA's best recommendations have been partially adopted, delayed, or simply ignored. With the notable exceptions of pitot changes and the decade-long march to better aircraft tracking systems, safety reforms have been piecemeal. In some important ways, particularly cutting back training for new pilots, the industry has regressed. In addition, recurrent hands-on training continues to be limited and does not address the more challenging scenarios that are considered low probability. In light of more recent accidents, it's possible that the BEA-recommended addition of standby angle-of-attack indicators could happen. This single change might be the enduring legacy of the intrepid French agency's outstanding analysis of an accident that could have been prevented.

CHAPTER 10
Crime Scene

While agencies like the BEA and the NTSB investigate accidents and issue lengthy reports, parallel criminal or civil cases represent the interests of the victims' families. Civil actions are typically settled out of court with the airline's insurers. The size of these settlements can be relatively small in countries like China and much higher in the United States, although all can be limited by the provisions of international treaties such as the Warsaw and Montreal Conventions. In some countries such as France and Italy, the courts treat airplane accidents as manslaughter cases. Conviction can lead to major fines and, in rare cases, jail time. While the criminal cases can go on for 15 years or longer, the civil cases are generally settled within a few years. Even after the civil cases are settled, the victims' families remain a party to the manslaughter action, presenting evidence at hearings and working hard through victims associations to press for aviation safety reforms.

While the BEA completed its Air France 447 report, a court investigation directed by Investigative Magistrate Sylvie Zimmerman led to hundreds of interviews conducted by airport police fanning out across Europe, Africa and South America. From air traffic control centers in Senegal to a morgue in Recife, these dogged experts pursued every angle imaginable. Technical consultants grilled the manufacturer and its subcontractors, while Air France management, operations officials and maintenance experts were interviewed at length. The final 700-page report released in 2012 documented the airline's failure to notify flight crews of the 2008 Madagascar A330 emergency that served as a dress rehearsal for flight 447.

Following the first investigation by court-appointed experts, Airbus sought a "Contre-Expertise" rebuttal with a new team of experts including just one French aviator. Lawyers representing Air France, the Association of Families of Victims of Flight 447 and an Air France Pilots Union tried and failed to appoint another expert of their choosing from a court-approved list. Their request was rejected by investigative magistrate Zimmerman. She ruled that adding one more expert would slow down the "urgent" case and lead to further delays triggered by translating proceedings into all languages spoken by victims' families residing in 32 countries from China to Brazil.

After the technical experts filed their "Contre-Expertise" highly favorable to Airbus in 2014, the Family Association and Air France moved to overturn it with support from one of the unions representing the airline's pilots. They argued that the exclusion of airline and family-chosen experts from a special Airbus 330 check ride attempting to simulate Flight 447 violated French criminal code.

The plaintiffs insisted that their experts were entitled to ride along on this flight with the "Contre-Expertise" team. The Family Association, with the help of its technical expert, retired Air France A320 captain and union leader Gerard Arnoux, sought additional technical investigations on unanswered questions about the Airbus's performance after certain anti-stall protections were lost.

This request and a motion to dismiss the "Contre-Expertise" was turned down in early 2015 by Zimmerman's successor, Investigative Magistrate Sabine Kheris. Air France and the Family Association, which includes family members suing the airline for damages, appealed.

In late 2015 the criminal investigation moved to a new "mass disaster" court division with a long name, Pôle Santé Publique et Accidents Collectifs du Tribunal de Grande Instance de Paris. Established in December 2011 in Paris and Marseille, this new court department focuses on mass accidents including airplane crashes. Judges with expertise in these kinds of cases, similar to American class actions, hear these matters. The department also handles cases involving crimes against humanity.

The first big French aviation case to go before the judicial mass disaster division, Air France 447 could set important precedents. In the past, aviation cases have not always been heard by judges with broad technical expertise. In 2016, well-qualified judges Nicolas Aubertin and Emmanuelle Robinson ordered further investigation of the Airbus 330 crash. The new mass disaster court judges can recommend manslaughter prosecution of Airbus and Air France, or conclude that there is insufficient evidence to prosecute the case in a French criminal court. Judges Aubertin and Robinson also approved a portion of the Air France 447 Family Association's request to investigate potential system failures that may have contributed to the accident

The 42-page appellate court decision released in November 2015 overruled Kheris's order on the "Contre-Expertise" because Judge Zimmerman violated the right of Air France and the Family Association to include an expert of their choosing. In addition to nullifying the "Contre-Expertise," the ruling struck from court records all evidence, testimony and exhibits gathered from the date of the overruled order. All this research is inadmissible in further proceedings.

"We are pleased that the court has annulled the 'Contre-Expertise' [because it] did not comply with legal requirements," said Danièle Lamy, president of Entraide et Solidarité AF447. "The families expect a fair trial that establishes responsibility and sanctions the perpetrators without delay."

The Family Association also asked the new judges to close the investigation, arguing that the original 700-page technical report adequately covers the matter. If Robinson and Aubertin agree, they could move the case to a trial court. Airbus can also move for a new "Contre-Expertise" in the mass disaster court. If this motion is rejected, Airbus could appeal. Should their attorneys prevail, a new team of experts might include investigators selected by opposing parties. As one of the attorneys representing victim's families explained:

"Given the appellate court's decision, the Family Association and Air France would be expected to select their own experts from a courtapproved list to join the second 'Contre-Expertise' team. That means we would become a party to this investigation with all the rights enjoyed by Airbus. We'd also be able to include an expert of our choosing on any check rides or test flights, submit new questions, request additional research, and ask any questions we want. In addition, we could potentially challenge the manufacturer on every point. None of this happened on the first rejected 'Contre-Expertise.' Only Airbus was a party to that investigation."

Portions of this review would challenge Airbus's position that technical difficulties outlined by the BEA report did not contribute to the crash. Anticipating this possibility, the family association's technical expert, Airbus Captain Gerard Arnoux called the appellate court's decision, "a victory that will keep the Air France 447 investigation going."

He prepared a five-page list of new conclusions for the mass disaster court and its future technical experts. Some of these key issues have not been previously explored by the BEA or previous court investigators. His bill of particulars suggests that many actors share the responsibility for this accident. A system designed to protect passengers failed, in Arnoux's view, to do what it was supposed to do. Here is his own summary of the causes and contributing factors submitted on behalf of the

French and German victims' family associations and the Air France flight attendants' unions.

Needless to say all of the parties identified here dispute Arnoux's opinions and conclusions. Each one maintains that the accident was not their fault. Here is his analysis:

On June 1, 2009 at 02h 10mn 05s, following the icing of its pitot probes generating unreliable airspeed indications, this Airbus 330 entered an aerodynamic stall in less than one minute, could not be recovered and subsequently crashed into the sea four minutes later.

Here is Arnoux's analysis. It represents his opinions and not necessarily those of the authors. It is offered here to give readers the opportunity to understand and appreciate his point of view:

• Causes linked to the failure of on-board systems to work "per design" (Airbus's responsibility) that made it impossible for this experienced crew to recognize the situation, analyze the problem, and consequently apply any related procedure. This led to inappropriate reactions, an poorly controlled flight path and finally the loss of control of the airplane.

• Preamble 1: The CS-25 requires, in part 2-F-47, regulating ECAM Airbus-type warning systems to the flight crew (electronic centralized aircraft monitor) stipulates that the failure of warning systems related to potentially catastrophic consequences should be extremely improbable.

• Preamble 2: Moreover, the Regulation EU 216/2008 in annex 1 & 1.c.4 indicates that essential information for the safe conduct of the flight and information relative to dangerous situations should be provided to the flight crew in a clear and pertinent manner, with no ambiguities; systems, equipment and controls, including the signals and announcements, should be designed and localized to minimize errors that could contribute to dangerous situations and potentially make them worse.

• Comprehension, analysis, and procedures: ECAM failure. All emergency procedures recommended by the Airbus FCTM (flight crew training manual) begin with identifying and announcing an ECAM alarm (there are around 500 possible warnings on this aircraft type), or such obvious aircraft mishandling that it can be referred directly to a printed checklist. The ECAM alarm associated with the loss of air data readings following the obstruction of the pitot probes is called "per design:" "NAV ADR disagree; SPEED...X check" which means "Air data reference units disagree, crosscheck airspeed." It is established (by the BEA report on this accident) that this alarm, directly correlated with airspeed discrepancies, popped up far too late at 02h12mn44s, which is 2mn39s after the beginning of the event (02h10mn05s) when the aircraft was already in a deep aerodynamic stall and thus in free fall for 1mn30s. This ECAM alarm, which is designed to warn pilots of unreliable airspeed indications and lead them to the appropriate procedures to correctly deal with this situation, should have been shown on the ECAM warning display from 02h10mn07s onwards before the aerodynamic stall began (at the latest this alarm should have taken place at 02h10mn14s). As a matter of fact, this warning did appear in a timely fashion during some previous instances of unreliable airspeed, but did not appear in some other incidents. This was demonstrated by the AF 447 criminal investigation. The absence of this alarm is a severe Airbus failure that misled the flight crew into an inappropriate response.

• Incorrect trajectory control and inappropriate responses were due to wrong altimetry and vertical-speed indications. These erroneous indications called for an ascent, thus justifying the pilot in command's first decision to pull up (due to lack of mach correction). This defect was known only on the model A330-200, not the -300 model or four-engine A340. As a result of this poor design, the erroneous indication calling for an ascent led to the pilot pulling back on the control stick to initiate a climb, thus causing the initial trajectory destabilization of the aircraft.

• Poor flight-control law programming led to loss of longitudinal stability at low airspeeds and high altitudes. Alternate law 2B can lead to an excursion of the flight envelope where the aircraft no longer has any protection against stall. As a result the plane flies not only with less protection than very old previous designs (no stick shaker, no stick pusher either), but the trimable horizontal stabilizer (THS) keeps working in auto mode and helps (forces) the pilot to get out of the (protected) flight envelope. This Airbus design flaw was pointed out by the first team of judicial experts in the criminal investigation of the crash and corrected accordingly on the new A350.

• Failure of the Flight Director (FD) contributed to the crash because the FD did not work "per design." (These defects were corrected by four subsequent Air Safety Agency Airworthiness Directives issued between 2010 and 2012.) The original failures of the FD led the command bars to reappear unexpectedly in reverse mode by giving primarily pull-up directives to the pilot saturated with contradictory information. This Airbus defect contributed to a primary flight display error and subsequently led the pilot to keep climbing.

• We detected a failure and regulation nonconformity of the stall-warning alarm. This, too, was Airbus's responsibility. As the start of the stall occurs at 02h10mn54s, only one stall alarm was heard (regarded unreliable by most crews, according to the inquiry) since the beginning of the event at 02h10mn11s. The alarm should have rung several times after that (the activation threshold of the stall warning was previously exceeded between 02h10mn14s and 02h10mn20s). Instead, the stall alarm stayed silent at a critical moment, probably due to the failure of the IRS 1 (contributing to the crew misunderstanding of the situation of the aircraft).

• The stall alarm that discontinued once the aircraft was already in a deep aerodynamic stall is non-compliant in violation of the CS 25.207 (which caused the pilot flying to primarily maintain a pull-up motion during the descent, preventing any attempt to recover the aircraft.)

• Stall alarms — 25.207 (c) Stall Warning. Once initiated, stall warning must continue until the angle of attack is reduced to approximately — that at which stall warning began.

• Expert's comment: It is not established that the requirement of certification CS25.203 is met as regards the load factor being still active when approaching stall.

• The requirement of certification CS25.207 is not met.

• The programming for the stall-warning system does not meet the certification standards and can actually operate in a "reverse" mode under certain conditions. During the accident flight, the stall warning was triggered when the pilot flying the aircraft made the correct control input to lower the nose of the aircraft, and the stall warning continued to sound until the pilot reversed that control input and pulled the nose up, thus aggravating the stall. This programming flaw and "reverse mode" of the stall-warning system added more confusion to the flight crew's mishandling of the aircraft's actual flight condition.

• The design, installation, and certification of the pitot probes was defective. Responsibility for this falls to Airbus, DGAC, EASA, and BEA. Under JAR 25 standards, the pitot probes should have been evaluated for their vulnerability to icing and ice crystals, and should have been tested to ensure their proper functioning under these conditions (ACJ 25.1419.4).

• Airbus and EASA failed to remove and replace the defective Thales AA pitot probes despite being aware of numerous failures on other aircraft. These failures likely followed the decision by Airbus to replace the Probe Heat Computers (PHC) without having conducted any safety evaluation beforehand. At the same time, flightcrews were not made aware of the possibility of pitot blockage, and they were not provided with limitations and procedures to follow in the event of pitot blockage or failure. This was a violation of JAR 25 sections 1309(a) and (c), section 1524, and section 1585.

• The risk associated with inconsistent airspeed indications due to pitot obstruction was not classified correctly. Additionally, no qualitative risk assessment was conducted by EASA and Airbus; rather, they relied on quantitative evaluation (AMC 25.1309).

• Airbus and EASA violated regulations by failing to correct an unsafe condition (the defective Thales AA probes) when a solution was readily available (the Goodrich probes, available since 2001).

• Airbus was careless in asserting prior to the accident that training pilots to handle stalls at high altitude was not necessary.

• Air France's response operational feedback from its flight crews was insufficient. The airline's Office of Flight Safety, Flight Division for the A330/A340, and the training department should have disseminated the knowledge gained by flight crews.

• There were a group of ergonomic flaws in the aircraft cockpit displays and controls that contributed to the accident.

• This lack of coordinated feedback is an ergonomic flaw that can prevent flight crew coordination when both pilots are manipulating the controls.

• This ergonomic flaw can prevent the flight crew from understanding that the aircraft is in a deep-stall condition and thus prevent them from taking correct recovery actions. The AOA sensors have been installed on all A320 aircraft since the type's first flight, but has not been connected to a cockpit display by any operators.

• The flight path vector (FPV) display was not capable of providing the flight crew with sufficient information to allow them to visualize the aircraft's instantaneous descent angle (a hair-raising 40 degrees, at one point). Without this piece of information, it was difficult for the crew to understand what was happening to the aircraft.

• Checklists and procedures tend to be too complex for incidents such as unreliable airspeed indication. Complex and cumbersome checklists do not adequately satisfy the requirements of CS-25 regarding flight crew response to major failures, and constitutes a violation of European Regulation 216/2008 & 1c4. Meeting these requirements was the responsibility of Airbus, DGAC, and EASA.

• The DGAC was negligent when it failed to produce and disseminate an operational directive or safety information in 2008, despite the OCV having recommended it do so.

• Air France should have paid more attention to the composition of the flight crew, and should have better defined the procedures for task sharing and in-flight crew change-out.

• Air France's maintenance department, department of safety, and department of quality failed to sufficiently evaluate the continuing airworthiness of the A330 in light of warnings and reports from Air Caraibes.

• Air France did not respond sufficiently to a prescient alert from its pilot union in 2002. The union had requested Air France training classify stall recovery an as emergency procedure that demanded pilots respond using memorized procedures instead of written checklists.

- The BEA failed to adequately investigate, or make any recommendations, after getting reports of many similar unreliable airspeed events beginning in 2008. This constitutes a violation of the law (99-243).

- Prior to the Air France 447 crash, neither DGAC nor BEA followed up on safety reports regarding unreliable airspeed indications. In particular, Air Caraibes and DAC Nord had provided an exhaustive report on ACA's incident, but there was no adequate follow-up by DGAC and BEA.

- The DGAC should have acted more vigorously following the decision by Airbus and EASA to take the Rosemount pitot probes out of service in 2001 due to the failure of those probes under similar conditions.

- There was a lack of follow-up by DGAC on NTSB Recommendation A-96-56. This 1996 recommendation asked that aircraft manufacturers provide pilots with some means of determining when their aircraft might be operating in icing conditions that exceed the aircraft's certification limits.

- Similarly, DGAC failed to follow up on a recommendation by German authorities (BFU Recommendation 01/99) that pitot probe certification standards be revised.

The crash of Air France 447 could have been prevented. There were many points along the way at which one decision made differently or one action properly executed would have broken the chain of events that led to the accident. Tragically, it took the loss of 228 lives for the EASA and Airbus to take the final, definitive action to remove all of the defective Thales pitot probes from service. Indeed, EASA did not issue an Airworthiness Directive on this until 2015.

Only after Air France 447 took its final fatal plunge did the BEA analyze all the precursor events that had accumulated in its data. Only after the accident did the BEA come to understand that most flight crews did not apply the manufacturer's unreliable airspeed procedures because the crews did not comprehend that they were in a situation where their airspeed had become unreliable. Sadly, this situation had been pointed out during the 14th Safety Conference held in Barcelona in 2007.

Only after 228 people lost their lives did the BEA realize that there was nothing in the cockpit to give pilots sufficient warning of icing or blocked pitot tubes. After the tragedy, the BEA finally recommended changing the certification standards for pitot probes.

Only after the crash did Air France finally decide to take steps commensurate with the situation to improve training, safety management, and intra-company communications regarding safety.

And it was only after the AF 447 disaster that Airbus finally classified stall recovery as an emergency procedure. It took this accident for Airbus to begin improving the ergonomics of its latest airliners (the A350 series). The newest models have better cockpit and control layouts, and better flight-control law programming even in abnormal-law mode.

In the end, it is clear that the tragedy of Air France 447 could have been avoided if EASA, Airbus, the DGAC, the BEA, and Air France had fulfilled their missions and responsibilities to ensure the safety of aviation."

CHAPTER 11

The Blame Game

Modern professional air safety investigators believe that assigning blame does not prevent future accidents. When people worry they may be held liable for their actions they are far less likely to be forthcoming and share information that could be vital to preventing a future disaster. Further, the science of causality and human cognition make it clear that the legal notion of negligence misses the point. The outcome of an event is only clear in hindsight. If a person knew that a certain action or inaction would lead to an accident, only an insane person would continue on that course. Unless the person was intentionally trying to cause an accident, they were actually making a critical decision with incomplete information. If investigators only viewed the information pilots had *at the time of this decision,* flight crews would be blameless.

The legal profession takes a different view. Whether it is based on Napoleonic law (which forms the basis of the law in countries such as France, Germany, and Italy), or the English Common law (which underlies the law throughout much of the U.S.), prevailing legal code holds that when something goes wrong, someone is "at fault." Although this approach is not likely to prevent a future accident, it can reveal valuable new information. Each Airbus accident triggers a look back at previous crashes in an attempt to provide useful clues.

The launch of the A320, christened by no less than Princess Diana and Prince Charles, was a critical turning point for Airbus and the French aviation industry. Although fly-by-wire aircraft with computer-managed flight control systems were created for military jets and the supersonic Concorde, the new jet was the first subsonic commercial jet to go this route. Here was a chance for the European manufacturer to get a step ahead of Boeing and other commercial airplane manufacturers. Clearly Airbus offered flight technology unavailable from any of its competitors.

The protections built into fly-by-wire controls limit pitch to no more than 55° nose up, restrict bank to 67°, and nose-down pitch to 15°. There are also underspeed and overspeed protections.

These protections reduce the pilot's workload by automatically adjusting the plane's trim for airspeed and configuration changes or banking up to 33°. With continuous pilot input it is also possible to bank between 33° and 67°.

The problem, argues retired Boeing test pilot John Cashman, is that these protections prevent pilots from using their skills in rare situations where these limits need to be exceeded: "When you fully automate and protect the system, you have to take away some of the capability. It makes no sense to us to limit the pull-up capability, say to miss another airplane or the ground. We feel that the pilot should have the capability and should be able to achieve it by use of normal controls, providing cues that he is getting close to those limits but letting him exceed them if necessary."

In theory, it is possible for an Airbus pilot to do this by literally turning off the computer system and flying manually. However, in some emergency situations, following the procedures necessary to accomplish this changeover can take longer than pilots would like. For example, in a loss-of-control incident where the initial rate of descent is relatively low, pilots may choose to exceed the kinds of climb restrictions built into

Airbus jets for safety's sake.

Cashman cites the case of a China Air 747 that was falling rapidly out of control toward the Pacific in 1985. In this case, the pilots lost control of the airplane during cruise flight after an engine shut down. They were distracted with the engine and did not realize that the airspeed was decreasing. The autopilot attempted to hold the wings level and was not disconnected until it had reached its maximum limit. The airplane rolled over and into a steep dive and into a cloud layer leading to further problems.

During their recovery from the dive and roll the airplane experienced forces of more than four times the force of gravity (normally referred to as 4gs), "a feat that would be impossible with fly-by-wire limitations" according to Cashman.

Absent from this argument is the fact that this maneuver also greatly exceeded the airplane's design limitations of 2.5 times the force of gravity and also exceeded what is termed the ultimate design load. In other words, the airplane could break apart under such force. Further, there is no evidence to support the contention that more than 2.5gs was necessary to recover. It is worth noting that the Airbus computerized flight-control system likely would have prevented this loss of control. Here is a case where fly-by-wire protections could have avoided a near-fatal incident that resulted in significant structural damage to the aircraft.

A more realistic concern is low-speed protections. When they sense an approach to stall, both Airbus and Boeing airplanes will automatically lower the aircraft's nose to protect the aircraft. In December of 2012, an Airbus A330 had an unusual event where the angle-of-attack vanes froze.

Normally, the angle-of-attack vane readings are fed into the envelope protection software to warn of stalls. In this case they froze below the low-speed stall threshold but above the high-speed stall angle. This discrepancy meant that the flight computers were receiving false information. While the plane climbed to cruise altitude, the frozen angle-of-attack vanes misled the computer system, which incorrectly commanded a nose-down dive. As the plane descended rapidly the plane accelerated. To avoid a potential overspeed, the pilots disconnected their flight control computer, solved the problem in manual flight and prevented a disaster. An Emergency Airworthiness Directive was issued regarding the event, which states (in pertinent part):

• When Alpha Protection is activated due to blocked AoA probes, the flight control laws order a continuous nose-down pitch rate that, in a worst-case scenario, cannot be stopped with backward sidestick inputs, even in the full backward position. If the Mach number increases during a nose down order, the AoA value of the Alpha Protection will continue to decrease. As a result, the flight control laws will continue to order a nose down pitch rate, even if the speed is above minimum selectable speed, known as VLS.

Despite the arguments against fly-by-wire protections that limit pilot discretion, a design preventing loss of control is beneficial. In fact, following recommendations from the U.S. Commercial Aviation Safety Team, Boeing included envelope protection features on its fly-by-wire aircraft. However, in the above scenario, even with the added protections, the Boeing pilot has the edge.

In the Boeing aircraft, the pilots are met with ever-increasing control forces as they might attempt to fly into a bank or pitch that is potentially unsafe. While these forces can be very high, with sufficient force a pilot can override them to roll the airplane upside-down or into a very steep nose-up or nose-down without the need to actually disconnect the flight control computers. Boeing uses "envelope protection", as opposed to the Airbus "envelope limiting". To prevent a dive, a Boeing pilot can just pull back on the controls; unlike an Airbus pilot who first has to turn off computers, a time-consuming action that can distract a flight crew from the critical job at hand. When seconds count this is a big advantage, although potentially it can take a lot of force.

The Boeing fly-by-wire design is seamless for the pilot. In fact, most pilots forget that they are not flying an airplane with conventional controls. Many pilots see this positively. They might argue in a perfect world it is best to have the pilot forget the reality of the environment in which they are operating—a digital world as opposed to really controlling the airplane. However, it is also possible that this could detract from a pilot being fully aware of the situation. Digital flight controls have some unique characteristics and failure modes. Just because there has not been a problem with the Boeing fly-by-wire so far does not mean there could not be some surprise in the future. There are scenarios where the flight-control computers need to be switched off on the Boeing also, one of which involves unreliable airspeed. While none of the envisioned failure modes require an immediate response, that does not mean that there is zero possibility of a scenario that does; after all, if every accident scenario could be envisioned, we would be able to eliminate them.

Certainly no country is more central to this debate than the place where fly-by-wire technology first captured the complete attention of the aviation community in 1988—France. In the same way that brave Aéropostale aviators flying out of Toulouse launched South Atlantic aviation, it was French pilots who introduced the fly-by-wire breakthrough destined to find its way into thousands of commercial jet cockpits. While some pilots and their unions expressed misgivings about this new technology, Airbus pioneers embraced it. Their self-confidence mirrored the image of French pilots around the world. You can see it in advertising for French airlines, hear it during the cabin announcements, and see it when saying *au revoir* to your immaculate captain while disembarking at your final destination.

The pilot may have been flying for 12 hours, but their uniforms are perfectly pressed and wrinkle-free. The men and women in charge of hundreds of lives appear to be immune to jet lag.

The families of the victims of Air France 447 filed suit against Airbus, Air France and other parties following the accident. Their technical expert, Gerard Arnoux, participated on both the civil and criminal cases. A pioneer A320 pilot at Air Inter and later Air France, he has a history of questioning the logic in the Airbus fly-by-wire technology. Thanks to the insistence of his union, the first A320s flown at Air Inter came with Angle of Attack indicators. Later this option was dropped by the airline and its successor, Air France. In 1999 Arnoux was the captain of an Airbus A320 that was involved in a collision with a glider. While both aircraft miraculously landed safely the incident raised some questions in Arnoux's mind. He described it this way, calling into question the benefits of the fly-by-wire controls: "On Boeing you can bank as much as you want. If you fly a Boeing you can go upside down. An Airbus I was flying collided with a glider on February 12, 1999. I was given an honor by the Minister of Transport—an award of high distinction, the *honneur et patrie* (ranked just below the Legion of Honor), for avoiding a fatal accident."

Arnoux's perception at the time of this event is fascinating: "The sidestick limits the rate of roll to 15 degrees per second, while Boeing lets the pilot roll as quickly as the airplane is able to. We could have very easily avoided a collision if it were not for the design limits. If we could have banked faster we could have avoided the glider."

Does Arnoux's memory of the event withstand numerical analysis? As is often the case, the issue is complex because there are many variables that can support various points of view. The 15°/sec rate limit on an Airbus may actually not be different than a Boeing. A review of flight data recorders appears to show that the collision occurred just as the 15°/sec roll rate was reached. This means that the roll rate limitation *per se* would not have played a part in the outcome.

Nonetheless, it is still worth asking if the fly-by-wire system may have contributed to the collision. Should the Airbus have been engineered to allow for faster roll rates? A very fast roll rate could trigger a pilot-involved-oscillation, now generally referred to as Aircraft-Pilot Coupling. The pilot gets out of phase with the way the aircraft is responding, resulting in a rapid back-and-forth action which can occur in roll, pitch or yaw. The human reaction time mixes with the aircraft response to the flight controls to make the situation difficult to stop absent some techniques that seem very counter-intuitive to the pilot involved. Even very experienced test pilots can be challenged in such a situation. Like high-altitude stalls, most pilots have never received training to counter or recover from such an event, which in extreme cases can lead to a loss of control.

What matters here is not simply aerodynamics but the way a pilot reads the situation, his basic airmanship. Considering the fact that pilots come to their jobs with a wide variation in experience and training, aircraft designers adjust for the norm. While the typical pilot thinks his skill set is above average, the typical designer is thinking about pilots who may not be experts like Arnoux, or simply flying under challenging conditions when they happen to be having a bad day.

As our book shows again and again, actions taken in the moment can be a far cry from the way they look in a simulation or accident analysis. It took the BEA's top team three years to fully understand what went wrong on Air France 447. This does not diminish Arnoux's analysis of the crash but highlights a fundamental issue in safety management—the difference between what a person perceives intuitively and what comes out of objective analysis after an event.

What matters in a critical moment is the pilot's perception of what the airplane will do or not do. Arnoux will be the first to tell you that just before impact he was not thinking to himself that his A320 was forcing him into a crash that he could have certainly avoided if he was flying a Boeing 737. He was entirely focused on flying his Airbus to the best of his ability. He knew exactly what his plane could and couldn't do and was working toward on the safest possible outcome for his passengers. Exceeding the A320's design limits was not an option and he proceeded accordingly. Fortunately he did his best to minimize impact with the glider and no one died.

Clearly designers have to balance many factors to ensure the airplane handles well and that the average pilot won't get into trouble. Looking at the worst-case scenario, they build in protections whenever possible. From a human factors standpoint the number one factor here is pilot reaction time. The problem, as accident analysis shows again and again, is that a pilot only knows what he or she sees or feels, often filtered through our imperfect memory. Considering the financial limits forcing cutbacks on training, a pilot may have never experienced a once-in-a-lifetime occurrence like Arnoux's event on a simulator, let alone actual flight.

It is one thing to walk away from an accident, analyze the event, and put all the blame on the design of the machine. For example, Arnoux is possibly correct that a faster roll rate could have prevented his run-in with a glider, but it is hard to say as the real limiting factor here may be innate human response time, not the roll rate. But what about another, less experienced pilot on a different day?

All of this points to the continuing challenge of understanding events that involve multiple "actors." As soon as a designer introduces more than one component, be it more than one person or computers, the interaction between these components can become challenging. They may not speak the same language. A perfectly designed component may not play well with another component resulting in unanticipated consequences.

For example, there is a significant difference between the

way an aircraft handles in a roll during normal law and alternate law. When a pilot enters a roll during normal law, the computer system handles everything perfectly. This makes the pilot's job much easier. The pitch is controlled via the flight control computers to make sure that the "g" load is not excessive thus insuring passenger comfort and load limitations. The pilot (or autopilot) command is filtered through the flight control computers which then interpret the command to provide a specific rate of change. In pitch they directly control the elevators (movable surfaces hinged to the horizontal stabilizer at the tail of the aircraft), and, in turn, the entire stabilizer can be adjusted. Thus the elevators act as short term, immediate change devices, while the stabilizer is adjusted to hold it for a longer term thus freeing up the need to hold an input from the elevator. This has the additional advantage of reducing the aerodynamic drag so the aircraft is more efficient.

When a pilot adjusts the pitch and roll in alternate law, as in Air France 447, the aircraft responds much differently. Effectively, in the pitch mode, the trimmable horizontal stabilizer continues to trim the aircraft to reduce the aerodynamic loads but the system no longer has envelope protection in pitch or roll. The roll axis has additional differences. In alternate law, says the Airbus manual, "the rate of roll is generally higher than with normal law and at first the aircraft appears to be very sensitive." These factors are discussed cryptically in the Airbus manual and are typically not taught in training and the amount of pilot attention to counter the "very sensitive" roll can lead to less attention to other factors.

In alternate law the aircraft continues trimming the horizontal stabilizer in the same manner as in normal law. When the pilot pulls the stick backwards to enter sustained climb or descent, the trimmable horizontal stabilizer moves to hold the forces constant allowing the elevators moving to the faired position—aligned with the rest of the stabilizer. The horizontal stabilizer lags behind what the pilot or autopilot is commanding and only starts to move after the elevator input has been made. The movement is slow by design, as it is only intended to even out forces and it would not be desirable for the entire stabilizer to move rapidly in a transport aircraft. This means that if the airplane is in a climb and the pilot decides to push the nose down and reverse it, the plane may continue to climb until the horizontal stabilizer catches up with the pilot's intentions. In other words, the system can inadvertently help the pilots exit the protective flight envelope. The consequences of this problem were obvious when first officer Bonin attempted to descend in the middle of the Air France 447 crisis. According to the BEA report, 13 seconds after Bonin pushed forward on the sidestick at two-thirds of full deflection, the aircraft continued to climb at the rate of 1,700 feet a minute.

This very slow response time added to Bonin's confusion, precisely at the moment the flight director's bars unexpectedly reappeared in reverse mode. Like a GPS rerouting a driver who has just missed a turn, the erroneous flight director appeared to be telling Bonin that his climb was right when in fact the plane was approaching stall conditions (a flaw corrected by four subsequent EASA airworthiness directives). Not only did this unexpected horizontal stabilizer problem compound Bonin's difficulties, it deepened the aerodynamic stall.

"When critics of this flight crew maintain that that this event was pilot error they are demonstrating that they have not read the BEA report," says Arnoux. "The fact is that at the precise moment that this unpredicted and untrained-for anomaly was happening, these pilots were effectively flying an aircraft that had become extremely difficult to save. The truth is that they were no longer flying a state-of-the-art plane. Even a 707 or DC-8 was better protected at this point."

Air France didn't teach these facts of Airbus life to its flight crews because the carrier assumed that the plane could not enter a stall at high altitude. When the unexpected happened, the pilots had no frame of reference for what was happening to their aircraft. They were in the dark when it came to understanding why the plane was descending at such a steep rate.

Humans are uniquely adapted to adjust to the variations they encounter with machines, whether those variations are mechanical or software in nature. We have had millions of years of evolution to learn how to adapt to other living organisms around us, in particular our fellow humans. Computers, on the other hand, will react consistent with their design—even if that conflicts with how the designer intended them to act. Machines do what they are programmed to do and can't think for themselves in every difficult situation.

Absent proprietary Airbus information, such as any algorithms that might enhance or diminish the initial entry into the roll itself, it is hard to definitively analyze Arnoux's event. The amount of information required is far more than the "back of the envelope" calculations possible with data that is publicly available. In any case, Arnoux remains a valuable gadfly promoting safety and keeping the pressure on to investigate the root issues in these accidents and incidents.

An Airshow Tragedy At Habsheim

Prior to the crash of Air France 447 perhaps the most controversial disaster in the airline's history was the June 26, 1988, A320 tragedy at Habsheim, a small town near the German/French border. The appearance of the airline's first fly-by-wire aircraft was, in its way, a national event that generates controversy nearly three decades later. The plane, which had been delivered to the airline just two days earlier, represented a key technological breakthrough for the manufacturer.

Test pilot Bernard Asseline's last takeoff for Air France took place on June 26, 1988, and was destined to become one of the most infamous flights in France aviation history. As the plane left the runway at the French border town of Mulhouse, the 130 passengers in the cabin included children and disabled guests. Also along for the ride in the cockpit were off-duty flight attendants who were personal friends of the pilot. They were part of a proud and storied tradition of French demonstration flights dating back to the earliest days of aviation. Before they were truly famous in America, the Wright Brothers dazzled crowds in Paris. While Boeing management has never been big on these public events, the French companies loved them. Not content to merely bring in military aircraft and stunt pilots, organizers began recruiting French airlines.

Airshows at the La Ferte-Alais outside Paris dazzled crowds as pilots flew French 747s, Concordes and other commercial jets breathtakingly close to the ground, almost near enough to see what the vendors were dishing up for lunch.

"It was done for many occasions because it was considered fun," suggested Pierre Sparaco. "It was a stupid French tradition. It was totally crazy."

Even more controversial was the decision of Airbus's Asseline and his copilot, Pierre Mazieres, to take off with their full load of passengers on a short flight from Mulhouse organized by the Habsheim Aero-club. As the brand-new A320 neared the crowd, the captain turned off the autopilot, taking manual control of the aircraft. He then also turned off the auto-throttles. Alerts triggered when the plane descended to 1,000 feet and the copilot began questioning his decision.

Captain Asseline, with more than 10,000 hours of flying time behind him, took the plane down to just 30 feet. Because the auto-throttles were off they did not provide their normal protection against being too slow, and with the power at idle the engines could not respond quickly. An attempt to climb out quickly failed, the plane brushed trees, crashed and exploded. Three passengers died in a fire, 34 were injured and 93 escaped without injury, including both pilots. The aircraft was a total loss.

The pilots, two Air France managers and the president of the Habsheim Aero-club were indicted. In court the prosecutor presented more than 20,000 pages of documents detailing the case against the pilots and the airline. Defense experts and former Airbus acolyte Asseline insisted that the crash was caused by unanticipated flight control and engine problems. Convinced that the French government was trying to protect the future of Airbus's promising fly-by-wire aircraft, some critics accused the authorities of a cover-up. They insisted that the local chief of France's Direction Générale de l'Aviation Civile (DGAC) had surreptitiously replaced the plane's voice and data recorders. In a widely publicized attack, they claimed these bogus replacements were designed to pin the blame on the pilot and exonerate Airbus in a desperate attempt to save the company's fragile fly-by-wire A320 business. This conspiracy theory, offered by a former union leader and widely circulated, was backed up with alleged photographic evidence of the "real" flight recorder being taken away from the crash scene.

In court, Captain Asseline, once a true believer in fly-by-wire technology, argued that the aircraft had failed to keep his crew and passengers out of harm's way. But the BEA report blamed the crash on pilot error.

By now the tragedy was turning into a spectator sport that rivaled the French air shows. Multiple venues offered aviation buffs their choice of Air France trials. A libel suit was brought by directors of the nation's two top airline agencies, the DGAC (France's FAA) and the BEA (France's NTSB) against pilot Asseline and author Norbert Jacquet after they published an expose on the alleged cover-up that assigned all blame in the crash to an Airbus malfunction. That trial ended in a verdict against Asseline and Jacquet.

Analysis of the accident shows that a contributing factor in the Habsheim tragedy was stall protection preventing the low-flying pilot from pulling up to avoid trees. The catch is that pulling back on the stick to raise the nose would have probably made the situation worse, as the aircraft would then have actually stalled or at the very least increased drag.

Appearing before the accident investigation team, the captain argued that had he been flying a traditional aircraft, the crash wouldn't have happened. The investigators and the BEA ruled otherwise. Increased drag would have apparently been greater than thrust, a momentary benefit. But it appears that this would have only slightly delayed the inevitable. In this case, the accident would have happened whether or not the flight crew was operating a fly-by-wire or conventional aircraft.

It's one thing to blame everything on the pilot. But from the pilot's point of view, in this case an exceptional test pilot flying a new kind of aircraft, perception can make a critical difference. Here the pilot hit the throttle expecting the airplane to respond like a traditional jet. He thought the engines would spool and accelerate to his touch. But fly-by-wire protections are designed to protect a pilot from himself, from accelerating in a way that would potentially put the aircraft in harm's way. This means he is not directly moving the controls the way he would on a conventional airplane.

All of his commands or sidestick inputs are filtered by a computer system designed to rule out pilot error. The point is that in a perfect world it's best to have the pilot focused on controlling the plane, regardless of the automation package on board.

Aircraft should always be operated based on a fundamental understanding of aerodynamic principles, not hypotheticals. Pilots shouldn't be distracted by secondary issues or waste time troubleshooting machinery having a bad day. It was a mistake to put the plane in a potentially hazardous situation. The very low altitude fly-by at Habsheim would have been worthy of a stunt pilot in a small plane. It was not appropriate for a big jet.

In the criminal trial, co-pilot Mazieres was exonerated because of a cockpit transcript proving that he questioned the pilot's decision. He moved on to work as a postal pilot. Asseline, who insisted he was flying by the book and made no errors, was convicted and sentenced to nearly a year in jail. After his release, the most famous Airbus pilot in France moved to Australia and then the United States where he was hired as a pilot, serving until his employer learned of the Habsheim crash.

As a direct result of this tragedy, Air France and Airbus ended the French tradition of low-altitude passes at air shows. But French technology continued to occupy an important place on every plane in the sky. The Habsheim tragedy was a learning experience for Airbus, says John Lauber, Vice-President of Safety and Technical Affairs at the National Academy of Sciences. A former National Transportation Safety Board member and Airbus executive, Lauber points out that the pilots intended to fly over the air show at 100 feet with their gear down. The problem was triggered by the pilots' decision to buzz the crowd at less than 30 feet. The plane was flying to low and too slow. As the new Airbus 320 headed for the trees, the captain added power to climb but it was too late. The fly-by-wire protections prevented a stall, but it was impossible to clear the trees. Even if the pilot could have raised the nose more, the increased drag would quickly have overcome any increase in lift, leading to a crash.

Clearly automation can be both friend and foe. The critical difference is the pilot's knowledge and skill. A pilot who understands the system knows when it needs to be disconnected. Equally important is that he understands when disconnection can lead to a bad outcome. Knowledgeable pilots should not encounter an unexpected outcome, but if they do, they have the know how to return an aircraft to safe flight.

Retired Air France pilot Gerard Arnoux has long championed the importance of airmanship. In his apartment office on Paris's Rue Voltaire, he gazes out over the small mountain of data he has compiled on the Air France 447 accident. This Airbus captain worries that a new generation of pilots will not have the resilience necessary to successfully confront challenges outside scripted airline curriculum.

"The man who invented the auto assembly line to build the Model T, Frederick Winslow Taylor, said this is not a job, it is a task. You want people who are doing the same thing all the time. This is the same thing they have done with fly-by-wire pilots for the past 20 years."

Arnoux believes it is a mistake to put all the emphasis on procedures at the expense of independent thinking necessary to deal quickly and efficiently with challenges outside the scope of training. He is especially concerned about training that omits critical issues such as handling convective storms. On a takeoff from Nice he asked a young copilot how she would handle two looming thunderheads separated by a small gap. The captain expected her to suggest going upwind of the bad weather.

"When she suggested flying through the gap between the storm," says Arnoux, "I realized that her procedural training simply ignored meteorology. That would have been very bad because we would have been flying through dangerous downdrafts. Too many young pilots have no respect for thunderstorms. They don't realize how dangerous this bad weather can be. Too often they obey a mistaken controller's orders instead of circumnavigating a storm for safety.

Arnoux is dismayed by what he calls, "Taylorization of the mind and training." He believes that the airline industry is "putting down layers of laws and procedures and telling pilots what they have to do. We have the data recorders that analyze each flight. If you make a turn at 500 feet they will call you in after the flight and ask why you have done that. You better have a good explanation, like conflicting traffic. Pilot discretion has to be justified."

Modern data tracking is standard across the airline industry. A set of parameters the airline wants to track is entered into the computer. These are based on a study of problems that have led to accidents and incidents. When a flight exceeds one of these parameters it is sent to an analyst for review. The analyst, an expert on this type of aircraft, reviews the data to see if there is some justification. For example, if the airplane was flying too fast on approach the analyst might note gusty winds required a faster air speed. However, absent any justification, the analyst will arrange for the pilot to be contacted.

This call is not supposed to be a "threat" to the pilot. The purpose is to gather information and learn from it. For example, at the Orlando, Florida airport it was discovered that pilots were often approaching too high and too fast on one runway. A review of the data and interviews with the pilots showed that the problem was the design of runway approach which forced pilots to exceed the normal parameters for descent rates and speeds. The procedure was redesigned and the problem disappeared.

As Arnoux argues, the rigid focus on conformity does not guarantee system safety. Airlines use the metrics from these reporting systems to "see how well they are doing." Lower numbers are seen as a big plus. But what is this really telling us? Is the data getting better or is there just less reporting of abnormal incidents? Perhaps pilots are inadvertently being "trained" to avoid certain things that will "trigger" a report, making the data look good while latent hidden risks grow. The danger is that pilots are being trained with a lack of knowledge or skill sets to fly beyond the very narrow parameters in scripted training. The concern is that flight crews may not have the resilience and ingenuity to come up with solutions to unexpected challenges.

Arnoux is concerned about the gap between the training of new pilots and veteran pilots. The older ones learned in a different era where the guidelines were less clear.

They encountered situations outside of the established parameters that are in force today. Performance relied on knowing how to handle unscripted problems beyond the scope of their training. Their success required them to create innovative solutions in real time. Creativity and independent thinking were essential to handle events beyond the scope of ground school and their in-flight training. Good decision making on the fly meant knowing how to handle one-off emergencies.

Enforcing standardization and proceduralization has reduced accidents. However, in the process industry is creating a new generation of pilots that has never needed to think creatively or acquired the skills to do so. Undoubtedly the industry has benefited from a combination of the old and new. Pilots who learned how to fly in the less rigid world certainly benefit from better flight automation. But as we've seen with Air France 447, advanced automation doesn't mean the industry can afford to cut back on training. Even great automation can contribute to unexpected problems that require good airmanship executed in a timely manner.

Automation in modern airliners was developed on the assumption that proceduralizing was the best path forward. Around the world, training centers place less emphasis on making sure pilots understand what their flight automation systems are actually doing. Pilots are taught to rely on the electronic procedures that display automatically or can be selected in the event of any problem. Flight schools focus on following commands issued by the automated system. The emphasis is on not intervening unless absolutely necessary. The problem is that pilots have little training on how to handle situations that are not programmed into the system, such as an unexpected low-altitude bird strike that knocks out both engines.

Other French inventions used in both classical and fly-by-wire aircraft remain controversial. One of the most important is century-old pitot technology, which has been embraced by airplane manufacturers since 1915.

Invisible to passengers, these devices mounted on the front

end of the fuselage are critical to flight safety. Updated and modified many times for the jet age, pitots continue to be a source of controversy. The European Aviation Safety Agency (EASA), which oversees flight certification for 31 member nations, is particularly concerned. The issue is that the two leading brands, Goodrich and Thales, have both been the subject of official inquiries. The French-made Thales pitot has also been the subject of an important Airbus/Air France controversy.

"The Thales and Goodrich pitot tubes are very similar," says EASA's Daniel Holtgen at his riverside office in Cologne, Germany. "It is hard to understand why one would be more prone to icing than another. Also we are not clear why so many of these problems have been reported by Air France pilots."

Further complicating the pitot issue is the fact that accidents related to pitot icing keep happening. A few months after the crash of Air France 447 another A330 with Goodrich pitots operated by a Qantas subsidiary, ran into problems. While the erratic speed indication on an October 29, 2009, flight from Tokyo to Gold Coast, Australia, was brief, it underscored the ongoing concern of pilots and airlines about this safety problem.

Adding to this dilemma is the lack of uniform regulatory standards. Arnoux points out that the regulation is different in Europe and the U.S. While the FAA classified the emerging pitot icing problem as potentially "catastrophic," in Europe it was considered as a "major failure" which did not require immediate corrective action for a European airline. This may explain why EASA has claimed diplomatic immunity in the Air France 447 case.

Iberia Airbus A320 first officer Fran Hoyas says his fear about the crash of Air France 447 is that "the focus will be on protecting the status quo, the system we have in place now, instead of increasing safety. Sometimes economics play a role that interferes with the final results of the investigation.

For example, the airlines did not want to add training for the kind of event that is now believed to have contributed to this accident—how to fly a jet when there is a loss of speed indication. Training is always heavily time constrained and it is not possible to add everything. Items deemed to present the most risk are given priority, and sometimes that risk assessment turns out to be flawed.

"There is a lot of pressure on these investigations," Hoyas says. "When there are accidents or incidents, the manufacturers are very worried. Recently there was an incident with a commuter plane in Switzerland. The pilot had to do an emergency descent. The first guy there after the pilot landed was from the manufacturer, talking to the guy investigating the incident. He was thinking, we can't go public because we won't sell any more airplanes."

Another problem is replicating accidents that occurred at a particular airline. This is both a legal and technical challenge. Creating a somewhat accurate scenario in a simulator takes a lot of work. Flight data is entered into the algorithms and must be subsequently tested, smoothed and refined. Assuming that can be done to a reasonable degree, there is inevitably a major hurdle surrounding legal approval required to present this scenario to pilots.

Hoyas, who has previously served as head of the industrial affairs department of the 38,000 pilots belonging to the European Cockpit Association, states cause for continuing concern: "You can't duplicate the Air France 447 crisis situation to show other pilots exactly what happened. This is coupled with the problems of pilot training.

"We are facing an industry where pilots have less and less experience. Some airlines hire inexperienced people who have never flown an airplane in their life. I was in the Air Force Academy for five years, trained in the U.S. Air Force and then flew for the military for ten years and piloted corporate jets. It was 16 years before I flew for Iberia.

"Today there are pilots flying with me who have only had 200 hours of experience. It used to take three years for pilots to qualify for a license. Nowadays you can do it in one year. All you need is 155 hours in a simulator, 40 hours of actual flying and you can get a type rating that qualifies you for the right seat of the aircraft.

"Today we have more and more junior captains with less flying experience and technical knowledge. You have a procedure to follow when the autopilot switches control of the flight to the pilots. If you go to page three and follow the emergency procedure you may be right today. You may not be right on another day. If you do not have a clear idea of what is going on in the aircraft you may not be able to handle an unusual situation that is beyond the scope of your hands-on training."

Although many airlines have far more stringent requirements than the ones Hoyas is worried about, even experienced pilots get short shrift when it comes to simulator training.

"Depending on the airline," says Hoyas, "you may get two to four hours of simulator training per year. The amount of manual hands-on training can be as little as half an hour to an hour per year."

In today's highly-automated flight environment, the emphasis is on staying with the autopilot even in turbulent conditions. This means when emergencies force the pilots to take control, they may not always have the experience necessary to quickly get out of a dangerous situation.

"The problem with automation is to a certain extent it prevents the pilot from keeping basic flying skills sharp," says Hoyas. "We've seen a big increase in loss-of-control aircraft accidents in recent years. Unfortunately, the simulator training does not accurately reflect important emergency situations you may have to handle in your job. You can't learn how to do this if you are only flying manually in a simulator for an hour a year."

"There is a tendency right now to lower certification standards for simulators because they are expensive. The airlines and manufacturers are encouraging the development of less-expensive simulators that do not have the same technical performance as the planes we fly. Instead of mirroring reality in emergency situations they are going for simulators that are stationary. They don't rock. Without motion you can't create the cockpit environment to resemble what the pilots of Air France 447 were going through that night.

"My PC is not the same as a simulator, even if I have three screens. You can't simulate real danger, real situations, real physical conditions and vibrations. Sometimes you can't read the numbers because it's so turbulent. The other day I was taking off from Cairo on a very bumpy runway, trying to read the engine temperature gauge to make sure it was safe. You must learn how to manage this kind of situation properly in a simulator. It is an essential part of our ongoing training."

If the pilot was at rest during the time of pitot failure another problem could have interfered with flight management. Pilots who fly for the British Royal Air Force train for loss of airspeed indication on simulators at least once a month, says Hoyas. One, who joined a simulation of the crash for a British law firm says:

"In recreating the Air France 447 incident we learned that when you leave 'normal law' and go to 'alternate law,' the captain's primary flight display went blank because of problems with the ADIRU computers. Following the emergency checklist, the pilots switch the first officer's primary flight display to the screen of the captain flying the plane manually with predetermined power and pitch settings."

Captain Hoyas points out that Bonin, sitting in the right seat on Air France 447, would have had to lean over in turbulence to read the instruments on the left seat display. "Flying in the vicinity of a powerful storm without the benefit of air traffic control communication or surveillance" made the job harder.

Adding to the degree of difficulty was the unexpected

failure of airspeed monitoring system.

"At the time of the crash there was no simulator training for the simultaneous failure of three pitot tubes," says European Cockpit Association vice-president and XL Airways Deputy Chief Pilot and Airbus fleet manager, Francis Nardy.

"This is not supposed to happen," adds Air France A320 pilot Patrick Magisson, executive vice-president for technical and safety standards for the International Federation of Airline Pilots. "But in 2008, when we simulated the failure of two or three pitots, the computer's polling (voting) system was wrong. It assumed that two airspeed indicators in agreement were correct and the third speed indicator in the minority was wrong. In fact, the pitots for the first two speed indicators had failed and the third indicator was correct. This is where the pilot has to take control."

A related issue at 35,000 feet is the fact that the Airbus A330 is tail heavy. A tail fuel tank linked to a fuel transfer system is designed to continuously adjust the plane's center of gravity aloft to conserve fuel.

"We don't know the exact physical reaction of a plane with an aft center of gravity stalling at high altitude," says Magisson. "Because of the flight envelope protection, we are not trained on how to handle this. The experts are still researching this and trying to figure it out.

"Unfortunately, when you test a plane for certification it is impossible to test all situations. The new planes are so complex that this is not feasible. We don't always know what the plane's behavior would be in any specific situation. This would take years and years of flight tests. You can't really train for every situation in a simulator. We are not sure they are correct."

Magisson, who flies the A320 for Air France, explains that nothing is certain when pitot tubes fail. "When you are flying any Airbus plane such as the A320 or 330/340 in 'alternate law,' you are not truly hand flying. The flying control computer still manages the pilot's input.

"When you certify a plane you don't say, 'this will never happen.' You say this *might* happen but the odds are so low you don't have to take it into account because it has a very low rate of probability. It may stall, it can stall. But you need to degrade the status of the plane to such an extent that it is not included in the certification process. The Boeing 777 is near to this, and some business jets use the same philosophy.

"As Airbus pilots, we are trained to recover from a near stall but we are not trained to recover from a full stall. This is the problem with flight simulators: no flight simulator is able to give good feedback behavior of the aircraft when it is completely stalled.

"It is very difficult to train someone on a pattern of behavior that doesn't respond to reality. We are able to give a good mathematical model of behavior that goes near a stall, but not a full stall. We are trained for this in small planes as student pilots. But as soon as we are flying larger aircraft, this is not the case."

Instead of hand-flying, pilots are taught to rely on automation. "Manufacturers tell you to follow the checklist. But as a pilot you have the authority to overrule the computer. There is a good reason for this.

"If you are really sure that you are correct, you don't have to follow the checklist and procedure. You can overrule the computer and take command. In this case we know that the computer has been tricked. We can turn off flight control computers that are incorrect. The pilot has full authority to make a decision to save your life."

In February 2017, a French mass disaster court named three experts to conduct a new contre-expertise on the Air France 447 case. The experts—Gilles Le Barzic, Patrick Pastor and Jean-Yves Grau—were appointed by judges Nicolas Aubertin, Emmanuelle Robinson and Fabienne Bernard to review the June 1, 2009 crash.

Le Barzic, an expert witness appointed to both the court

of appeal in Aix-en-Provence and the French Supreme Court, is a retired engineer, test pilot and training pilot. Pastor has worked as a chief pilot and flight instructor on the Airbus 330. Grau, a human factors expert, has extensive experience with the French Army's Aerospace medicine health service. He is also cofounder of SynRjy, a company that does human factors work for corporate clients.

The criminal court has asked the experts to review many of the same issues covered by the French accident investigation agency BEA including loss of speed indication due to pitot failure, inconsistent and confusing stall alarm warnings, an unexpected and untrained-for high-altitude stall and numerous human factors issues.

In addition, for the first time since the case began, the court has asked the experts to compare the performance of the Thales pitot tube on AF 447 against widely used Goodrich tubes. The vast majority of aircraft reporting unreliable airspeed events at the time of the Rio-Paris crash were equipped with the Thales pitot tubes.

A contre-expertise highly favorable to Airbus's position regarding the causes for the crash was thrown out by the mass disaster court in late 2015 because this study failed to include representatives of Air France on test flights and failed to address many questions. That report, concluding that the main cause of the crash was pilot error, was rejected by representatives of family victims and Air France. Subsequently, the mass disaster court judges canceled the contre-expertise. All its findings and conclusions were removed from the files.

The previous 2012 and 2013 reports on the Air France 447 crash were based on thousands of pages of documents and interviews in Europe, Africa and South America. They paralleled the BEA's conclusion.

The court's decision also appears to indicate that a 700-page expert's report filed with Investigative Magistrate Sylvie Zimmerman in 2012 and the complementary expertise made at plaintiffs' request by the same experts in 2013 would be allowed to stand and remain part of the case.

The 2012 accident investigation agency's 38-month analysis attributed the worst airline crash in French history to multiple causes. The tragedy was attributed to incorrect flight director indications, loss of angle-of-attack protection and display to pilots, lack of Air France safety management and training on how to handle abnormal airspeed indication, the absence of any visual information to confirm approach to stall after the loss of limit speeds, erroneous airspeed messages from the electronic centralized aircraft monitor (ECAM) and a stall-recovery procedure not in line with Airbus recommendations.

Some recommendations based on the BEA's analysis have been implemented. Many others, such as the long overdue airline adoption of standby angle-of-attack indicators found on most military aircraft and many business and general aviation planes around the world, have languished.

A 42-page appellate court decision overruled Kheris's order on the contre-expertise. This ruling held that Judge Zimmerman violated the right of Air France and the Family Association to include an expert of their choosing.

In addition to nullifying the contre-expertise, the ruling struck from court records all evidence, testimony and exhibits gathered from the date of the overruled order. All this research is inadmissible in further proceedings. Following this ruling the case was also moved to the mass disaster court.

The family association has previously submitted a five page list of new questions for the mass disaster court and future experts. Some of these key issues have not been previously explored by the BEA or previous court investigators.

It's possible that some or all of these new issues could become part of the second contre-expertise.

One question mark for the new contre-expertise is the issue of another live stall test of the A330. It is not possible to reproduce the startle effect because the flight crew doing the test flight will certainly know what to expect during the demonstration.

In addition it is impossible to entirely recreate the 2009 A330's performance because of upgrades to the computer system. A 2017 A330 is not the Air France plane that crashed into the Atlantic. Earlier in the investigation, the court did not accept a request from a German attorney to keep a 2009 A330 computer in custody.

The mass disaster court judges can, following submission of the second contre-expertise and review of all the testimony and evidence, recommend manslaughter prosecution of Airbus and Air France or dismissal of the Flight 447 case. If the case against Airbus and/or Air France goes to trial all seven technical experts, including four who worked on the 2012 and 2013 expertise report to the court, could join Le Barzic, Pastor and Grau in court.

CHAPTER 12
Stalling

As the manslaughter investigation moves through the French courts, the slow pace of safety reform in commercial aviation underscores key challenges in pilot training and simulator programming. Pilots are only as good as the instruction they receive. If they are simply handed a recurrent training DVD where they grade themselves on a multiple-choice test, or are rushed through a short class that skips over critical details, they may not have the skills needed for a once-in-a-lifetime challenge. Likewise, simulators only work when manufacturers have the fundamental data required to make these machines effective for training. An inadequately trained pilot or an incorrectly programmed simulator can lead to unexpected consequences.

The BEA report on Air France 447 focused on these key issues that have a critical impact on the future of air safety. After the 2008 Colgan Air crash outside Buffalo, New York and the 2009 disappearance of Captain Dubois's Airbus A330, the industry meticulously reviewed stall-recovery procedures. In the process, regulators, manufacturers and training departments agreed that stall-recovery training for many pilots was based on little or no understanding of the dynamics of high-altitude commercial jets.

Recognition of this problem has begun to revolutionize flight training. But before pilots could be correctly retrained, simulators needed to be upgraded in two ways. One problem was making sure that ground-based simulator motion accurately replicated the sensations of flight. This upgrade would help pilots develop a much better feel for the way their big aircraft handled.

A second problem was the absence of critical data on how these modern swept-wing jets behave in a stall. Without correct parameters there was no way to accurately program a simulator. A classic example was incorrect simulator training that misled the pilots of an American Airlines Airbus 300, which crashed shortly after takeoff from New York's JFK in November 2001. The accident investigation revealed that a procedure created in an airline simulator recommended a new approach to handling an unexpected roll. The standard technique, using the aircraft's ailerons, was replaced with rudder deflection. Here, best intentions worked great in theory and failed dramatically in the air. Concepts that worked in a simulator (that was not correctly modeled) contradicted the manufacturer's advice.

To explain this as simply as possible, with the A300, like other conventional airplanes, roll is normally controlled via the ailerons, which are moveable surfaces at the trailing edge of each wing. Traditionally the control wheel is turned in the direction of desired roll. In the case of a fly-by-wire Airbus aircraft, the control stick is moved in the chosen direction.

On one wing a panel moves upwards, decreasing lift. On the opposite wing a panel moves downwards, increasing lift. In addition, on large airplanes there are spoiler panels, which deflect upwards on a wing to decrease lift. For a rapid turn, panels on the downward moving wing will be deflected upwards to further decrease lift on that side.

Airplanes can also be turned via the rudder control, the large moveable surface at the trailing edge of the vertical stabilizer, and, in fact, this is the only control for some model airplanes. It creates a roll by something called "dihedral effect" and it can be very effective but in a large aircraft it can also put very high forces on the vertical stabilizer.

In the case of American Airlines, it looked perfect on a simulator. Unfortunately, the airline's training simulators were not programmed to replicate the excessive forces that could be encountered on a bigger plane.

On departure from New York's JFK airport, the crew of American 587 ran into wake turbulence from a previous departure. Their Airbus A300 rolled to the side and the first officer, who was flying, reacted as he was trained on the simulator with a rudder input to counter the roll. The airplane rapidly rolled in the opposite direction. To stop that roll he reversed the rudder, making successive rudder inputs. Each time the nose swung, it was followed by a roll. This sideways motion put more force on the vertical stabilizer. As it swung the opposite way, the pilot made another input that backfired, doubling the force on the vertical stabilizer. Both the motion of the aircraft and large rudder input combined to drastically exceed the design limits of the vertical stabilizer. The stabilizer broke, leading to a total loss of control and crash.[11]

This tragedy showed that these simulator-trained pilots had a poor understanding of the structural limits of their airplane as well as other transport airplanes. This hidden danger was not covered in their manuals or instruction because engineers did not consider the possibility that a pilot would make this fatal error. Clearly the American crew had been misled by their simulator instruction.

A related problem is that most pilots learn recovery procedures in light planes that experience a different and far easier to recognize type of stall. On these classic planes the aircraft generally recovers itself unless the pilot interferes with stall recovery. The plane will not remain in a stall as long as the

11. The NTSB did find that the design of the Airbus rudder control contributed to a scenario where full rudder deflection was relatively easy to obtain. The strength of the vertical stabilizer was not an issue as the forces generated were well above the expected failure point for any transport aircraft, regardless of manufacturer.

pilot refrains from actively pulling back on the control wheel or stick.

Many pilots have assumed that the same was true for larger transport airplanes at any altitude. Manufacturers, airlines and instructors believed that years of experience ensured that pilots could make a similar recovery on big jets. After all, stalls on transport aircraft were a rare event.

Until recently, training programs for transport airplane crews required pilots to add thrust and "power out of the stall" without losing altitude. This exercise was done in simulators and by test pilots checking a plane after maintenance. Transport jets have a big weight range depending on their fuel and passenger/freight loads. When the stalls were performed in the simulator or during flight tests, they virtually always took place at a relatively light weight. This approach was chosen because at higher weight the "power out" technique would fail. Also, the tests were done at lower altitudes.

Given these limitations, the old technique worked on jet aircraft for two reasons. First, the pilots recovered as soon as the first approach to stall warnings occurred – long before the airplane actually stalled. Also, under these conditions, there was so much excess thrust that the aircraft was able to accelerate to a lower angle of attack. In addition, these stalls were part of a planned training maneuver. Thanks to a heads up well in advance of the event, pilots would intentionally and knowingly pull the aircraft into a stall. There was no "startle effect." Like good actors, crews fully rehearsed every step of this procedure.

Because few pilots enter a full stall during training, they don't have a good feel for this occurrence. Lacking first-hand experience, they see this kind of stall as a remote possibility. Another problem is the effect of a low-altitude scenario where actual speeds are reduced. Here the atmosphere is more forgiving because the aircraft can safely fly at a higher angle of attack. The catch is that handling a full stall at a higher altitude in a commercial jet demands a different kind of training. Without it, even the most experienced pilot is at a disadvantage.

By definition a full stall in a transport airplane is any combination of the following:

A nose-down pitch that cannot be readily stopped (pitch break). It may be accompanied by an uncommanded rolling motion.

Strong buffeting, not to be confused with turbulence, that effectively prevents an increase in angle of attack.

The pitch control reaches the aft stop for two seconds. No further increase in pitch attitude occurs when the yoke or sidestick controller is held full aft, an action that can lead to an excessive descent rate.

Activation of a stall identification device (e.g., stick pusher).

Many pilots when encountering or considering several of the above listed items without knowing they are associated with a stall may be misled and believe they are an indication of "Mach tuck," an issue in the early jets. This is a common misunderstanding that likely contributed to the Air France 447 accident. In Mach tuck, the wing design can lead to a shock wave that becomes stronger as the aircraft approaches the speed of sound. This leads to an abrupt loss of lift toward the leading edge of the wing, causing the airplane to go into a dive. Modern wings are not susceptible to this problem. They are designed to operate as the air moves over the wing at supersonic speeds under normal cruise conditions. Unfortunately, like the misconceptions that led to the crash of American 587, most pilots are not educated on this key point.

In a classic straight-wing airplane, it is fairly easy to identify a stall. Generally there is considerable aerodynamic buffet. There is also a stall "break" where the wing fails to develop lift forward of its center of gravity. In this case the aircraft pitches forward and naturally reduces the angle of attack, ending the stall.

This is not the case in a modern swept-wing jet transport flying above 30,000 feet. On these planes, the rear section of the wing, which is aft of the center of gravity, stalls first. As the air begins to separate toward the back of the wing, the forward section continues to develop lift. This discrepancy between the front and back of the wing can lead to the plane slowly pitching up as a stall is approached. While the airplane remains stable in a classic sense, the flight controls of the fly-by-wire system in the alternate law mode lead to the aircraft pitch remaining constant or even pitching up to maintain one "g" if a descent develops. In level flight this will slowly increase the angle of attack towards stall. The situation changes radically for an aircraft that is in a climb. Here the angle of attack increases rapidly without sufficient thrust. This infrequent and unexpected event, which contributed to the Air France 447 aerodynamic stall, is beyond the training of many pilots.

Airbus optimists tried to convince regulators that the probability of pilots encountering a stall was so low that there was no need to demonstrate stalls during the aircraft certification process. The incorrect assumption was that this kind of stall was nothing to worry about. The FAA correctly denied this request.

Unfortunately the manufacturer's overconfidence meant that key high-altitude stall issues were skipped in airline training on the theory that state-of-the-art commercial jets couldn't stall at cruise altitude. One key mistake was failing to teach pilots how to distinguish between severe buffeting and turbulence. Unless pilots expect the possibility of buffeting, they may miss this critical stall cue.

Another confusing element for pilots is the fact that buffeting encountered on small aircraft during stall recovery training is relatively mild. Many pilots aren't taught that buffeting on a big jet is far stronger, similar to the kind of turbulence they may have encountered on many previous flights. Because they have never flown or trained on an approach to stall at high altitude, crews may not recognize what is going wrong.

It's impossible for pilots to recover from a stall if they don't realize they are in one (absent an unintentional recovery, which has occurred on several occasions.) It's relatively easy to understand why even an experienced pilot with a perfect record might not recognize a stall. As humans, our brains filter out information that seems irrelevant. This protects us from becoming overwhelmed by too much information. Recognition also depends on our perception of the progress we are making toward a specific goal. If the cues for a stall don't match our expectations, we may have trouble sorting them out and assigning them a high priority.

There is a certain irony here. Warning systems are built to send instant cues designed to keep humans out of trouble. When these systems behave abnormally, we may tune these warnings out. On the other hand, crews can overreact to a nonexistent problem. A spurious warning, such as a defective nose-gear warning light, might distract a flight crew from the fact that their plane is unexpectedly descending. This actually happened to a 1972 Eastern Airlines flight that crashed in the Florida Everglades.

Several accidents demonstrate another computer-related problem in training. An American Airlines crew stalled an Airbus A300 in 1997 and luckily averted a crash. In that case the pilots did not notice that the auto-throttles were reducing airspeed as they focused on avoiding the worst of several thunderstorms.

Fortunately the aircraft rolled over and recovered from the stall naturally, with the pilots pulling out of the resulting dive. While not ideal, the rollover may have saved them as neither pilot recognized the plane had stalled. In 2014, an Air Asia Airbus A320, captained by a veteran pilot, crashed into the Java Sea after stalling at high altitude. He was busy trying to trouble-shoot a faulty electrical system while flying through a convective storm.

The same year an Air Algérie MD-80 also stalled and crashed in similar weather. In this case, the engines were not putting out enough thrust due to icing over of sensors measuring pressure for the engine fuel controller. Like a carburetor, the controller uses the pressure to determine the proper amount of fuel to meter into the engine.

Unfortunately, the crew did not notice the airspeed decay, probably because they were focused on convective storms ahead. These and other crashes in recent years took place on planes flown by experienced test pilots and veteran airline captains. Accident analysts were surprised that these flight crews did not quickly recognize that they were stalling. What went wrong in training?

A flight simulator utilizes the same instruments and control systems found on a real airplane. While simulators are designed to replicate flight, all those computers running ones and zeros will never fully match reality, even in ideal conditions. Instead of duplicating the real world, they create a hypothetical flight. Equally important, you can't die in these forgiving machines. Simulators give pilots second chances. Airplanes do not.

Ideally, simulators try to replicate how an airplane flies as well as the way aircraft systems operate. The same switch that turns on a real hydraulic pump in the airplane activates a computer program in the simulator.

Simulating flight is far more challenging. Airplanes react to all kinds of anomalies. Small variations in temperature or a few insects smashed on the wing will subtly alter the way the air flows over the wings. Fortunately the impact here is minor. By contrast a small amount of ice adhering to the wings can make a major difference. Layer on more problems like pilot fatigue or design defects and the issue becomes a bigger challenge.

Regulars at an airport might talk about how that aircraft hangar alongside the runway can make the landing "squirrely."

Winds coming from a certain direction, and the hot air rising from a parking lot on approach, can prompt a last-minute landing control adjustment. The aircraft reacts in ways that are not always predictable. It's impossible to anticipate these seemingly minor issues that quickly add up to major challenges.

Out of necessity, the aerodynamic model for a simulator is much simpler than the real world. Manufacturers do a reasonably good job of mimicking real airplane behavior as long as they have reliable data. When a company is not required to provide data for their airplane in certain regimes (e.g., a full stall at high cruise altitude), that data is nonexistent. Even if they do the testing, they may not have retained the data or, if they have, be willing to share it. Guessing what a plane will do can be very dangerous, as the disturbing accident report of the previously mentioned 2001 American Airlines flight out of JFK demonstrates.

A major challenge is that today's simulators have no way to warn instructors or pilots when they have exceeded known parameters. Also, a perpetually grounded simulator's motion is, necessarily, limited. For example there is no way it can replicate a prolonged "falling" sensation. Other forces are similarly compromised to varying degrees.

In the aftermath of Air France 447, FAA experts worked with Airbus, Boeing, and other manufacturers to obtain better stall modeling data for programming flight simulators. In the fall of 2014, these experts were able to ride in the cockpit with Airbus test pilots as they entered full high-altitude stalls at high Mach numbers. Airbus had previously argued that such a scenario—a stall occurring while in alternate law mode—was of such low probability that it need not be a concern.

Because each plane has different handling characteristics, the FAA did similar tests on other models such as the Boeing 737. The resulting data was used by the FAA to improve simulator fidelity for training these dangerous scenarios. The new data package was installed on the FAA A330 and B737 simulators at the vast FAA Mike Monroney Aeronautical Center complex in Oklahoma City. These advanced packages were not yet available for most carriers, but by the spring of 2016 a few American carriers began making the necessary upgrades.

The Monroney Aeronautical Center also administers certification of pilots, medical records, and reviews aircraft certification. In addition, it is home to the FAA Academy, the training facilities for air traffic controllers, FAA inspectors, and other employees. Scientists also study human cognition and physiology at the FAA CAMI (Civil Aerospace Medical Institute) Research Center. Several full-motion simulators are based here.

With the new package installed, the A330 simulator could now, for the first time, correctly replicate the last minutes of Air France 447. Of course, the pilots flying this simulator had a tremendous advantage over Dubois, Robert, and Bonin. The simulator trainees knew they would be stalling and were not "flying" in a confusing South Atlantic thunderstorm in the middle of the night.

Despite these advantages, co-author Shem Malmquist, a veteran training pilot with comprehensive knowledge of the accident, discovered it was harder than expected to recover from a high-altitude stall on the A330 simulator at the FAA's test facility in Atlantic City.

In February 2016 he became the first author to actually recreate the event on a correctly modeled simulator. His journey began in the left seat, flying at 35,000 feet at Mach 0.82, or 82% of the speed of sound. The simulator operator programmed in the failure of all three pitot systems. Airspeed indications disappeared, and that was immediately followed by an autopilot disconnect and numerous alerts.

Lateral control was surprisingly challenging as the aircraft proved quite sensitive in the roll axis. As the aircraft's roll control entered alternate law mode, the pitch control was in alternate 2 law, a mode lacking normal law protections for high-and low-speed flight. The big Airbus proved surprisingly nimble. While this was an advantage in routine flight, it proved to be an unexpected challenge in this situation. Airspeed was deliberately reduced to pull the airplane into a stall. As it slowed, the automatic trim system kept moving the trim control upward to hold the nose up. Now the flight crew could not easily lower the nose to regain lost airspeed.

An initial stall warning was ignored and the nose of the airplane stayed up with the altitude kept constant. As the aircraft entered the stall, Malmquist had to correct for major oscillations in roll despite the fact that no turbulence was programmed into the simulation. With speed decreasing, the roll control became more sluggish, lagging behind aircraft motion. Significant buffeting shook the plane violently, just like major turbulence. Then, at a predetermined point, Malmquist was commanded to recover from the stall.

When he pushed full forward on the side stick, the plane kept rolling left and right. Finally the nose began to drop. As the stall continued, the airplane plunged into a steep dive, with the nose dipped nearly 20° below the horizon. Time seemed to expand as the plane dropped.

In real life, this drop would be a horrifying emergency for all but a few experienced test pilots. Although the simulator could not recreate the low g-forces that would occur as the airplane began to drop, the event was unlike any training flight Malmquist had ever flown.

"I almost feel like I am in slow motion," he told his FAA instructor as the plane slowly began picking up speed.

After an excruciating nearly 10,000-foot fall, the plane accelerated to a point where it was safe for Malmquist to recover from the dive and pull up. Even though he expected this crisis and was an experienced instructor for large transport jet airplanes, the stall recovery maneuver was slow and treacherous. Recovery from an actual stall in a real aircraft under those conditions would be far more challenging.

Prior to the new simulation packages created via the recent work of the FAA and manufacturers, it was not possible to accurately do this type of training. These studies based on actual high-altitude stalls replaced licensing assumptions created with theoretical models. Nearly seven years after Air France 447, airlines are now finally able to replicate the reality of a stall in these swept-wing airplanes currently dominating commercial aviation.

New and badly needed training can teach pilots how to recover from stalls in different scenarios that lead to loss of control. This training is designed around actual upset recovery events where a pilot will be surprised by rolls and extreme nose-high and nose-low conditions, as well as stalls at both low and high altitudes.

For stall recovery, the new guidance developed by the FAA and EASA is to immediately reduce angle of attack until the aircraft is unstalled, followed by rolling the wings level. This is true for any altitude, although the experience is far more challenging at higher altitudes. At cruise, the stall angle of attack is critical due to the high speeds involved, plus the aircraft recovers much more slowly.

This important work is designed to create a solution to the stall-recovery problem identified by the BEA. Adoption of these new higher standards in the United States, Canada, Europe, Australia, and the Middle East has begun. Although the American carriers have three years to upgrade their simulators, some carriers, such as Alaska Airlines and Southwest Airlines, are completing this important work well ahead of the 2019 deadline. No one knows if this critically needed training will expand to other carriers around the world before there are more accidents triggered by high-altitude aerodynamic stalls.

CHAPTER 13

Weather or Not

B etween 2009 and 2014, three commercial airline crashes that took the lives of 506 passengers and crew have pinpointed a growing problem challenging outstanding legacy airlines and lesser-known carriers alike. Two of these tragedies took place in 2014, five years after the traveling public was alerted to this challenge by the disappearance Air France 447. Is something going wrong at aviation schools, flight academies and airline training programs?

For Professor Debbie Schaum, now in her 20th year teaching meteorology at Embry Riddle Aeronautical University in Daytona Beach, the answer is obvious:

"Most pilots, many dispatchers and air traffic controllers are not taking meteorology classes taught by meteorologists."

As she works with students from around the world, Schaum, who also served as an Air Force meteorologist for 17 years, believes a majority of pilots around the world are not getting the training they need in weather science.

"If you take a weather class that is not taught by a meteorologist you do not get the depth of understanding you need to be a good pilot."

As planes take off and land at the adjacent Daytona Beach airport, Schaum sounds a bit like a missionary straining for her voice to be heard.

Is it possible that events like Air France 447 in 2009 could have been avoided entirely if the copilots in command had a deeper understanding of high-altitude icing conditions that can shut down a plane's automation in seconds? Are there other problems such as an inability to correctly read on-board weather radar and mistakes being made by controllers?

Schaum notes that foreign pilots who come to American schools like Embry Riddle on scholarships "lack the depth of understanding needed because training requirements in their countries are not as stringent as ours. It's also clear that training for dispatchers and air traffic controllers is not as in-depth as it should be. "

"You can blame as many people as you want to," says Professor Schaum as a student enters her campus office to discuss a paper. "But it's obvious that meteorology training in many parts of the world is falling behind the needs of today's pilots and their airlines." While Air France, and Air Algérie operate on vastly different business models, it's clear that in each case special challenges presented by adverse weather in the intertropical convergence zone were misunderstood by inadequately trained flight crews.

Hundreds of thousands of passengers fly through the intertropical convergence zone (ITCZ) every day. Few realize that even the best pilots find special weather conditions here that go well beyond their experience in the classroom and in the air. It doesn't matter whether you are in your first year of flying or have many thousands of hours behind you, chances are your airline training did *not* offer special instruction on the unique challenges faced in this potentially deadly zone. Even now, in the wake of these three devastating accidents, training at many carriers fails to address this important challenge.

The ITCZ is a constant presence in the world and as Professor Schaum explains: "If you haven't taken an aviation weather class from a meteorologist chances are you probably don't understand the dynamics of thunderstorms and heights to which structural icing can impact aircraft in this area of the world."

On a map, the ITCZ looks like a floating equator. Its latitude depends on the season. In the summer the ITCZ is north of the equator and during the winter it moves south with the greatest variations in the western Pacific and Indian oceans. Typically the active parts of the ITCZ form over warmer waters where storm activity varies depending on the season. In the summer the ITCZ is very active in the Atlantic north of the equator and during the winter it is a strong force in the Southern Indian Ocean.

For pilots, the significance of this zone can not be overstated. For example, most Atlantic hurricanes get their head start in the ITCZ off the coast of Africa during late summer and fall. And during the winter, all hell breaks loose in the Indian Ocean, south of the equator, creating cyclones in Australia as well as scary convective storms in Africa where clouds top out at 50,000 feet.

"The problem," says Schaum, "is that most pilots, dispatchers and air traffic controllers don't understand the dynamics of these weather problems. This is a problem that the best automation and engineering design can't eliminate. Even the newest plane in the sky equipped with the latest on-board weather radar can run into trouble here. One storm in the ITCZ could be a once in a lifetime phenomenon that tests the skills of even the most experienced pilots."

Why is there so little aviation training on the impacts of the ITCZ on flight? "We concentrate a lot over land because of the dynamic forces caused by land," says meteorologist Schaum. "Since the water is smoother, oceans normally get much less attention in training. We gear much of our flight instruction in the U.S. for the northern hemisphere and the mid latitudes where icing caused by thunderstorms doesn't reach the altitudes it can in the ITCZ.

"Except for the summertime over the Atlantic we don't

really deal that much with the ITCZ in the northern hemisphere. In the parts of the world where the problem exists, flight crews don't get adequate instruction."

The three ITCZ-related accidents in the southern Atlantic, the Java Sea and Africa are well known. But Schaum is quick to point out that "many other flights also encounter these conditions which cause significant icing at high altitudes where they are not normally expected. Because more planes are flying these ITCZ routes, this problem is magnified. Until pilots, dispatchers and controllers are trained to recognize the subtleties of these hazards at altitude this dangerous problem will continue.

The first of these three ITCZ accidents, Air France 447, was triggered by pitot icing in a June 1, 2009 convective storm. Two of the three pilots had extensive experience crossing the ITCZ. Unfortunately, none of them had the necessary training to fully understand why it was critical to avoid the dangerous weather that shut down the plane's autopilot.

For several years prior to Air France 447, company pilots at this carrier and its competitors had been reporting a series of icing issues in the ITCZ. In many of these incidents, an autopilot shutdown put the plane into manual mode forcing pilots to hand fly the plane at cruise altitude. While the pilots duly reported these incidents, the carrier failed to effectively share this information with their pilots or provide special training on how to handle this anomaly.

On August 16, 2008, Air France 373 flying from Paris to Tananarive was "almost a dress rehearsal for what happened on doomed Flight 447," says one French flight safety analyst. The ninth in a series of 2008-2009 Air France Airbus 330/340 unreliable airspeed incidents triggered by frozen pitot tubes, the Flight 373 event began in an ITCZ storm over Ethiopia.

When the flight crew lost reliable airspeed due to pitot tube icing, they did not set mandated power and pitch or maintain level flight as prescribed by the Air France emergency procedure checklist. Determined to avoid heavy turbulence above, the captain immediately descended 4,000 feet, ignoring a malfunctioning flight director's climb order. In the process he learned something that every pilot crossing the ITCZ needed to know.

After the flight landed the captain wrote a blistering report and sent it to his airline. He warned Air France that the flight director appeared to be working on this Airbus when it fact it was not. Had it not been for his decision to avoid turbulence above his flight level, he might have followed the corrupted flight director's misleading instructions and climbed into an aerodynamic stall.

Had he been flying for an American airline, the pilot's blistering critique might have been widely shared with flight crews through the industry's anonymous incident reporting system. Unfortunately, the Flight 373 captain's critical warning was never shared with other Air France pilots.

Is it possible that the Madagascar-bound pilot's superiors failed to understand the special weather hazards posed by the ITCZ? Professor Schaum believes that some decision makers lack the training and experience to understand complex meteorological events like the one encountered by Flight 373. Had the airline correctly analyzed the special icing conditions that triggered this crisis the company might have alerted flight crews to this hazard and how to handle it. The key was not to climb but to follow standard procedures for an unreliable airspeed incident by setting power and pitch until the ice melted and the pitots began sending reliable data.

Had managers realized the hidden dangers in the ITCZ, it's possible that the airline might have issued a bulletin to its own pilots and the European Aviation Safety Agency. Clearly the crew of Air France 447 did not understand the hidden ITCZ risks when they took off from Rio on the evening of May 31, 2009. Had they realized the hidden dangers in the weather ahead, they might have chosen a safer route across the southern Atlantic.

Like many other flights headed for the ITCZ on the night of June 1, 2009, the three-man crew of Air France 447 anticipated rough weather. Briefed by dispatch before taking off from Rio on the 12-hour flight to Paris, the pilots believed cockpit radar would help them navigate around dangerous convective storms commonly found in the South Atlantic during the summer months.

Had these towering storms been over land, it's likely that ground-based radar systems feeding continuous updates to air traffic controllers might well have helped the French crew avoid the storms entirely.

Three years earlier the FAA, working with the National Center for Atmospheric Research and United Airlines, had successfully tested a satellite-based system designed to warn transoceanic pilots about these dangerous storms. With cloudtop heights monitored from above, the satellites were able to pinpoint dangerous Pacific storm systems well beyond the reach of on-board radar.

Using cockpit map printers, this approach gave pilots more than an hour warning on these storms, plenty of time to change their route and avoid these ice-producing weather systems that could corrupt critical airspeed and altitude data being fed to the autopilot. Although the projected cost of the system was only about $1 million per plane, the FAA suspended the research program in 2007 due to budget constraints.

Without this warning system the Air France 447 crew was routed through the challenging the ITCZ where other crews had been reporting high-altitude ice crystals during 2008 and 2009. This dangerous phenomenon was little known at the time and is still not fully understood.

The ITCZ is particularly worrisome over oceanic areas, or other regions with very high moisture content such as the Amazon basin. Due to high relative humidity in this equatorial zone there is a tremendous amount of moisture aloft. In other areas the tropopause serves as a cap limiting the growth of the storms. But in the ITCZ the clouds can reach heights over 50,000 feet. Unlike a storm over Kansas, most of the rain does not exceed the freezing level.

One theory is that as the water freezes in the ITCZ it gives off latent heat. Because the newly warmed air is a bit more buoyant any frozen particles are now held aloft.

Studies have shown that ITCZ storms over warm tropic waters or rainforests during monsoon season tend to have a weakening of the updrafts in the 20,000 foot range—an area where storms in other parts of the world are quite violent.

While a storm over Kansas can push liquid water 20,000 feet or higher due to their extreme energy, the majority of liquid water in an ITCZ storm remains at relatively lower levels. At higher levels closer to cruise altitude, there is significant water frozen into crystals or graupel. This explains why ITCZ storms tend to produce less lightning, making them harder to spot and avoid at night.

In daylight the storms are very easy to visually avoid. Unfortunately, they do not "paint" on the radar unless the beam is tilted very far down, scanning in the 20,000-foot region and below with the gain turned all the way up.

As a result, these storms are incredibly easy to miss on the radar, particularly at night. New radar systems do incorporate algorithms that can compensate for these factors to an extent, but there is no substitute for pilot training in understanding weather.

Nobody is expecting pilots to pore through scientific meteorology papers to gain the depth of understanding necessary to fully understand these concepts. Nonetheless, training could easily be improved to include these scenarios and integrated within the footprint of current curriculum.

"Sadly, the crew of Air France 447 did not have the benefit of this critical knowledge, and who could blame them?" says Schaum. "Few pilots even today have an understanding of these factors because they have not been trained by aviation meteorologists."

Fortunately, some hopeful signs began emerging in 2017 at the FAA. New flight testing to provide on-board weather forecasting system via satellite was a hopeful sign. Delivered by satellite to the aircraft's onboard wifi, this approach, being tested at carriers like Lufthansa, can help pilots anticipate and avoid convective storms hundreds of miles ahead. With this important aid, pilots would be able to fly around formerly hidden danger zones that might harbor convective ice.

CHAPTER 14
The Loss of Resilience

"Design of human-operated complex systems can easily surpass operator capabilities. When the operator is the safety feature of last resort, the operator's systems knowledge should surpass the 'how' behind normal and irregular procedures, and explain the 'why' of system behavior. Good design allows the operator to troubleshoot problems with speed and confidence."

Terry Wilcutt and Tom Whitmeyer
NASA Safety and Mission Assurance

Due to retirements, the number of airline pilots with hands-on flying experience at high altitudes is shrinking rapidly. Today, most of the time, in those rare cases pilots hand-fly at cruise altitudes they do so with augmented controls that make the airplane easier to handle. Current training regimens focus on procedures and the ability of pilots to follow them. Making sure airline pilots are versatile aviators well-qualified to handle the unexpected with stick and rudder skills is a much lower priority.

Economics is one of the challenges that contributes to this risk factor. Passengers want low fares. Airlines want to remain competitive with each other, as well as with trains and automobiles. One way to keep costs down is to standardize training around automation.

193

In the past, pilots were often encouraged to trust their autopilots and not try to fly their planes manually; however, today the emphasis is that even with "hand flying" the pilots should follow procedures scripted by people sitting in offices and cubicles.

The airlines benefit economically because they don't need to train pilots for special conditions. Even weather, one of the biggest challenges pilots face, is given short shrift in training programs that lack training in how to use weather avoidance tools (such as weather radar) or convey an understanding meteorology itself.

Jet airplanes are most fuel efficient at higher altitudes. At the same time, higher weights limit the ability of the wings to develop enough lift for the higher altitudes and engine thrust can also be not enough to maintain the required speeds. Any wing design will be most efficient at a specified angle of attack. The speed required for that angle of attack is a function of aircraft weight. As weight increases more airspeed is required to keep the plane airborne.

The key is to reach a sweet spot short of the speed sound where efficiency begins to decline. In most cases the optimum cruise altitude falls between 30,000 and 40,000 feet. As air travel grows at a rapid clip, traffic is constrained by a shortage of available altitudes.

Another challenge to high-speed flight is the accuracy of the altimeters. You might be surprised to know that older altimeters were more error prone at higher altitudes due to the effects of the thinner air. This challenge plus faster closure speeds between aircraft persuaded regulators to increase vertical aircraft separation.

At altitudes below 29,000 feet, the separation for two airplanes flying in opposite directions was 1,000 feet, with easterly flying airplanes flying at odd altitudes (21,000, 23,000, etc.) and westerly flying airplanes flying at even altitudes (22,000, 24,000, etc.). Above 29,000 feet, they were separated by 2,000 feet to compensate for potential altimeter deviation in thinner air.

Under the old rules planes lacking an autopilot could, if necessary, be dispatched on long transoceanic flights. Hand-flying for hours at a time was a burden for crews.

Some motivated pilots sometimes would spend some time using their stick-and-rudder skills to hand-fly up to cruise. This gave them a chance to stay current should they suddenly need to take over the flight.

Their approach was a departure from the norm in an industry where new pilots might just hand-fly up to cruise once during training. However, many pilots still gained experience due to the nature of the flying and the fact that autopilots did not always work.

Between 1997 and 2005, growing traffic led to more flight delays. The only way to alleviate the pressure was to add more flights into airspace that was already densely packed. One solution was to allocate more altitudes for airplanes to fly, however that required more precision. The solution was found in new criteria. More stringent regulation of altimeters, new altitude monitoring systems and better autopilots and flight directors persuaded the FAA to reduce vertical separation to 1,000 feet as long as the aircraft were properly equipped and pilots properly trained. To ensure compliance and rule out surprises, a new rule took effect. Most airlines required pilots to fly on autopilot during flight above 29,000 feet.

Initially this change seemed inconsequential since veteran pilots, especially those with military training, carried their hands-on high-altitude flying skill set and experience with them. Then a series of accidents, beginning with Air France 447, prompted pilots' unions, manufacturers and regulators to call for more hands-on flying on the assumption that lack of airmanship was to blame. Arguably, lack of flying skills was part of the problem, so this push made sense.

The industry's call for more hand-flying, particularly on

simulators, was an important shift from the dawn of highly automated aircraft. Even so, most pilots still limit hand-flying to a relatively short time after takeoff, perhaps to 10,000 feet or so, and then use their autopilot until they are on approach to their destination. Some pilots hand-fly even less than that.

Workload influences this procedure, particularly on approach. Pilots do not want to "load up" monitoring in a modern cockpit with only two pilots. The standard procedure for most airlines is to have the pilot monitoring run the checklists, talk on the radio, communicate with the company, check landing performance to ensure the runway is long and safe enough, check that navigation systems are properly configured, and monitor and configure the aircraft systems.

When the autopilot is on, the pilot flying the airplane generally sets assigned headings and altitudes with the other pilot monitoring and confirming those settings. Pilots will generally leave the autopilot on during busy phases or poor weather to lower the workload for the pilot monitoring.

As a result, the only "real" opportunities for hand-flying in difficult situations are aboard flight simulators. Unfortunately, at best simulators only partially replicate the reality of flight. They are a bit like dress rehearsals minus sound or lights. You know what you are doing but you may not be able to see or hear everything that is going on. Assuming the simulator has the correct and accurate data programmed, it will react like the airplane given the conditions in which it is "flying." The problem is these conditions are not the real world. At best, a simulator gives you an incomplete picture of real flight.

Slight disturbances of the air burbling across a ridge line or uneven heating as it rises from a mix of parking lots and wooded areas create turbulence, temperature variations and wind shifts. Local bodies of water change the temperature and moisture content of the air. Slight variances in the way flight controls drag on a pulley or the way a slightly leaking hydraulic actuator reacts typify the variations that can lead to making every flight a different experience.

Up in the air, a pilot naturally learns to adapt to these subtle differences; a small bit of extra pressure here, a relaxation there. A small power adjustment offsets the updraft or change in windspeed. Adjusting to these differences is what pilots have done for more than a century to compensate for the natural world.

A simulator does not work that way. It can only do what it is programmed to do. This machine is built to the aircraft's design specifications, modified for on-the-ground performance by its programming. Even failures are choreographed by the programmers. The air never varies. The turbulence is generally "on or off" and, while it is mixed enough to appear random, bumps are scripted. Even randomly generated turbulence remains at a predictable level set by the simulator operator.

In the real world a confluence of temperature and orographic effects can create a small and almost impossible to forecast pocket of strong turbulence similar to "sneaker waves" at a beach.

A simulator never demonstrates these unexpected emergent properties. One-off surprises don't come out of nowhere. Similarly, the pilot in the simulator will only experience problems the designers imagined might happen.

Failures are modes that have occurred in the real world. Scenarios not forecast in various risk assessments won't be programmed into the simulation. As a result, pilots can learn to "fly" a simulator with grace and beauty. Like a love affair, this relationship may have a tricky moment or two, but there is great trust between the partners.

Landings become routine as the "variables" remain consistent. Once a pilot has figured out the "formula," he just flies a familiar pattern again and again. An instructor might take someone who is not even a pilot into a heavy jet simulator and say "just hold it steady until you hear '30' (30 feet), reduce the power, raise the nose two degrees and the landing will be perfect."

While the simulator replicates the routes and procedures to follow for instrument flight, the mix of different air traffic, controller techniques, other traffic and radio congestion are all missing. The variations in accents and radio procedures from controllers in different regions of the world is not heard, nor is the chatter in various languages across the radio. These are critical aspects of flight training central to any air journey.

It can also be challenging for simulators to faithfully mimic aircraft motion. A device fixed to the ground can only reproduce the accelerations of real flight within small variations. Typically a simulator leans back in an attempt to replicate forward acceleration or nose pitch up. It leans forward for a deceleration or pitch down.

Unfortunately, the simulator is unable to fully model very high and low pitch, or sudden speed changes. Even worse, combining these two problems on a simulator is beyond the range of the machine and its programmers. Similarly, a ground-based simulator leans to one side to match the outward force of a turn. An airplane can "skid" this way in flight but this is less efficient than banking into a turn. Yes, the simulator will also bank a bit to replicate a roll into a normal turn. But once again it is hard to mimic all these forces on a machine that doesn't fly.

Again and again simulators fall far short when they are programmed to demonstrate extreme situations. All too often pilots are unable to train on these expensive machines for unanticipated surprises. When it comes time to demonstrate emergencies, simulators all too often fall short.

Sound is another big problem. Peculiar noises can be the first sign of an emerging problem. On a simulator the sound will never match the real world. An engine failure will never sound like an explosion. The sound of wind moving across the windshield, the sound of rain, the sound of hail, or the lack of sounds are all absent on a simulator.

Yes, the various cockpit warnings work, but that is really the only thing that you can always count on. The 3D visual systems are impressive but lack realism when it comes to detail beyond runway markings and lighting. Attempts to match fog or low clouds are problematic, lacking the ability to fully combine related common real-world variables such as rain, ice and snow. Sometimes, multi-million dollar simulators misbehave. These "sim-isms," such as wacky motion and visual systems that abruptly switch on and off, are unique to the simulator itself.

At times these surprises verge on the comedic. For example, during a simulated approach to the Almaty Airport in Kazakhstan, conditions were set to a cloud ceiling of 500 feet. On approach the pilot broke out below the simulated ceiling and correctly saw the airport. Suddenly the runway visual began shifting and the pilot had to turn and chase down the airport!

In another session on an older Boeing 727 simulator, the system went bonkers and initiated an extreme climb. The altimeters wound higher and higher. Even with the power pulled back the simulator began climbing at 6,000 feet a minute, quickly passing through the real aircraft altitude limit of 42,000 feet. The plane soared past 50,000 feet, then 60,000, 70,000 and finally "leveled off" at over 90,000.

Stuck at more than twice its cruise limit, the Boeing 727 simulator began to revolt. All three engines flamed out along with the controls being completely ineffective, as one would expect when trying to fly in such thin air. Now in high overspeed with mach buffet and the overspeed warning "klacker"[12] sounding, the plane entered a stall with the "stick shaker"[13] warning. Controls were unresponsive and the simulator instruments (but of course not the motion-limited simulator itself) showed the aircraft plunging into a forward oscillating dive before it finally shut itself down.

12. The "klacker" is installed on the Boeing 727 and other models. It makes a loud constant "clack, clack" sound like a woodpecker pounding on hollow wood.

13. The stick shaker vibrates the control column rapidly to indicate a stall condition. It is a common stall indicator used in a variety of transport airplanes.

Obviously the entire training session was a bad joke.

There is a final, but no less trivial consideration. While a simulator pilot may be stressed out due to the knowledge that she is being evaluated, there is no fear of an actual crash. This kind of training never raises the possibility of dying. Stripped of real fear, there is unlikely to be an adrenalin rush that shuts down senses and changes the blood flow. Simulators are a useful tool, but they remain, at best, a window to possible outcomes. Real flight training forces pilots to move well beyond theoretical training.

Even the best simulators are only a step toward the kind of quick decision making that comes from real hands-on flying.

At their best, simulators are not a substitute for aggressive real-world hand-flying on a variety of aircraft. Since airplanes are expensive to operate, some companies, especially business and charter flight operators, are training pilots on smaller tail-draggers to give them a chance to freshen up on stick-and-rudder skills.

For example, Rick Fiddler, a veteran pilot and head of aviation at Alticor (formerly Amway), home of one of America's largest corporate aircraft departments, was astonished to discover how his own hands-on flying skills had deteriorated after years of automated flight. Determined to address the problem, he bought a small tail-dragger to make sure all his pilots had a monthly chance to brush up stick-and-rudder skills.

Fiddler's approach is one way to make up for the lack of real-world hand flying. Alas the cost of using a commercial jet for this purpose is prohibitive. Not only are big airplanes expensive to operate but airlines can't afford to pull them out of revenue service.

Why don't airlines follow Rick Fiddler's example at Alticor and opt for stick-and-rudder training on smaller aircraft? While pilots would love it, airlines believe little planes don't present many of the aerodynamic challenges present on big jets. For example, Pipers have different stall characteristics than Boeing or Airbus aircraft.

A good example is a high-altitude approach to stall that would be well beyond the operating range of that small piston-powered Piper or Cessna. Training for a real stall at 35,000 feet requires either a jet or a specially configured simulator. Fly-by-wire[14] technology adds to the complexity of this challenge.

In traditional aircraft, the pilot makes direct inputs, even if the controls are working through hydraulic actuators. Part of the pilot's job is adjusting for small variances previously described.

If the aircraft weight is distributed a bit forward, they know it requires more control input to change the pitch. If the weight is aft, the aircraft controls can be lighter and possibly lead to overshooting the pilot's intended target.

An updraft might push the plane up, increasing the angle of attack, causing the plane to pitch forward, and a downdraft might do the opposite. A gust might cause it to roll. Handling these issues are familiar territory for stick-and-rudder flying.

On a fly-by-wire airplane the pilot is directing the airplane through flight control computers that translate what the pilot is "demanding" to the airplane. When the pilot pulls back on the controls, the computer delivers the appropriate pitch "rate" or, at faster speeds, a certain amount of "g" force (or in some designs commands a flight path).

If no control input is made the computers "hold it steady," similar to cruise control on your car. What about all those gusts, updrafts and other factors that pilots normally compensate for when they fly hands-on? Once again computers automatically compensate for these variables. The pilot is now the "ace of the base" and his plane becomes easier to fly. It does not matter if the air is thin at high altitude or if there is some ice on a wing. The fly-by-wire system will attempt to compensate for these challenges.

---

14. Fly-by-wire is a system where the pilot controls are connected to a computer which then creates a command to the aircraft controls.

How does that impact pilot skill? A pilot dependent on this automated control system may lose the resilience required to handle the controls absent all these built-in protections.

The real challenge begins when the system fails. Pilots have very little experience flying these aircraft without full augmentation, in "direct law," where cockpit flight controls directly command the flight control surfaces. Instruction for this anomaly during initial and subsequent recurrent training is rare. Airlines don't think it's worth spending the money to teach pilots how to handle this "low probability" event.

Of course, lack of in-flight experience with system failures at high altitude can challenge any pilot. Reduced vertical separation requirements prevent pilots from keeping current on their hand-flying skills above 29,000 feet. Due to retirements, the number of pilots who practiced stick-and-rudder skills prior to the new rule is diminishing. This means that younger pilots might lack the training and experience for unexpected control problems at cruise altitude.

One possible solution is an "augmented" training aircraft. This airplane comes with a fly-by-wire control system that can be designed to mimic the response of virtually any other airplane's control system. The fly-by-wire controls interface directly through a computer. This gives pilots the ability to manipulate flight control surfaces as they would be required to do in direct law or with various system failures.

Calspan has created several aircraft designed for this needed training. The catch is that this approach must be used on a large airplane that matches the amplitude of the high-altitude stall buffet. The control system must be designed to create these forces.

The long length of a large airplane creates a scenario where the cockpit moves quite a bit for a given amount of buffet due to the flexing of the fuselage. If airlines are willing to ante up for this valuable training approach, their pilots would be able to realistically mimic degraded flight modes, such as alternate (or secondary) law and direct law. The money spent would be a wise investment given the recent history of high-altitude loss-of-control crashes.

As discussed in our previous chapter, the lack of meteorology knowledge presents similar challenges. The problem extends to air traffic controllers vectoring pilots around convective weather and airline dispatchers who also lack this critical classroom training. Talk to any pilot who has been routed through a thunderstorm with 3,000 foot per minute updrafts and you'll understand the consequences of this short-sighted training policy.

Without the training they need from economy-minded airlines, pilots will not correctly understand the limitations and capabilities of their systems. Air traffic controllers will not know how to best utilize their systems to assist pilots, and airline dispatchers will be similarly handicapped. The only way to avoid these hazards is to provide them with the training necessary to stay out of harm's way.

In each of these examples (and many more not discussed here), if we want and expect pilots to be able to avoid and recover from real hazards and unexpected problems, we must provide the system, weather and flying training necessary for them to be able to do so.

CHAPTER 15

Deja Vu: The Night Flight From Paris

In late May 2016, an EgyptAir Airbus 320 takes off from Paris, heads south to the Mediterranean, makes two sudden turns and then dives, with no Mayday call, into the deep blue sea. Experts from around the world scramble to find the plane resting 4,500 feet below the surface. Grieving families gather in airport briefing rooms to learn the latest from the airline their loved ones trusted to bring them to the ancient land of the Pharaohs. Once again a submarine equipped with "golden" sonar ears struggles to detect pinger signals from the downed plane in a 40 square mile search zone. Cryptic satellite messages, effectively the plane's last will and testament, raise disturbing possibilities. Was this catastrophe triggered by a fire in the electronics bay, electrical failure, a stall, a tablet's flaming lithium battery, sabotage, even a bomb on a plane staffed with three air marshals? As families grieved, a new BEA team immediately launched an investigation in the deep blue sea. While the case remains open, it is currently portrayed by the Egyptian government as an act of terrorism.

The loss of this EgyptAir flight on a redeye from Paris to Cairo documents the attention deficit disorder plaguing the management of a transportation system serving over 3.5 billion passengers annually. The worldwide aviation community's inability to apply lessons learned from past mistakes creates yet another valuable opportunity to listen to the BEA, the National Transportation Safety Board and other first class accident investigation agencies that put human lives ahead of industry profits. To be fair, these investigative boards are, by charter, tasked with providing recommendations regardless of the cost that might avert a future accident. In the real world, we make decisions all the time where we balance safety against operational efficiency, even in our own lives. The choice to drive a bit over the speed limit to get to an appointment on time, or, perhaps in a better example, to get a loved one to hospital, is really no different than the types of decisions that are made in the aviation industry. The only way to be completely safe from an aviation accident is to not fly at all — and even then there is a risk of being hit by a plane while on the ground. The key is to find better ways to create the resilience in the system necessary to prevent accidents, and that remains a human component.

Unpredictable failures and preventable accidents continue to plague good and bad airlines alike, and need to be addressed just as aggressively as terrorism. Since 2009 when Chesley Sullenberger and copilot Jeff Skiles landed US Airways Flight 1549 in the Hudson River, there have been nearly 100 commercial airline accidents. This is hardly reassuring for the airlines, the manufacturers or the traveling public.

There is a great deal of confusion and uncertainty because, as we have seen with Air France 447, easy-to-implement and affordable recommendations such as real-time tracking of aircraft that would have led to quick recovery of the EgyptAir flight, have not been implemented worldwide. Every one of these delays on the BEA's Air France 447 recommendations potentially contributes to more accidents. At the very top of the list is the industry's failure to do more hands-on training for pilots. Better aircraft tracking, especially over the oceans, isn't far behind.

The slow process of tracking the EgyptAir flight eliminated the possibility of recovering any survivors. The longer the delay, the harder it is to put the pieces together. Whether or not the BEA and the Egyptian government ultimately confirm terrorism on this crash, numerous other events including the 2015 Egyptian bombing of a Russian Metrojet flight, and the 2014 shooting down of a Malaysian Air jet over the Ukraine, document the industry's inability to manage risk, effectively share security information between carriers, and prevent sabotage.

The unresolved mystery of Malaysia Air 370, another flight lost in the ocean and still missing, further documents the industry's inability to apply the lessons learned with Air France 447. How many crashes does it take for the industry to spend the money necessary to adequately track planes? The price of this worthwhile retrofit would amount to a small fare increase for passengers.

The industry's collective failure to implement the critical recommendations from accident investigators who have studied the June 2009 loss of Air France 447 means more avoidable accidents are inevitable. Even turning on preinstalled angle-of-attack indicators, as simple as flipping a pin setting on many commercial aircraft rolling off assembly lines around the world, has been held up. Most airlines don't want to pay for the requisite pilot training (a few hours at most) and government leaders refuse to make it happen. A few carriers have added angle-of-attack indicators to portions of their fleet. Unfortunately most airlines have not incorporated the comprehensive training required to use this safety enhancement on every flight. There is no excuse for not taking advantage of this technology that has been standard in the military for decades and more recently on business jets flown by pilots who love it. Even some operators of small single-engine planes use this helpful tool.

Most passengers feel safer flying on carriers based in the United States, Canada, Europe, Australia and the Middle East, which can be as much as 20 times safer than choosing a third world airline. This sounds good until you consider the fact that carriers with very good safety records, such as Air France, Lufthansa's German Wings unit and, until recently, highly regarded Malaysia Air have all had crashes in recent years. All of these statistics mask the fact that the safety of a particular airline is often not entirely within the control of the airline itself.

How can the industry make better safety management decisions? Are traditional safety analysis systems up to the task? Boeing estimated the risk of a lithium battery fire on their state-of-the-art 787 to be just one for every ten million flight hours. In reality, two occurred in the first 52,000 hours. What went wrong?

Leading researchers such as Dr. David Woods at Ohio State, Dr. Nancy Leveson at MIT, Dr. Erik Hollnagel and Dr. Sidney Dekker and others have been studying new approaches to understanding risk in complex systems, from modern airliners to nuclear power plants. Can we use these ideas to do more realistic probability analyses?

How do we use these lessons to predict where we need to be in research and training to prevent the next accident? Why did the aviation industry need to wait for a series of controlled flight into terrain accidents to rule out this avoidable problem by installing ground proximity warning systems? Decades of experience proves that loss of control accidents can be prevented by anticipating the problem with angle of attack indicators that protect pilots from accidentally flying into harm's way. What if those lessons were so profound that they could help us predict other scientific challenges in our complex world, such as lead contamination in a public water system or global warming. Systems that merely react to predictable failure at a cost of many lives are misleading and obsolete.

Preventing accidents means anticipating new problems that can compound one another. The best fix is built around the idea that probability analysis is a bad way to save lives.

Expertise can't always be dependent on hypothetical models. Instead of just certifying new systems based on the latest risk study, we need to give professionals the training and expertise they require to solve the latest challenges creatively. Computers that have been put on board to automate flight make it appear that pilots have little to do. In fact, these technical systems create complex interactions between computers. In addition, automation is unable to solve traditional problems like the one that confronted Sully and Skiles. Today, heroic pilot airmanship is more critical than ever. Of course these complex computer interactions also impact us in our day-to-day lives. The quicker we apply lessons learned in aviation the better.

Scientific progress creates new opportunities. It can also backfire when good work is compromised by unseen contingencies like convective storms. As we've seen, refusing to model pilot training on successful outcomes can lead to more human tragedy. Focusing curriculum around one-off accidents that may never happen again can be counterproductive.

Dozens of modern aircraft computers run millions of lines of code. The fact that an average of one out of 30 lines of software code has an error may not affect links under normal conditions. Unfortunately when pilots confront a novel situation like three pitots failing due to icing, these errors may contribute to a dangerous computer malfunction. It's only a matter of when, not if, there will be another critical upset requiring a resilient flight crew to save the day.

A critical problem, one that demands a call to action, is the collective failure of the industry, the regulatory agencies and the traveling public to put safety ahead of low fares. Demand for lower fares puts pressure on management to continually try to get more out of less. While this strategy can lead to efficiencies, it can also lead to turning a blind eye to risks that don't appear to be life threatening. Like a swimmer who worries more about a low-probability shark attack than a riskier motorcycle ride to the beach, many people have difficulty objectively assessing risk. Forecasting accidents can be hard for people who believe luck is perpetually on their side.

Instead of looking at where things went wrong in the past, some scientists believe it would be more profitable to study how things have gone right. Pilots prevent many accidents every day by adjusting to unexpected variables. Studying their routine successes might be a path forward to accident prevention. Training based on what the industry is doing right, instead of past mistakes, helps pilots develop the skills they need to handle unanticipated emergencies. Consider the pilot deciding whether or not to land on a runway with a thunderstorm overhead while balancing a low fuel situation. The correct solution is dynamic and requires pilots to consider a combination of factors where there is perhaps no "right" cookie-cutter answer. The scenario is easily modeled with training based on good pilot performance. This can be far more productive than limiting training to past runway accidents in thunderstorms.

Unfortunately, too many airlines have cut back on long-overdue hands-on training. Even when carriers push hand-flying, the effort is far too scripted to be of much value. Adding dynamic training can add costs. This conflicts with the corporate goal of cheap tickets. As their profits soar thanks to increased demand, bag fees and higher change fees, as well as cheaper fuel, far too many airlines have significantly lowered pilot salaries. Traditional aviators are treated as systems managers who become a problem if they deviate from the scripted regimen created by a boss sitting at a desk. This push, backed by statistics, is creating a latent risk within the airline industry. Of course, when avoidable accidents happen, industry cheerleaders all too often use bad news as an opportunity to proudly tout statistics documenting aviation's safety record relative to other forms of transportation.

This doesn't provide solace to those who have lost a relative or a friend, nor does it set a good example. Aviation has an opportunity to take a leadership position in the world of safety management by implementing the concepts championed by deep thinkers such as David Woods, Erik Hollnagel and Nancy Leveson. Unless or until this happens, more unpleasant surprises like Air France 447 are inevitable. Working together, we can leave an important legacy insuring that people have the knowledge and training to protect us from trusted machines that are having a bad day.

APPENDIX A
The Independent Safety Review Team for Air France

Findings and Recommendations Overview

R. Curtis Graeber, Chair Erik Hollnagel, John Marshall Jean Pariès Nick Sabatini Geoff Sartori, Roger Whitefield David Woods

The Independent Safety Review Team (ISRT) was formed in December 2009 at the request of the CEO of Air France—KLM as part of three initiatives to enhance safety performance atAir France. The membership was selected from a broad spectrum of industry and academic expertise with a remit to study: how well Air France identifies and addresses safety issues; how well safety issues are perceived and acted upon by Air France personnel on a daily basis; and to identify strengths, weaknesses, and short and mid-term improvement opportunities for implementation within Air France. The ISRT employed a methodology of interviews, Focus Groups, letters sent to a confidential website, and observations of operational situations, training, and safety management processes. To validate the hypotheses formed from these activities it developed a Safety Management Assessment Questionnaire (SMAQ) to obtain representative safety perceptions from 5800 operational employees as an empirical basis for comparing interview and Focus Group data. The ISRT analyzed the full set of data using its collective expertise from flight operations, safety and human factors science, and regulatory practices. It also compared procedures and policies used by other carriers about which it had in-depth knowledge, as well as industry standards and major established organizational safety principles. Air France is a longstanding European airline with a distinguished history; it operates in accordance with all EASA standards and is an IOSA registered carrier (part of IATA's Safety Oversight Program).

While the ISRT did not conduct a safety audit, it did compare Air France against the safety attributes of a modern, safe and efficient airline which its ex-airline members and ex-regulator collectively described: SMS Implementation, a Proactive Approach to Safety, Management and Governance Structure, Safety Culture, Training and Human Factors, Flight Data Monitoring, and Organizational Resilience and Reliability.

As is usual in this type of review, the ISRT found areas and activities in Air France that were excellent in comparison to other carriers, some that were well within the norm, and others where Air France was at variance to the norm and which needed improvement. The ISRT believes that if Air France embraces the 35 recommendations in this report it will have made a positive step to address the differences. For this summary the findings have been grouped into three main areas: Organizational Structure, Culture / Behavior, and Individual Responsibility.

Organizational Structure

Air France's safety governance structure is overly complex, leading to an overlap and blurring of the lines of responsibility, roles and the activities of company's safety organizations. There is a lack of clarity in the minds of many frontline personnel as to which managers are responsible for which aspect of safety. Most carriers have one executive responsible for all safety programs within the company, including worker safety, reporting to the Accountable Manager. At Air France the Corporate VP Safety does report to the Accountable Manager, but the other safety managers have a reporting line to their departmental head and no direct reporting relationship to the Corporate VP. Air France also has a structure in which operations post holders report to a Directeur Général Délégué Opération (DGDO) — the Accountable Manager — for regulated matters, and to the CEO for other matters. Although this structure meets the requirements of the DGAC and EASA and the statutory delegation of power to the four operations post-holders is clear, (as is the manner in which they report to the Accountable Manager and the issues on which they report) most other carriers' post-holders report directly to the Accountable Manager for all issues under their responsibility. This is a simpler structure which makes the lines of responsibility for safety clear to the organization's workforce. Air France needs to undertake a review of its safety governance arrangements starting at the top. It should consider a simpler structure with clear responsibilities and reporting arrangements and with the Corporate Safety department at the center responsible for policy and coordination. This structure should have an independent Board Safety Subcommittee providing oversight of the whole system. Air France should also clarify the roles, hierarchy and responsibilities of Corporate Safety, Group Safety, and all Operational Divisions' safety organizations (e.g. Flight Operations Prevention and Safety, the Flight Analysis Department, Ground Operations, etc.) and ensure that each division's safety department has a reporting line to Corporate Safety. The ISRT believes that in general there is an absence of the strong safety leadership at all levels of management needed to guide proper consideration to safety in daily actions and decision making. When interviewed and asked about flight safety, Air France senior executives clearly state their commitment to safety and present safety as the airline's highest and undisputable priority. However, this message does not appear to have penetrated the workforce. "Safety first" is not commonly heard. This may lead some employees to believe that safety considerations are secondary to commercial considerations. The CEO and senior management need to drive safety from the top by providing more visible and clear leadership in terms of the strategic safety vision, policy development, implementation and most importantly personal and visible delivery. The ISRT found that Air France has pockets of excellence in risk management, comparable to other carriers, using formal processes to identify risks and apply appropriate mitigation strategies. However, the data flow and feedback loops in the current safety management system are not obvious and indicate an overly complex process. Air France is currently defining its SMS according to industry standard and implementing most of the industry's standard safety management tools. An improved, more structured, risk assessment process has been progressively implemented enabling incidents to be examined for their potential to cause a more serious event, and major changes to be assessed for their safety implications. The ISRT strongly supports Air France's effort to develop these more predictive methods of risk identification. However, these predictive processes are not yet mature, fully implemented nor consistently executed and applied in a systematic manner across the operational sector. Through attendance at various safety meetings as well as interviews with key personnel, the ISRT also confirmed that, outside the safety expert community, the safety culture at various levels of the Corporate and Flight Operations department is still primarily event driven and reactive (it strives to prevent similar events from occurring again through eradication of their causes) rather than proactive and predictive (trying to understand the event as a symptom of a poor system safety design and to anticipate safety risks).

Our survey revealed that the majority of front line employees trust the confidentiality of the open reporting systems and report safety-related events when they occur. Given the fundamental importance of such trust for any safety management system, this is encouraging. In relation to other forms of hazard identification, Air France has had a well-established Flight Data Monitoring (FDM) analysis section since 1974.

Unfortunately FDM is seen by some pilots as a "policeman" and not as a proactive tool to improve procedures and safety. Therefore, it has less than the desired impact on safety management. Over the years the FDM program has been an industry leader in development and innovation; however, the original protocol that governs the use of the data requires urgent updating to ensure that the safety lessons can be applied as judiciously as possible. This will align Air France with other major carriers. Air France has a formal process for change management (Concerto Majeur), but there is evidence that it is not being systematically applied. There is also is evidence that the final step of a mature SMS—"Review and Monitoring"—is often absent. The outcome of poorly monitoring the effects of change can increase the risk of unintended consequences. The introduction of a mandatory safety risk analysis currently being developed for any new equipment or operational process change is a positive development.

Culture And Behavior

The next group of findings and recommendations is about aircrew culture and behavior. The lack of adherence to Air France regulations and procedures by a small minority of pilots reported to the ISRT is of serious concern and reflects on flight deck discipline in general. The General Operations Manual allows Captains to deviate from Air France procedures, if necessary, for the safety of the aircraft and passengers. Similar authority is universally accepted internationally and is phrased "if a greater emergency exists". Unfortunately there is a small percentage of Captains who abuse this general guidance and routinely ignore some rules. It should also be noted, based on responses to the SMAQ, that employees believe that AF staff (not only pilots) sometimes take procedural short-cuts or use expert workarounds. While such actions may be necessary to adapt to operational variability, the ISRT believes the issue needs to be better understood and managed. Other departments, mainly Maintenance and Cabin Crew expressed a difficulty relating to pilots (captains) who treated them in an autocratic and arrogant manner. Once again this may be a small percentage of pilots, but the effect on morale, discipline and Crew Resource Management (CRM) is entirely out of proportion to the number of offenders. Air France needs to address this and other cross departmental frictions swiftly. We were repeatedly told by pilots and others that line managers are not empowered to hold pilots accountable for improper actions. Hence, the ISRT believes that Flight Operations must assure that these managers have all necessary tools at their disposal to effectively carry out their pilot management responsibilities. This refers not only to support and empowerment from senior management, but also to the fundamentals of selecting the right/best person for the role and providing effective training in managerial skills. A side-effect of the compliance problems at Air France is the tendency to "fix" such problems by adding to the procedure rather than disciplining the individual. The ISRT believes that this has contributed to the complexity of AF procedures being substantially higher than among its counterparts. Air France's procedures need to be simplified with clarity of purpose including the use of Original Equipment Manufacturer manuals and procedures as the company standard. A number of selection issues were raised during our review in relation to roles of flight instructors and entry-level pilots. The ISRT believes that the selection processes for flight instructors and evaluators must become more substantiated, open, and transparent. A review of initial pilot selection and training programs may provide an opportunity to develop a more team oriented, less elitist behaving pilot workforce. The quality of training received by flight crews affects their ability to carry out their line duties satisfactorily. CRM training is a key element of that training. We were told by both cabin crew and pilot Focus Groups that classroom CRM training was ineffective, too conceptual, and too routine. While the ISRT believes that CRM has lost its effectiveness in Air France, it may be that it has not evolved as much as other airlines programs have. Regardless, CRM training should be updated with a focus on establishing an integrated link with simulator training and integrating the knowledge gained from SMS and LOSA data.

Individual Responsibility

The third group of findings relates to individual responsibility. The ISRT believes that the culture at Air France does not reflect the level of trust and cooperation that senior management would like to see and that is typically seen at best performing carriers.

This lack of trust generates unnecessary and time-consuming crosschecking, repeated questioning of others' work product, and a refusal to accept that someone from another function has the ability, training and professional commitment to perform his or her duties accurately and completely. The culture also includes low trust of managers by employees. A broadly recognized and key feature of high reliability organizations is an appropriate level of mutual trust along the hierarchical chain. Therefore, in order to enhance safety as well as efficiency Air France should be striving to establish an inclusive culture where all departments work together as a team. To do this trust needs to be re-established across the various departments with an emphasis on cross-departmental teamwork. It is vital that, as individuals, each member of Air France feels a part of the Air France family and strives to do all they can to improve the safety and well being of passengers and staff alike. Team building exercises, particularly cross-department, will reinforce this behavior, as will strong and visible safety leadership from the Chief Executive down through all levels of management. Having an inclusive culture is also dependent on union support for safety issues. The high number of pilot unions makes it difficult to reach consensus. Unfortunately an unhealthy relationship currently exists between management and workforce unions partly as a result of Air France's "social peace at any cost" approach to the unions. The ISRT believes there is a potential risk to safety because union tension, particularly among pilots, has invaded the operational domain. Air France does not have the right place and way to discuss safety with the unions. So in practice, safety is officially outside, but implicitly inside, the scope of labor management discussions. Operational policies, rules and procedures should not be the subject of any form of union negotiation, but well researched union technical data and input should be welcomed as at other carriers in a collective debate. Beyond recent efforts such as the formation of the CMP, this situation has to be addressed if Air France is to improve the working relationship with the unions and ensure that the unions are "partners in safety" with management. The working relationship with outside parties including the DGAC was the subject of ISRT attention as part of the review. Some issues were identified with respect to the experience level of the DGAC inspectors and the resulting problems that arise during oversight activities. The ISRT is aware that air carriers who embrace a "working together" relationship with the regulator experience higher levels of safety performance. This requires that there be an open sharing of safety data and partnering with the regulator to capitalize on its experience in identifying risks and implementing corrective actions. The clear direction that resulted from our examination of the relationship is that a more "working together" attitude from both parties would be of great benefit to both organizations.

SUMMARY AND CONCLUDING REMARKS

The formation of the Independent Safety Review Team in a public manner and providing it a represents an example of safety leadership rarely seen in today's international aviation industry. Each member of the ISRT feels honored to have been asked to assist Air France in this important endeavor and sincerely hopes that our report will be taken in the way it is intended – an honest, forthright examination of the fundamental underpinnings of flight safety and a sincere attempt to offer helpful and valuable insights and recommendations that will enable Air France to become a world leader in aviation safety. The reader should bear in mind that we did not examine major portions of Air France, nor did we conduct a safety audit. Because of these intentional omissions and the nature of our effort it would be irresponsible to attempt to link this report and its findings with any accident past or future. As both employees and managers repeatedly told us, this report offers Air France a accordance with its historic position in international aviation. There are a number of ways by which Air France can improve how it manages the safety of its operations, both at the formal (system design) and practical (real work) levels. Our recommendations are designed to help, and we believe that they should be implemented as soon as possible. We are particularly pleased that Air France has already begun to implement four of them including establishing a Board Safety Subcommittee and conducting a LOSA to better understand flight deck operations. We strongly believe that the ISRT report should be directed to the Board Safety Subcommittee and hope that they will accept the responsibility for overseeing the implementation of the recommendations going forward.

We are particularly pleased that the pilot unions have joined together through the leadership of the CMP to support carrying out a LOSA. It is a credit to them and Flight Operations management that Air France will be the first major airline in Europe to conduct a LOSA using an external independent organization. We hope that such a dramatic demonstration of trust by pilots will set the example for re-establishing trust across the entire workforce. While some recommendations will be relatively easy to implement, others will require considerable effort by both the management and workforce and will take almost a decade to become totally effective. This is not a recipe for short-term remedies. Strong and effective leadership will be required for success.

Especially challenging will be the need to redefine the relationship between management and the unions, particularly the pilot unions, in terms of how they can work cooperatively to improve safety. Teamwork and mutual trust must be the foundation of safety to ensure lasting change. With our focus on championing lasting change, we believe that Air France needs to review its traditional project-based approach to change and consider establishing change agent teams beyond the typical two-year lifespan. The already established Comité Mixte de Propositions (CMP) and Programme Trajectoire are two such efforts that could provide significant benefit to safety enhancement in the future. We also strongly believe that recurrent administrations of the SMAQ over the next several years will enable Air France senior management to monitor the impact of our recommendations as well as other actions on improving the safety culture of Air France. The results should also enable management to better understand what safety themes (see star diagrams) need more attention in which operational areas. After spending a year interacting with Air France's managers and workforce, we believe that major safety improvements are possible, but if, and only if, it is driven from the top. We collectively wish them well and thank them for the open and cooperative attitude that they have shown us throughout.

List of recommendations

Air France should establish a Sub-Committee of the Board of Directors that deals exclusively with safety. In order to provide: Independent oversight, visible safety leadership, assistance to the Board in fulfilling its corporate governance responsibilities in regard to operational safety and risk matters, and compliance with legal and regulatory obligations relating to safety and risk. It should be comprised of at least three members, including the CEO and at least two Non-Executive Directors, and chaired by an independent Non-Executive Director. The Sub-Committee will confirm that management has established and operates a risk management system, which identifies, assesses, monitors and manages operational safety and risks.

Air France should establish leading and lagging performance indicators of the Safety System based upon analysis of the rolled up safety data and the risks they pose in order to make informed decisions about the indicators to be tracked.

Establish safety oversight of Wholly Owned Subsidiary airlines, in particular, those carrying the Air France brand. Oversight should specifically include those airlines' safety performance indicators.

The COMEX should reinforce and develop the effectiveness of its company-wide communication plan that explains and reinforces its commitment to safety and its expectations for employees and managers.

The safety policy which communicates AF's safety objectives should be produced at the CEO level.

In order to simplify the company's safety governance structure and reflect safety governance structure best practice, Air France should examine alternate structures that would:

6a   Modify the company's governance structure to have the Nominated Postholders reporting to the Accountable Manager;

6b   Establish a formal hierarchy of safety meetings within each Division from the local level through to Board Safety Subcommittee;

6c   Ensure that the linkages between the meetings are, at least, the Corporate Safety department representative and a common database.

Air France should communicate and explain the roles, hierarchy and responsibilities of Corporate Safety, Group Safety, and all Operational Divisions' safety organizations (e.g. Flight Operations Prevention and Safety, the Flight Analysis Department, Ground Operations, etc.), and ensure that each division's safety department has a reporting line to Corporate Safety.

Managers' roles, responsibilities, and authority regarding safety should be clearly described in writing, as relevant, in their position descriptions, and their performance should be evaluated on at least an annual basis.

Air France should ensure that the safety data gathering and analysis methods used by all Safety Departments are consistent and that they are communicated clearly to all the staff.
Review and update the Flight Data Monitoring Protocol so that:
10a The process is streamlined to ensure that investigations are closed before the next meeting whenever possible;

10b   The involved crew members are required to participate in the investigation if needed;

10c   One well-trained and informed pilot represents all the unions per fleet;

10d   Air France management has the ability to determine whether events are attributable to a single individual over time or multiple individuals

Air France should continue to develop their proactive management of safety data, wherein attempts are made to understand the event as a symptom of system design and to anticipate risks before accidents occur, and also pursue their effort to achieve a predictive state, where risks are anticipated, weighted and mitigated before symptomatic events have occurred.

Air France should ensure that change requirements intended as risk mitigations affecting frontline operators are monitored to confirm that the required behavioral change is achieved.

AF should reinforce Concerto Majeur (is this the right term?) implementation, and ensure that formal operational cross-divisional safety risk analyses are conducted at the start and at relevant phases of all projects (not just those involving operational issues), that identified risks are mitigated satisfactorily before proceeding in accordance with SMS requirements, and that mitigations are monitored to ensure that they are having the intended effect.

Air France should ensure that it has a suitable process to manage and support weak performers in operational areas to eliminate unacceptably low performance.

Institutionalize LOSA as a reliable tool for monitoring routine flight operations. The outcome and follow-up actions should be overseen by the Board Safety Subcommittee.

Consider extending LOSA-type observations to other operational areas and using all additional available information channels (e.g. incident reporting, instructors feedback, front line management feedback, etc.) to build realistic indicators of real work, daily operations which in turn can guide decisions about procedures, competences, teamwork, and work contexts.

Fleet Managers must be and feel empowered to manage safety and standards and to take disciplinary action when necessary to hold their staff accountable.

The process of the "no fly" list should be managed in a consistent way across the fleets. The list should be used to provide feedback and to address inappropriate behaviors, not to avoid them.

Air France should implement a leadership development program for managers in Flight Operations. AF should establish a pool of high-potential aircrew for future management positions. Members of the pool should be given broad-based management training and evaluated over a period of time (2-3 years). These individuals can become source for selecting future pilot managers.

With the goal of assuring the highest quality candidate, the selection process for Flight Operations Management positions must be open and transparent.

With the goal of assuring the highest quality candidate, the selection process for flight instructors must be open and transparent and promotion must be based upon performance.

Initial pilot selection and training programs should be reviewed and, if necessary, changed to develop a more team oriented pilot workforce which behaves in a non-elite manner.

Air France should continue its efforts to simplify policies and manuals across operational areas including the use of Original Equipment Manufacturers' manuals and procedures in English as the company standard.

Air France should communicate, explain, and illustrate the areas and circumstances in which Captains may exercise discretion.

Air France senior management must clarify and promulgate its position and policy on disciplinary action for non-compliance in order to strengthen procedural compliance and assure that safety is being managed effectively on a daily basis.

Air France should improve the overall quality and standardization of its flight instruction by:

25a   Improving the instructor selection process

25b   Standardizing training delivery and content

25c   Conducting recurrent training in instructional techniques for instructors

25d   Monitoring of the flight instruction process, including thorough feedback from trainees

25e   Requiring inclusion of CRM principles in training delivery and evaluation

25f   Ensuring that lessons from incidents and identified risks are integrated in a realistic manner into the training program so that the risks are effectively mitigated as determined by Corporate Safety.

Air France should review and update CRM training in order to establish a strong link between simulator training, CRM training and the SMS monitoring and LOSA outputs, and ultimately embed CRM as a cross-domain platform into all parts of the operations including training :

26a   Use a detailed questionnaire to all crews to assess and understand strengths and weaknesses of the CRM training;

26b   Reinforce references to CRM skills in the pilot ab initio selection and hiring criteria, in the pilot's performance assessment, and in the flight instructor selection criteria;

26c   Reinforce skills for observing CRM issues, as well as for CRM issues briefing and debriefing skills, in the Flight Instructors initial and recurrent training, and recurrent assessment;

26d   Collect Flight Instructors feedback about CRM skills evolution among the trainees and provide it to CRM program managers, flight operations managers, flight operations safety managers;

26e   Involve CRM facilitators in a systematic collection and synthesis of critiques and suggestions expressed during CRM training session to improve such training;

26f   Reinforce cross-domain cooperation (e.g. with maintenance) issues during CRM sessions discussions;

26g   Incorporate conclusions from recent AF incidents, main LOSA outcomes, and AF risk management priorities into CRM sessions;

26h   Involve CRM facilitators/Human Factors experts (not just pilots) in the design of operational processes and procedures changes.

Ensure that the FAR project continues to address pre-flight processes that reduce pilot workload.

Air France senior management should make clear to operational personnel, including cabin crew, how they expect them to behave when pressures for efficiency seem to conflict with the need to be thorough to maintain high safety standards.

Air France should establish an effective Cabin Crew Safety Department to deal with cabin crew safety issues and have the same reporting structure as the similar bodies in other Divisions (a hard reporting line to Division manager and a dotted reporting line to Corporate Safety).

Senior leadership and all levels of management should demonstrate teamwork and emphasize the importance of teamwork, celebrating positive examples.

Air France should launch a highly visible, cross departmental team building initiative to break down the "walls" between organizations (e.g., BA's "Putting People First"). This initiative should provide opportunities for cross functional teams to work together on significant projects.

Operational policies, rules and procedures should not be the subject of any form of union negotiation, but well researched union technical data and input should be welcomed as at other carriers in a collective debate. Flight safety should be explicitly incorporated at the relevant level within the perimeter of discussions between management and pilot unions.

An official "locus" should be established for discussions about operational safety between management and unions, at different levels in the organization: technical committees at department level, and a more strategic committee at corporate level. There should be two unions' representatives at the corporate level nominated globally by the unions, not one per union. Union representatives should have knowledge and experience in aviation safety. Air France should assist them in gaining expertise (e.g. providing training) if required.

In order to define and communicate the boundaries between acceptable and unacceptable behavior and protect those who report errors and safety gaps, Air France management together with labor unions should develop and implement an approach, within all aspects of operations, that reflects current international aviation industry best practice using ICAO guidance on Just Culture as a model.

All Air France Unions should establish a common forum to routinely discuss inter-domain cooperation for flight safety.

Air France should develop a more cooperative "working together" relationship with the DGAC. For example, Air France should promote, encourage, and embrace participation of DGAC inspectors in their data sharing sessions, e.g., RX2.

APPENDIX B
A Short History of Pitots at Air France

In its bid for transparency on the controversial airspeed monitors that have been a focal point of the investigation of the Air France 447 crash, the airline's public relations department offers this candid summary that dates back more than two decades.

Numerous manufacturers, upgrades and modifications, as well as intense discussions between Air France and Airbus highlight some of the technical challenges that are part of the manufacturer's "fly-by-wire" system. Here, in Air France's own candid words, is an illuminating look at the challenges faced by an airline trying to solve a technical challenge that remains the subject of international regulatory investigation.

1988–February 2001
At the outset, all Air France short- and medium-haul A320s were equipped with Pitot probes manufactured by Badin Crouzet, which subsequently became Sextant Avionics, and then Thales Avionics. In 1999, due to the risk of water ingress and inconsistent speed data during heavy rain or icing conditions, Air France decided to replace these probes by Thales AA probes in compliance with a recommendation from Airbus. Even before the Airbus recommendation became mandatory on 4 December 2001, all the Air France A320s had been equipped with Thales AA probes on 8 February 2001.

August 2001

Following the fluctuations and inconsistency in aerodynamic speed indications on the longhaul A330 and A340 reported by some airlines, the French Civil Aviation Authorities published an Airworthiness Directive (AD) per type of aircraft to impose the replacement of the Rosemount P/N 0851GR Pitot probes, either with the Goodrich

P/N 0851HL probes, or by the Sextant (Thales) P/N C16195-AA probes. This operation had to be completed by 31 December 2003. The authorities did in fact attribute these incidents to the presence of ice crystals and/or quantities of water, which exceeded the specifications of the P/N 0851GR Pitot probes, manufactured by Rosemount (now a unit of Goodrich). In accordance with the Airworthiness Directive, the Sextant (Thales) P/N C16195-AA (Thales AA) probes, already fitted on the A320s, were installed on Air France's A340 fleet. In December 2001, Air France received its first A330s, already equipped with Thales AA probes so that this was the only type of probe on its Airbus fleet of aircraft. No inconsistency in speed indications was reported on the Air France A330s and A340s until May 2008.

September 2007

Airbus issued service bulletins, which recommended, on an optional basis and devoid of any context affecting aircraft airworthiness, the replacement of the Thales AA probes fitted onto all the A320/A330/A340s with a new Thales P/N C16195-BA model (Thales BA). This model was said to improve the performance of the probe by limiting water ingress during heavy rain and reducing the risk of probe icing. After examination, Air France's technical teams decided to modify the Airbus A320 fleet, which had experienced incidents involving inconsistent speed indications at low altitude during heavy rain. They decided to replace the probes on the A330/A340s with the new models only when a failure occurred, as these aircraft had experienced no incidents involving inconsistencies in speed data.

May–August 2008

The first incidents involving inconsistent speed data were

reported on Air France A340s, although no such incident had been reported beforehand.

Air France immediately questioned Airbus on the cause of these incidents and on the corrective measures to be taken.

September and October 2008

A great deal of discussion took place with Airbus' technical teams. Two new incidents were then reported by Air France. Airbus replied that the presumed cause of these incidents was the formation of ice crystals, which iced up the airspeed probes; the new Thales BA model had not been designed to address the problem of probe icing and could not therefore provide a significant improvement; the probes in place were perfectly compliant with and even exceeded the regulatory requirements in terms of airworthiness and flight safety.

November 2008

Subsequent to different follow-up messages from Air France's technical departments, Airbus amended its service bulletins of September 2007 in a memo dated 12 November 2008, cancelling the recommendation of September 2007. The revised version no longer recommended the installation of Thales BA probes to reduce the risk of icing. A meeting took place between the technical managements of Air France and Airbus, where the incidents involving inconsistent speed data were discussed at length. Air France asked for a rapid solution. Airbus once again confirmed that these incidents were caused by the icing over of the probes, that the Thales BA probes did not address the problem and that the probes in place complied with the airworthiness and flight safety requirements. Air France asked if it were possible to replace them with Goodrich probes. Airbus noted the request from Air France and indicated their desire to verify the feasibility.

February 2009

Faced with Air France's insistence on finding a solution, wind tunnel tests were conducted by Thales and Airbus on the behavior of the Thales BA tubes.

March 2009

At the end of March 2009, two new operating incidents were reported, including the first on an A330. This brought the total number of incidents to nine—eight on the A340 and one on the A330. Once again Air France appealed on several occasions to Airbus, who replied by confirming the presumption of probe icing, referring the airline to a maintenance procedure and to checks on the probes.

April 2009

In a letter dated 15 April 2009, Airbus changed its position: the Thales BA probe was not designed to solve the problem of probe icing but tests conducted by Thales revealed a significant improvement in its performance compared with the AA model. Given the limitations of the wind tunnel tests, Airbus suggested a trial on Air France planes to check whether the improvement would be confirmed in a real-life situation.

Without waiting for these tests, Air France decided immediately to replace the Thales AAprobes with Thales BA probes on all its Airbus A330s and A340s. An internal document launching the replacement procedure was issued by Air France on 27 April 2009. The probes were ordered from Thales. The start of the modification process was scheduled as soon as the parts were delivered, on the basis of several aircraft per week as from 1 June 2009.

May–June 2009

In May 2009, Air France asked Thales to speed up the delivery schedule for its probes. They were delivered starting on 26 May 2009. By 12 June, all the Airbus A320s, A330s and A340s operated by Air France were equipped with Thales BA probes.

July–August 2009

A study carried out by Airbus and presented to EASA prompted this agency to make it mandatory as from 7 September 2009 (Airworthiness Directive), as a precautionary measure, to equip the aircraft in all A330 and A340 fleets with at least two Goodrich PN 0851-HL probes. Consequently, in compliance with the service bulletin issued by Airbus on 30 July 2009, the entire fleet of A330s and A340s of Air France has been equipped with these probes since 7 August 2009. On 23 September 2009 The European Aviation Safety Agency issued an Airworthiness Directive (A/D) applicable on 23 September 2009, asking all operators of Airbus A330/340s fitted with Goodrich 0851HL Pitot probes bearing certain part numbers, to verify them. Air France wishes to point out that all its aircraft concerned by this A/D had already been checked, as requested, between 5-9 September 2009. This check was carried out on the basis of technical data provided beforehand by Airbus.

Bibliography

Books

Amedo, Fabrice (2010) *La Face Cachée D'Air France*. Paris, France: Flammarion.

Bartlett, Christopher (2010) *Air Crashes and Miracle Landings*. Buckinghamshire, UK: Open Hatch Books.

Bibel, George (2008). *Beyond The Black Box*, Baltimore, USA: Johns Hopkins University Press.

Gero, David (2010) *Aviation Disasters*, London: The History Press.

Heimermann, Benoît & Olivier, Margot (1994) *L'Aéropostale,* Paris, France: Arthaud.

Hewson, Robert (2002) *Airbus A330 and A340*, Shrewsbury, UK: Airlife Publishing.

Langewiesche, William (2009) *Fly-By-Wire*, New York: Farrar, Straus and Giroux.

Michaelides-Mateou, Sofia; Mateou, Andreas (2010). 'Civil Versus Criminal Liability Flying in the Face of Criminalization: The Safety Implications of Prosecuting Aviation Professionals for Accidents', Farnham, UK: Ashgate.

Mermoz, Jean (2001) *Mes Vols*, Paris: Flammarion.

Newhouse, John (2007). *Boeing Versus Airbus*. New York, USA: Alfred A. Knopf.

Sullenberger, Chesley (2009) *Highest Duty,* New York, USA: William Morrow.

Sparaco, Pierre (2006) *Airbus The True Story*, Toulouse, France: Editions Privat.

Tobin, James (2003) *To Conquer The Air*, New York, USA: Free Press.

U.S. Department of Transportation (2016) Federal Aviation Regulations/Aeronautical Information Manual. Newcastle, Washington: Aviation Supplies & Academics.

Documentary

Darlow Smithson Productions (2010). *Lost: The Mystery of Flight 447*. London: BBC.

Crash of Air France 447. Arlington, Virginia: PBS 2011.
www.pbs.org/wgbh/nova/space/crash-flight-447.html

Reports

Bureau d'Enquêtes et d'Analyses pour la Sécurité de l'Aviation Civile:

Air France 447 Interim Report July 2, 2009 www.bea.aero/docspa/2009/f-cp090601e1.en/pdf/f-cp090601e1.en.pdf Air France 447 Second Interim Report December 17, 2009

www.bea.aero/docspa/2009/f-cp090601e2.en/pdf/f-cp090601e2.en.pdf Air France 447 Third Interim Report #3 July 29, 2011

www.bea.aero/docspa/2009/f-cp090601e3.en/pdf/f-cp090601e3.en.pdf Sea Search Operation Phase One: June 10 to July 10, 2009

www.bea.aero/en/enquetes/flight.af.447/sea.search.ops.phase.1.php Sea Search
     Operation Phase Two: July 17 to August 17, 2009

www.bea.aero/en/enquetes/flight.af.447/sea.search.ops.phase.2.php Sea Search
     Operation Phase 3: April 2 to May 24, 2010

www.bea.aero/en/enquetes/flight.af.447/sea.search.ops.phase.3.php Sea Search
     Operation Phase 4: March 2011 to summer 2011

www.bea.aero/en/enquetes/flight.af.447/sea.search.ops.phase.4.php

Accident on 27 November 2008 off the coast of Canet-Plage to the Airbus A320-232
     registered D-AXLA operated by XL Airways Germany

www.bea.aero/docspa/2008/d-la081127.en/pdf/d-la081127.en.pdf Metron Search
     Analysis January 20, 2011

www.bea.aero/fr/enquetes/vol.af.447/metron.search.analysis.pdf

Ministry of Planning, Housing, Transport and Maritime Affairs, Investigation
     Commission concerning the accident which occurred on 26 June 1988 at
     Mulhouse-Habsheim to the Airbus A320, registered F-GFKC. Final Report, No-
     vember 29, 1989. Air France Pitot Probe Chronology corporate.airfrance.com/
     en/press/af447/pitot-probes/#c1983

Endnotes

1. Captain Shem Malmquist flew the Air France 447 simulation at the FAA's Mike Monroney Aeronautical Center, Oklahoma City in March 2016.

2. FAA Regulation took effect: Federal Register http://bit.ly/2uxlyYK

2. Carriers such as Alaska Airlines and Southwest Airlines have worked to implement the FAR 60 rule ahead of the 2019 deadline.

5. With more than: Sud Ouest, June 4, 2009, Felix Dufour interview with pilot Arnaud Lorente.

5. Rapoport interviews with Jacques Dubois, Paris, October 2015 and January 2017.

7. President Sarkozy's plane: *Guardian*, November 16, 2009.

9. Artificial intelligence is promising: http://bit.ly/2dH3FCH http://bit.ly/1zxa04h David Mindell, "Our Robots, Ourselves".

10. Rapoport interviews with Jacques Dubois in Paris and Jean-Louis Bonin in Bordeaux.

11. *Ibid.*

14. *Ibid.*

15. *Ibid.*

16. Rapoport interviews with Gerard Arnoux, Paris.

17. One of his aircraft's wing: *Time magazine* September 8, 1961 http://content. time. com/time/magazine/article/0,9171,872735,00.html and *Chicago Tribune*, August 30, 1961.

19. Rapoport interview with Michel Guerard, Blagnac.

20. Rapoport interviews with Pierre Sparaco, Paris, Aix- en-Provence.

21. Rapoport interview with the European Air Safety Agency's Daniel Holtgen, Cologne, Germany confirmed the waiver of the requirement to demonstrate that the new jet could recover from an aerodynamic stall.

22. Also all of the fly-by-wire Airbus jets: http://www.airbus.com/aircraftfamilies/passengeraircraft/commonality/

22. Airbus's optimism was seconded by accident investigators at the prestigious French Bureau d'Enquêtes et d'Analyses (BEA): Final BEA report.

31. On one 1930 flight: Heimermann, Benoît & Olivier, Margot: L'Aéropostale (Paris: Flammarion, 2001).

34. Among the parents: *Sunday Times* (London) November 15, 2009.

36. Because an electronically: Rapoport interview with Col. Xavier Mulot, head of research at the Interior Ministry's Air Transport Police, Roissy-en-France, 2010.

36. Communications via a 1940's vintage high-frequency network: This system was somewhat improved with single sideband from amplitude modulation, or AM, in the mid-1960s.

47. In 1996 : National Transportation Safety Board Safety Recommendation, November 15, 1996. Letter to Acting Administrator Federal Aviation Administration. https://www.ntsb.gov/safety/safety-recs/recletters/A96_141.pdf

51. In the spring: Hugues Houang memo. http://bit.ly/2gZOIh9

52. Air Caraibes quickly: Flight Global, November 6, 2009. http://bit.ly/2uxMwCk. By the early 21st century, when regulations started limiting: Silva, Saulo. "A Brief History of RVSM", (Montreal: International Civil Aviation Organization, 2010).

53. By the early 21st century, when regulations started limiting: Silva, Saulo. "A Brief History of RVSM", (Montreal: International Civil Aviation Organization, 2010).

54. Mach tuck: http://bit.ly/2eKVTJb

55. Could the stall warning be a false: Stall warning systems are based on angle of attack, not airspeed. FAA Advisory Circular 25-7C, 120-109A, presentation by Jeff Schroeder, February 2016.

56. Robert and Bonin can feel: As seen on the Flight Data Recorder VG trace in the 2nd Interim Report from BEA the aircraft was accelerating downwards at between 0.5 and 0.7 g for a large portion of the descent. This far exceeds what most pilots have ever experienced in a transport airplane.

58. During much of this time Bonin is holding the controls full back. While this may seem surprising the Airbus flight controls are designed to put the wings at an ideal angle of attack, enabling perfect recovery from windshear and other problems. Captain Sullenberger utilized this feature to enable a successful landing on the Hudson River. The problem is that this feature is not available with the degraded flight control situation they were facing. Was Bonin trying this trained response to the unexpected situation?

63. As the A330: BEA Report and Rapoport interview with Air France pilot and SNPL union official Érick Derivry, Paris.

63. Because the oceanic flight: BEA report, Authors interview with Col. Xavier Mulot, Roissy-En-France.

67. In a parallel tragedy: New York Daily News, June 11, 2009

73. Batteries powering the pingers: BEA report.

74. This explains precisely why: Rapoport interview with Arthur Allen, U.S. Coast Guard.

76. Olivier Ferrante: Rapoport interviews with Olivier Ferrante, BEA.

77. Underwater archaeologists: Michigan Shipwreck Research Associates, Northwest Flight 2501. http:// www.michiganshipwrecks.org/dc4.htm

77. Also missing: Aviation Safety Network, Flight Safety Foundation.

78. Even shallow bodies: Flight Data Recovery Working Group Report, BEA, December 22, 2009.

78. Of the 27: Search Analysis for the Location of the AF 447 Underwater Wreckage, Metron report to BEA, January 20, 2011.

82. A safety investigation: Rapoport interview with Martine Del Bono, Paris.

82. In their report: Ibid.

82. In addition to: Rapoport interview with Michael Kutzleb.

Endnotes

83. As you ascend: Rapoport interview with Johann Strumpfer.

84. Airbus maintains: *New York Times*, March 17, 2011.

85. We do not recognize: *Ibid.*

86. In an earlier meeting: Rapoport interviews with AF 447 victims' families.

86. There are at least: Rapoport interviews with IFALPA's Paul McCarthy and Pierre Sparaco.

87. All these possibilities: Rapoport interviews with John Clemes, Paris, London.

90. On his desk is a 2007 article: Safety First No. 5, December 2007.

95. We were not considered: Rapoport interview with Mike Purcell, Woods Hole, Massachusetts.

96. A long time ago: Rapoport interview with Mike McDowell.

98. It is hard to understand: Author interview with Dick Limeburner, Woods Hole, Massachusetts.

99. One wandered: Rapoport interview with David Gallo, Woods Hole Massachusetts.

99. Changseng Chen: Rapoport interview with Changseng Chen.

102. On the afternoon: Author interview with Mike Purcell, Woods Hole Massachusetts.

106. One problem: Rapoport interview with aviation insurance executive, Paris.

114. The crystal ice problem: BEA interim report, Rapoport interview with Dr. Debbie Schaum, Emery Riddle University, Daytona Beach, Florida.

119. Consider this warning: Rapoport interview with J. Walter Strapp, 'Environment Canada and Jet Engine Power Loss in Ice Particle Conditions', The High Ice Water Content (HIWC) Cloud Characterization Study. March 22, 2010, presentation, incorporated in http://www.tc.faa.gov/its/worldpac/techrpt/tc14-31.pdf

120. Simulators: Full-Stall Simulators Take Shape, *Aviation Week*, March 24, 2014. "The Real Cost of Simulated Stalls", *Aviation Week*, April 8, 2016. EASA and FAA will Improve Stall Testing, Avionale.

127. Some applicants: Rapoport interview with aviation students in Great Britain.

133. While the BEA completed: Rapoport interview with Xavier Mulot, Paris.

134. Following the first investigation: Rapoport interviews with Air France 447 case attorneys and relatives of the victims.

134. The plaintiffs: Rapoport interview with Gerard Arnoux, Paris.

139. The trimmable horizontal stabilizer: Absent normal law protections, in alternate law, the system may attempt to hold the aircraft to the demanded "g" force in cruise, so a neutral control would potentially hold the elevators up as the aircraft started to fall in an attempt to maintain one "g," as an example.

146. The problem argues: Seattle Post-Intelligencer, March 20, 2000.

147. When they sense approach to stall: http://bit.ly/2v4QZxL and the Airbus *FAST*, issue 23.

155. Prior to the crash: Ministry of Planning, Housing, Transport and Maritime Affairs,

Investigation Commission concerning the accident which occurred on June 26th 1988 at Mulhouse-Habsheim to the Airbus A320, registered F-GFKC. Final Report, November 29, 1989.

155. Humans are uniquely adapted: Malmquist discussion with Dr. David Woods.

163. The Thales and Goodrich: Rapoport interview with EASA's Daniel Holtgen, Cologne, Germany.

163. While the erratic: *Aviation Today*. November 9, 2009.

164. Iberia Airbus: Rapoport interview with Captain Fran Hoyas.

166. If the pilot: Rapoport interview with RAF pilot, London.

167. This is not: Rapoport interview with Air France pilot Patrick Magisson.

167. At the time: Rapoport interview with Airbus A330 pilot Francis Nardy.

173. After the 2008: National Transportation Safety Board Report, February 2, 2010.

176. Until recently, training: Croft, John, "New Training And Technologies Designed To De-Program Pilots". *Aviation Week* & *Space Technology*, March 24, 2014.

177. Unfortunately, like the misconceptions: Clearly the American crew had been misled by their simulator instruction that was itself a translation of experience gained on fighter aircraft that was inappropriate on an airliner not built for the resulting structural overloading.

177. Mach tuck. http://bit.ly/2eKVTJb

190. Like many other: Rapoport interviews with Bruce Carmichael, National Center for Atmospheric Research, Boulder, Colorado, Érick Derivry and Col. Xavier Mulot, Roissy-En-France.

190. Three years earlier: Rapoport interview with Dr. Bruce Carmichael, National Center for Atmospheric Research, Boulder, Colorado

191. Studies have shown: WXR-2100 MultiScan™ Threat Detection Radar 2011. Relationships between lightning flash rates and radar reflectivity vertical structures in thunderstorms over the tropics and subtropics, 2012.

194. In the past pilots were often encouraged to trust their autopilots: Asiana Accident Report, NTSB, 2015.

About The Authors

Roger Rapoport is the producer and co-screenwriter of the acclaimed feature film *Pilot Error* as well as *Waterwalk* and *Coming Up For Air* which will be released in 2018. He is also is a contributing editor at *Flight Safety Information*, a daily online magazine that reaches the aviation safety community worldwide. His many books include *Citizen Moore: The Making of an American Iconoclast* (winner of the Forward Magazine Gold Award for Biography), *Hillsdale* and the *I Should Have Stayed Home* trouble travel series which has sold over 200,000 copies in English and many foreign editions.

He has written for the *Chicago Tribune, Wall Street Journal, Miami Herald, Boston Globe, Dallas Morning News, San Jose Mercury News, The Independent* (UK) and the *San Francisco Chronicle*. His magazine work has appeared in *Harper's, The Atlantic, Esquire* and *Mother Jones*. Over the past eight years Rapoport has interviewed more than 300 pilots, executives at Airbus, Air France, officials at the French BEA, the FAA, the European Aviation Safety Agency, the National Transportation Safety Board, the National Center for Atmospheric Research, NASA, Environment Canada and numerous academic experts.

Captain Shem Malmquist has been involved in aviation safety work since 1981, working in multiple aspects of aviation safety, from charting procedures, aircraft design to human factors and weather avoidance. After leading a major accident investigation for his organization he became involved with the Commercial Aviation Safety Team (CAST) Loss of Control Joint Safety Implementation Team (JSIT), where he was the Automation and Human Factors team leader. Subsequently, he was asked to join the CAST Joint Safety Implementation Data Analysis Team and worked as Chairman of Safety for his pilots association, later moving from that role to the Aircraft Design and Operations Committee Chair position, during which time he was involved with several investigations in various capacities. In 2009 he became involved in another major aircraft accident investigation and although officially a member of the Operations group, he also performed performance, human factors and kinematic analysis to support that investigation. He was subsequently asked to join the CAST Aircraft State Awareness JSIT. Captain Malmquist is currently a 777 Captain flying routes worldwide including many in the Intertropical Convergence Zone that is central to the Air France 447 story. He previously served as a Line Check Airman on the MD-11 and served as a member of his airline's flight operations management.

He is an active member of ISASI, IEEE, AIAA, HFES, FSF, SAE and an elected Fellow of the Royal Aeronautical Society. He holds an MS in Human Factors in Aeronautics from the Florida Institute of Technology, a BS in Aeronautics from Embry-Riddle University and an AS in Commercial Flight from Mt. San Antonio College.

About Curt Lewis Aviation Books

Over the past 20 years Curt Lewis's *Flight Safety Information*, has become an indispensable daily read across the aviation industry. CEOs at airlines and manufacturers, heads of regulatory agencies, university faculty, and their students, accident investigators, Air Force Generals, lawyers, engineers, and frequent flyers worldwide consider his daily journal a must read. Thanks to his passion for air safety, he has become one of the most trusted names in aviation writers. Curt Lewis Aviation Books, launched in association with Lexographic Press and General Editor Roger Rapoport, offers readers the same kind of up to the minute analysis and writing they have come to expect with *Flight Safety Information*. Available in print or via the web worldwide, Curt Lewis Books offer a balanced look at critical aviation safety issues. All of our authors work with a veteran team of aviation editors, training pilots and academic experts.

Curt Lewis served with American Airlines/AMR Corporation (AA) for seventeen years, first as Corporate Manager of Flight Safety and Flight Operational Assurance (FOQA), then as Corporate Manager System Safety. Before his tenure at American Airlines, he was a Lead System Safety Manager for LTV Aerospace Company, a Product Safety Manager for Texas Instruments, a Flight Training Instructor for Boeing Commercial Airplane Group, and served as Chief Corporate Pilot and Safety Director for various industrial corporations.

He has in excess of 40 years of safety experience as a professional pilot, safety director, and air safety investigator. Dr. Lewis holds an Airline Transport Pilot License (ATPL), Certified Flight Instructor Certificate (Airplane Single, Multiengine & Instrument); with over 10,000 hours of flight experience. In addition, he has earned technical Bachelors degrees in Aeronautical Engineering and Physics, a Masters degree in Aviation & System Safety, and a Ph.D. in Business Administration (Specialization: Safety Management.

Acknowledgements

I am first grateful for the love of my life, my wife, Meredith, who allowed me the time to complete this work. In addition, it was at her suggestion that I delved deeply into the cognitive psychological aspects of human response which played a vital role in the analysis that went into this work. I thank all of my children for their understanding of the hours I needed to devote to the research and writing. I also must give a nod to Captain Jeff Kilmer, who started me on this road by asking me to work with Roger Rapoport and which led to this collaboration. Finally, I thank Roger Rapoport for his support and guidance.

Shem Malmquist

I am grateful to my friend Richard Harris who edited an early draft of this manuscript. James Sparling at Lexographic Press has been central to this book's publication from day one and also suggested writing the screenplay that became Pilot Error.

My co-author Shem Malmquist has diligently researched and written key sections of this book with an eye toward helping pilots everywhere benefit from the lesson of Air France 447. For more than 25 years his aviation writing has been valued by fellow professionals and it is a pleasure to introduce his talents to a general audience.

Megan Trank, John Likakis, Gerard Arnoux, Curt Lewis and Larry Kirshbaum all generously contributed their talents to the editing of this book. I am also grateful to pilots Robert Hesselbein and Michael Hahn who worked with us on this book along with Dr. Nicklas Dahlstrom and Olivier Fressard of the Bibliothèque nationale de France.

Additional assistance was provided by pilots Hank Austin, Gideon Ewers, Heinz Frühwirth, Paul McCarthy and Claudine Oosterlinck. At the BEA Olivier Ferrante and Martine Del Bono were both gracious with their time. Daniel Holtgen of the

European Aviation Safety Agency, the FAA's Ali Bahrami, and the National Transportation Safety Board's Peter Knudson answered many key questions.

In Madrid and Bordeaux attorneys Jean-Pierre Bellecave and Carlos Villacorta generously contributed their time to this project as did Daniel Soulez-LaRiviére and Eileen Gleimer who demystified their complicated law practices. Arthur Allen, Bruce Carmichael, Scott Kendall, Michael Kutzleb, Walter Strapp, and John Strumpfer carefully analyzed some of the factors that could have contributed to this crash. Thanks also go to Air France's Etienne Lichtenberger, Andrea Boiardi at Italy's ANSV Italy and Vincent D'Horne at the Le Bourget Air and Space Museum.

At the SNPL, the French pilots' union, captains Érik Derivry, Francis Nardy, Patrick Magisson went out of their way to shed light on this mystery. In Blagnac Airbus's Michel Guerard and his product safety colleagues offered a valuable overview of fly-by-wire and the A330. At Woods Hole Oceanographic Institute Mike Purcell, David Gallo and Richard Limeburner offered valuable insights and a chance to meet Maryanne and Ginger. A nod also goes to Changseng Chen at the University of Massachusetts Dartmouth campus. I am also grateful to Michel Groisne of IFURTA in Aix-en-Provence for welcoming me to their comprehensive aviation safety conference at the only law school in the world named for a dropout, Paul Cézanne who deserted the bar for an artist's studio. Aurelie Pouzerat, an able translator who did a superb job on interviews with the pilots' families, and Catheline Leoni both assisted with reporting on legal issues related to this case Nicola Clark of the *New York Times* also provided valuable assistance. I also want to thank Jacques Dubois, Elisa Dubois, Jean-Louis Bonin and Frederic Alline for the time they generously contributed to our research on the story of the flight crew. Special thanks go to John Clemes who has worked tirelessly on behalf of the victims' families

My wife Martha Ferriby is a library director with a wonderful sense of humor. She and her staff at the Hackley Public Library were kind enough not to run the other way every time I came up with another series of research requests. My three children, Jonathan and Elizabeth Rapoport and William Ferriby were all great sounding boards for this story.

Finally I would like to thank my father Dan Rapoport, a Misco and Howmet ceramic engineer in the aviation world for over 35 years. Although he never talked about it much, his name is on one of the company's key manufacturing patents. I will always remember the day he came home in 1957 to announce that American commercial jets, flying with Misco parts, had cut the route from New York to Los Angeles to just five hours.

He was intensely interested in this book and we had many long conversations about competing theories on the crash. While that may not sound like a very cheerful topic, both of us shared the view of many families of the victims. If lessons learned from this tragedy can lead to needed improvements perhaps the industry will be able to rule out similar events. It's a lofty goal and one worthy of the kind international teamwork described in these pages.

Roger Rapoport